Rudolf Vierhaus
Germany in the Age of Absolutism

RUDOLF VIERHAUS

Germany in the
Age of Absolutism

Translated by
JONATHAN B. KNUDSEN
WELLESLEY COLLEGE

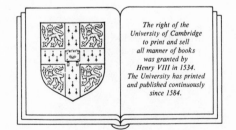

The right of the
University of Cambridge
to print and sell
all manner of books
was granted by
Henry VIII in 1534.
The University has printed
and published continuously
since 1584.

CAMBRIDGE UNIVERSITY PRESS

Cambridge

New York   New Rochelle

Sydney   Melbourne

Originally published as *Deutschland im Zeitalter des Absolutismus (1648–1763)*
© Vandenhoeck & Ruprecht in Göttingen.

Published by the Press Syndicate of the University of Cambridge
The Pitt Building, Trumpington Street, Cambridge CB2 1RP
32 East 57th Street, New York, NY 10022, USA
10 Stamford Road, Oakleigh, Melbourne 3166, Australia

First published 1988

Printed in the United States of America

Library of Congress Cataloging-in-Publication Data

Vierhaus, Rudolf.

Germany in the Age of Absolutism.

Translation of: Deutschland im Zeitalter des
Absolutismus (1648–1763).
1. Germany – Economic conditions. 2. Germany – Social
conditions. 3. Germany – Politics and government –
1648–1789. 4. Germany – History – 1648–1740. I. Title
HC285.V5313   1988   943.04   87–31970

British Library Cataloguing in Publication Data

Vierhaus, Rudolf

Germany in the Age of Absolutism.

1. Germany. Social conditions, 1648–1763
I. Title
943'.04

ISBN 0-521-32686-9   hard covers
ISBN 0-521-33936-7   paperback

CONTENTS

PREFACE

DIMENSIONS AND CHARACTER OF THE AGE

Germany in the Age of Absolutism – the title appears problematic in almost all its terms. It is difficult to ascertain what constituted "Germany" in the seventeenth and eighteenth centuries. For European diplomats and German imperial jurists it was undoubtedly the empire that still was called Roman; and many contemporaries agreed with them. Yet the empire encompassed many non-German peoples – especially in the lands of the House of Habsburg in the northwest, south, and southeast. In addition, Germans were excluded in the north and northeast. Moreover, certain German-speaking areas had once belonged to the empire and had since become independent or seceded, such as the northern Netherlands, Switzerland, and Alsatia. There was no German capital city; no common foreign policy affecting all Germans; and very little common history, but rather boundless local, regional, confessional, and cultural variation. Hence we cannot delimit precisely in geographical and political terms what belongs to German history in the period before us.

To accept this point, however, only means to be even more aware that the histories of the individual European peoples, states, and nations cannot be viewed or understood in isolation. If we still seek to write German history – even though Europe and its particular regions have both become much more sharply the focus of historical interest in recent decades – we must also integrate the gains of these two perspectives into our account. Nonetheless, it is also true that the individual cultural and political nations have been such fundamental factors in the development of Europe – and remain so today – that we must continue to explore and explain their historical development. "Germany" thus encompasses the empire and the German states, the cultural and political terrain, in which those matters occurred that were understood then to be part of German history.

Even more problematical, however, is the epochal term "Age of Absolutism." Here I adopt the conventional usage only because no other term of comparable appeal is available. Absolutism emphasizes a system of government and a principle of political organization that was not aspired to in all German states and was only partly achieved in others. It is certainly true that the policies of those princes who sought to gather absolute power about themselves represented the most dynamic political force in their day. The exercise of such power can be found before the middle of the seventeenth century, but this objection is not as critical to our use of the term as the other fact that monarchical absolutism had not come to an end by 1763. Indeed, in many states it only then acquired its sharpest features, albeit in an enlightened version. In this sense it does not seem justified to use the term as the signature of the era. With these limitations in mind, we can use the term Absolutism to encompass the one hundred and fifteen years between the end of the Thirty Years War and that of the Seven Years War.

That I use two wars to bound this account does not mean that I understand history to be the consequence of great "political" events, the course of which can be presented to us in narrative form, or that I presume great wars to be special caesurae in the historical development. In the seventeenth and eighteenth centuries, however, we can recognize an altered historical constellation at the end of each of these great wars, which was only partly due to the wars themselves. Particular historical forms and possibiities either had come to an end or had lost significantly in importance; others, on the other hand, were set free and now acquired formative power. The forces of continuity proved to be more significant than those of change, even as they were experienced differently in the various states of Germany and among the various sectors of the population. But there remains a clear difference in the overall historical shape of Germany after 1648 and then again after 1763. The era of confessional struggle and war came to an end with the Thirty Years War: At the center of the struggle within and among the states was the struggle for political power, its acquisition, exercise, and triumph. With the end of the Seven Years War it was not only decided that Germany would henceforth be divided into two rival political camps but also that economic, social, and cultural reform must become the agenda of the new epoch and that only political systems adapting to the new agenda would be able to assert themselves.

The character of an epoch cannot be determined from its temporal boundaries. We must ask instead after its special imprint. This is never a single individual, institution or idea, never a single event. An epoch is characterized by the particular way many forces interact. It is the intention of this book to reveal to the reader both their extreme complexity and their relative homogeneity. In order to achieve this – anything else would be an impermissable oversimplification – I have chosen a narrative form that reveals the great structures of historical life and thereby also makes visible their continuity.

MAP

(overleaf)

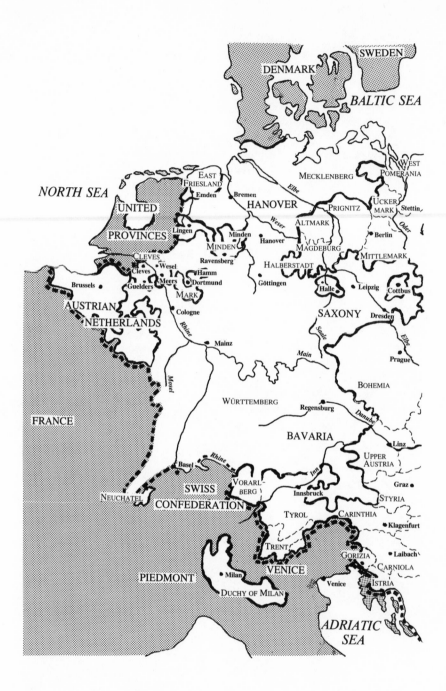

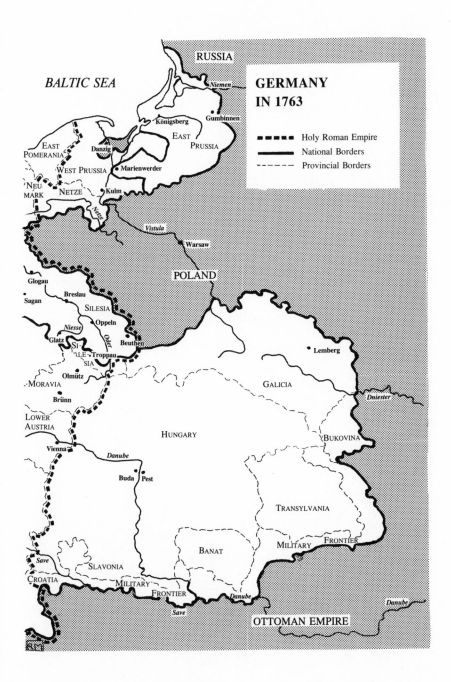

BALTIC SEA

RUSSIA

Niemen

Königsberg

Gumbinnen

EAST
PRUSSIA

EAST
POMERANIA

Danzig

WEST PRUSSIA

Marienwerder

NEU
MARK

NETZE

Kulm

Netze

Vistula

Warsaw

POLAND

Glogau

Sagan

Breslau

SILESIA

Oppeln

Niesse

Glatz

SI-

Oder

Beuthen

LE-Troppau

SIA

Olmütz

Lemberg

MORAVIA

Brünn

GALICIA

Dniester

LOWER
AUSTRIA

Vienna

HUNGARY

BUKOVINA

Danube

Buda Pest

TRANSYLVANIA

Save

SLAVONIA

BANAT

MILITARY FRONTIER

CROATIA

MILITARY

FRONTIER

Danube

Save

Danube

OTTOMAN EMPIRE

GERMANY
IN 1763

▪▪▪▪▪ Holy Roman Empire
───── National Borders
- - - - - Provincial Borders

—— INTRODUCTION ——

GERMANY AFTER THE
THIRTY YEARS WAR

————— · —————

SOCIOECONOMIC CONSEQUENCES:
COLLAPSE AND DELAYED DEVELOPMENT

"I do not intend to give the reader of this history, as it is often done, a mosaic constructed from an infinite number of individual accounts. [This method] perhaps aims more to arouse terror and compassion than to bring about a creative synthesis and inner understanding," wrote Bernhard Erdmannsdörffer. He was seeking to reconstruct the "material and cultural conditions" after the Thirty Years War in his still valuable *German History from the Westphalian Peace to the Accession of Friedrich the Great* (1882). He thought that such a synthesis was not yet possible, though "the new research in economic history" might one day make it so. Since then we have learned much more, but we still cannot give a general account of the war's consequences that is complete in detail and breadth.

The contemporary reports of the devastations of the Thirty Years War, and the accounts in the imaginative literature do not always rest on direct experience. If some of these works do not reveal the extent of the suffering caused by the war, others exaggerate. More importantly, the devastations were not spread equally throughout Germany. The war spared extensive areas largely or completely; in others, it passed through numerous times, bringing with it destruction, plunder, and impoverishment. If simply compiling the terrifying reports would give far too negative an impression, by the same token, statistics for the empire as a whole cannot come close to revealing the actual catastrophic losses that took place in a particular city or region. Trying to arrive at trustworthy, concrete information is still fraught with almost insurmountable difficulties. We cannot conclude that a population was destroyed just because a village was abandoned, since a part or all of its inhabitants might have emigrated elsewhere. Fugitives streamed continuously in and out of the cities, and vagabonds wandered about the countryside in great number. As with the murdered and killed, exact

1

figures are impossible to come by. Desertion was commonplace: Foreign mercenaries poured into Germany, and many remained, some in extreme conditions. There is no way of knowing about the birthrates in areas affected by the war for years on end. In some places the land remained uncultivated, while in others planting and harvesting was unaffected. Need and waste could exist side by side; many people were impoverished, while others made money. The war did not last for three continuous decades even in the areas hardest hit. There were long periods of apparent peace and even attempts – sometimes fruitless – at reconstruction.

Our efforts to assess the consequences of the war are connected with yet another difficult question that has still not been sufficiently resolved. Had economic decay already begun before the war, in the late sixteenth century, only to be accelerated and intensified by the war itself? If not, what macroeconomic meaning must be given to the earlier changes? We know that since the late fifteenth century individual population groups had been affected differentially by the steady, if uneven, rise in prices and wages known exaggeratedly in the scholarly literature as the "price revolution." Lords and peasants had both profited from it, the one from the increase in feudal burdens, the other from the higher prices; insofar as they produced for their own consumption, both had remained largely outside the price structure. Artisanal producers, on the other hand, especially craftsworkers, suffered a serious decline in real income, because wages rose more slowly than agricultural prices. The aggregate national product continued to climb until about 1620; but agricultural production, confined within the traditional agrarian legal system, could not keep pace with the rapid rise in the population, especially among the poorest orders in the cities, who increasingly were forced into beggary. We cannot reduce crafts and trade on the eve of the war to a uniform pattern. For instance, the great lower German mercantile houses, those representatives of early capitalism, experienced serious losses, while the capital market remained generally solvent, and capital even managed to spread and become more densely interconnected. If stagnation and decline had begun in a few cities, others prospered. Frankfurt blossomed around 1600, as did Leipzig; cities on the Rhine and in Westphalia that exported manufactured goods supplanted older sites; the textile trade in Saxony-Silesia, organized in manufactories, flowered; and the share of German goods in the colonial trade was considerable. But the economy became increasingly distorted, because the growth in productivity could not keep up with the growth in population and the increase in agricultural prices. As the macroeconomic system failed to alter, an active economic policy began to disappear within the territorial states, which became increasingly self-contained and hindered distant trade.

Thus if the economic situation in Germany on the eve of the war reveals a number of crisislike characteristics, there was as yet no general decline. The appearance of crisis resulted from a growing discrepancy among population, the development of prices and wages, the economic system, and the techniques of production. If Germany was economically backward after the war, then it was basically due to the war itself. The war generated enormous losses and postponed economic growth at the beginning of the seventeenth century for approximately another hundred years.

Just as the demographic catastrophe of the Black Death in the late fourteenth century led to a sharp decline in production and consumption, the loss of life from war in the first half of the seventeenth century also destroyed productive capacity and living space. The regions most severely affected toward the east were Mecklenburg, Pomerania in Brandenburg, the area between Magdeburg and Leipzig, and lower Silesia; toward the southwest, the areas extending from the Palatinate to Augsburg. Less severely affected were Saxony, northern Hesse, parts of Westphalia and the Rhineland, Upper Silesia, Bavaria, and Bohemia. The war largely passed over Schleswig-Holstein, large parts of lower Saxony, though not the edges of the Hartz and the Leine valley, most of Westphalia, the Rhineland, and the Alpine regions. But loss of life did not result simply from battle and material destruction. More devastating was the loss of life through murder and starvation, particularly in the last stages of the war, when unpaid soldiers plundered their way through the land. The armies stripped the land of food and made it impossible for crops to be planted. Epidemics also swept the countryside. From 1636 to 1640 the plague returned, attacking large parts of western and southern Germany. It is assumed that 45-50 percent of the rural population and 25-30 percent of the urban population was lost. In absolute terms the population is thought to have declined from 15-16 million inhabitants in 1620 to 10 million in 1650. For the first time, the population of Germany fell behind that of France. In qualitative terms this decline dramatically altered the age and geographical distribution of the population.

If population remained relatively constant in the areas largely unaffected by the war, it declined in the most severely affected areas by 60-70 percent. Only 50,000 of the 400,000 inhabitants living in the duchy of Württemberg in 1619 survived the war. Only 40 of 6,500 people survived in the Silesian city of Löwenberg. After the cities were besieged, captured, and plundered, the unprotected inhabitants of the countryside were the worst off. The lords could not prevent the survivors from abandoning the land. Many survivors forced their way into the walled cities even though there was no work for them. For those remaining in the countryside, it hardly paid to maintain the soil. The land under cultivation shrank, and villages were deserted. The livestock population rapidly declined, in certain areas by 90 percent. Buildings were destroyed or fell into disrepair. Only children and the elderly survived. Urban and rural trades declined even in almost intact regions because demand plummeted and because of the uncertain conditions of the long-distance trade routes and the unreliable supply of raw materials. Heavy contributions and ransoms demanded by ever-changing conquerors and allies alike plunged certain cities into long-term debt and forced a restructuring of landownership in the countryside.

This grim portrait needs to be corrected in certain ways. Money and goods expropriated by the military rabble were returned to the local economy. Military requisitioning created business opportunities. Officers in pacified areas bought estates cheaply and began new construction, while those in more fortunate areas profited from food shortages in other regions. Even though the nobility of the Niederlausitz was impoverished, the large peasant proprietors of Schleswig-Holstein prospered. With the disappearance of prewar overpopulation, shortages in the agricultural work force emerged. The price of grain sank significantly as demand declined; similarly, the value of land and estates declined. As agricultural production and, even more so, as industrial production gradually recovered, it became clear that international trade had not simply come to a temporary halt, but that the trade connections themselves were broken. There was too little money in circulation and too little capital for reconstruction. This meant that successful wartime speculators, coinage entrepreneurs, and Jewish court factors – those who had ready cash and could lend it at high interest rates – acquired an unprecedented influence.

Although agriculture was more seriously affected than trade or manufacture, the war intensified the agrarian character of the German economy. The German economy became even more detached from that of western Europe: Witness the relative insignificance of foreign trade, the comparatively modest standard of living maintained by the large majority of the population in the politically peripheral regions, and the lesser competence among artisans who therefore produced less for the wealthier orders. Hence the external impetus and financial means were often lacking for fundamental reconstruction. Furthermore, for a time, individuals and corporations lacked the will to begin. The Treaty of Westphalia did not bring immediate and universal peace. It took years for the old armies to disperse and retreat, even as new wars broke out on German soil in the next decades. For all of these reasons the postwar economic depression was extraordinarily lengthy.

It is in this context, significantly, that the territorial rulers and their governments began actively to intervene in the economy. We witness the beginning of a new phase in the development of political practice, a phase of mercantilism and cameralism that sought to strengthen the power of the state by supporting the economy.

SOCIOCULTURAL CONSEQUENCES:
EXHAUSTION, STAGNATION, PROVINCIALIZATION

Every general statement concerning the social and cultural consequences of the war is crude and inexact. Even if we do not portray life in the villages or on the estates, each residential or trading city had its own particular standard of living, education, religious life, art, and literature. The surviving written accounts give us only a narrow slice of that reality and are necessarily colored.

Once again we must take a short look backward to conditions on the eve of the war. In general the sixteenth century had brought increased prosperity, especially to the cities. Their wealth and spending for public buildings continued into the first years of the war. In many cases spending may even have increased, though the political clout of the cities within the emerging territorial states had already begun visibly to wane. Rich burgher families and the landed nobility demanded luxury goods and artistically crafted implements of various kinds, thus challenging the artisanate to great achievement. The rural nobility and the territorial princes actively supported new construction. Elias Holl began building the Zeughaus in 1602 and the town hall in Augsburg in 1615; Georg Riedinger started the palace in Aschaffenburg in 1605; construction of the Danzig Zeughaus began in 1600 and the town hall in Bremen in 1609. All of these, including the buildings of the so-called Weser Renaissance, expressed a secular urge to build inspired by the culture of the Italian Renaissance. Catholic and Protestant church construction blossomed at the same time, though Protestant construction began somewhat more haltingly with Paul Franke's building of the Marienkirche in Wolfenbüttel (1607-8). The early baroque Latin drama of the Jesuits reached a high point in the person of Jakob Bidermann, whose *Cenodoxus* was first performed in 1602. Protestant church music also flowered for the first time in the figure of Michael Praetorius, who became active in Wolfenbüttel from 1612 onward. The territorial states continued to found confessional universities into the first years of the war: Giessen (1607) and Paderborn (1614) were followed by Rinteln (1621) and Salzburg (1622). Imperial cities also established new universities: Strasbourg (1611) and Altdorf (1622 within Nuremburg territory). A late humanist Latin style was still cultivated within the universities, but legal-political theory had a contemporary orientation. In opposition to the teachings of Spanish late scholasticism, Althusius argued for the western European Calvinist conception of the political compact, and Arnisaeus elaborated the Lutheran conception of patriarchal godly grace. The oldest surviving newspapers date from 1609 in Strasbourg and Augsburg, attesting to the continued activity of public life in the cities.

The religious fervor and intellectual energy released by the Reformation had largely faded. Theological questions had become routinized, as had the confessional shaping of thought and social life. Lutheran orthodoxy unfolded within the Formula of Concord that had been achieved after lengthy negotiations in 1580. Catholic doctrine of the Counter-Reformation developed within the decisions of the Tridentine Council, though these had been accepted only haltingly within the individual German territories.

Both churches demonstrated a growing rigidification that still revealed the central importance of faith and the institutional church within social and political life. At the same time, the territorial princes and their legally trained councillors began to transform the churches into state churches by placing them under princely authority and integrating them into the institutional life of their territories.

It was the war that destroyed the material basis of a regional cultural life that was no longer as dynamic as it had been in the early sixteenth century but was still viable and prosperous. Construction came to a standstill in large parts of Germany. There was no longer a demand for craftsmanship and artistic creativity. Once construction began again after the war, urban burghers and the now impoverished and indebted landed nobility could no longer function as major patrons. Instead, the ruling nobility and, in Catholic regions, the church dominated reconstruction, and they often looked outside Germany to satisfy their needs. We also cannot overemphasize how low the cultural aspirations of the rural population had sunk in the war zones.

At the beginning of the war the opposing forces had been shaped largely by religious affiliation, and they had seen the war as a struggle over correct belief. But this view of the war was soon carried to absurdity. Although religious conflict did not disappear, it receded in significance in comparison to the property-holding classes' search for security and to the territorial princes' efforts to achieve a stable and expanded authority. Religious affiliation was largely maintained through an agreement in the Westphalian Peace to make 1624 the normal year. From then onward relations between church and state were essentially determined by the individual governments. German Catholicism entered a period of self-satisfaction with the fading of the Counter-Reformation, which also corresponded to a decline in the significance of the papacy. Within German Protestantism, on the other hand, the ruling orthodoxy loosened somewhat later, influenced by a Christian stoicism and pietism that in turn was shaped by English and Dutch sources.

The "great war" prepared the inward turn of religious life afterward. It did not bring with it either a sense of rupture or destruction in either secular or religious literature, but rather it challenged belief and created a turning inward. The war drove men and women to hope and despair. It was an occasion for jubilation and lament. It forced a search for meaning and created profound anxieties about the meaninglessness of existence. It brought forth eschatological hope, a deep feeling of sinfulness, and a search for worldly pleasure. Grimmelshausen's great novel *Simplizissimus* appeared in 1669 as a portrait of events and manners during the war years and as a moral-satirical allegory of human life: The world is inconstant, fortune is fickle, and human behavior is a type of madness from which we are freed only through renunciation and trust in our salvation in the next life.

After the war there was no longer a broad stratum of urban burghers who could create a self-confident, materially potent, and socially dominant literature. Except for the few spared or revitalized trading cities such as Hamburg or Leipzig, only the courts survived. There the poet became courtier and his work courtly verse. The learned character of the literature also intensified itself. It had already been present in Martin Opitz's *Buch von der Deutschen Poeterey (Book of German Poetry)* (1624) and in efforts of the Fruchtbringende Gesellschaft (Fruitbearing Society), founded in Weimar in 1617 by Prince Ludwig von Anhalt-Köthen, to support the German language and literature. The officials, clergy, and nobility wrote nothing with a popular appeal, for there was simply no resonance to be found in a self-confident and intellectually dynamic society.

The material decline and reduced sense of self-worth in the second half of the seventeenth century encouraged the increasing dependence on French modes, taste, and language. It became even more difficult with the complete parcelization of the empire into territorial states to construct a central location of political power, wealth, culture, and taste. In the midst of decline, the ruling groups and the educated sought to participate in the most progressive developments in Europe by adapting themselves to the standards of French civilization. For similar reasons they assimilated Italian opera by hiring foreign artists and architects, and they, especially the nobility, began to travel for cultural purposes to western and southern Europe.

Cultural and social life became narrower and more provincial in Germany at the end of the Thirty Years War. Social differences rigidified; the distance increased between the courts – as poverty-stricken as they were in comparison to others in Europe – and the life of the people in city and countryside. A living style developed at the courts that was enormously different from the life experience of the great mass of subjects. Though the pace and degree differed in the individual states, the nobility was either brought or was itself drawn to the courts. In addition, educated burghers increasingly sought positions, income, and prestige in princely service. Such service must also have become attractive because the expanding absolutist system had a growing need for manpower at the courts and within the bureaucracy. At the same time handicrafts, trade, and private service declined.

We noted that Germany in the sixteenth century had been a country with a dynamic and highly developed urban culture, with numerous regional and important supraregional cities. After the middle of the seventeenth century, however, it became a country, like Italy, of innumerable courts, of which few were of European significance. Many cities never regained their prewar population levels or earlier eminence. Life in these cities stagnated; with it the sense of burgher initiative and self-confidence declined; and communal independence was increasingly lost to princely administration. At the same time older and new princely residential cities grew in significance. The courts also acquired new social functions with their increased striving toward displaying their power and prominence. Similarly, the princely army and administration had a many-sided impact on the society. The social disciplining of the population through the patriarchal regime of the territorial sovereign and the church authorities, which had already begun earlier, now expanded much more fully because there was so much less resistance. This stamped permanently the social and political consciousness of the German people: It engendered those habits of servility, of appeal to authority, and of an absent public spirit that was so apparent to foreign visitors and German critics in the eighteenth century. Such values developed even in those states where princely authority proved unable to overcome the resistance of the estates.

Of course the pattern was similar elsewhere in Europe. Absolute monarchy asserted itself even earlier and more successfully in France; the monarchy degraded the nobility to a court nobility and suppressed the regional opposition of the estates. England was also shaken by civil and religious warfare, destroying the political order, and in Thomas Hobbes's view, bringing society back to the state of nature where each struggled against all. Indeed, crisislike tensions manifested themselves in all countries, so that historians speak of a "general crisis of the seventeenth century." But Germany was the only country to be so exhausted by war, so shaken to its biological and material foundations, so set back in its social and cultural development, and left to such alienation and retreat into narrowness and inwardness. The only comparisons might be to Italy in the sixteenth and to Spain in the eighteenth centuries.

POLITICAL CONSEQUENCES:
THE PARTICULARIZATION OF PUBLIC LIFE,
THE TIME OF GOVERNMENT

Naturally the political development of Germany since the mid-seventeenth century was not simply determined by the Thirty Years War or even by the Peace of Westphalia. The treaty agreements of Osnabrück and Münster did not simply seal the results of the war, but they must also be seen within a wider historical context of confessional pluralism and a shift westward in the political center of gravity within the European states system. This process had begun long before the beginning of the war and was still incomplete at its end.

The signing of the peace treaty brought a legal conclusion, though not yet a practical one, to the open war that had begun as a struggle for Bohemia and had spread to Europe. The original causes played only a subordinate role at the end. Rulers and generals had been exchanged, and most men living at the beginning either had not survived or could not remember a time of peace. There were so many powers involved, interests at work, and problems to resolve. Delegates from almost all European nations took part in lengthy, wearying negotiations that continually threatened to collapse. In the end they were unable to achieve the perpetual peace they had sought, since they were unable to neutralize the dynamic of the European system of states or satisfy the ambitions of the German dynasties. Even so, the provisions of the peace dealing with the constitution of the empire survived until the empire collapsed in the Napoleonic Wars. The Instrumenta Pacis Osnabrugense et Monasteriense was accepted in the Jüngster Reichsabschied on 17 May 1654 as "eternal Law and sanctio pragmatica, gleich anderen des Heil. Reiches Fundamental-, Satz-, und Ordnungen" and as "perpetual judge and eternal norma iudicandi."

One part of the territorial arrangements in 1648 only confirmed long-existing realities: The Netherlands and Switzerland were excluded from the empire and France annexed the Lorraine bishoprics of Metz, Toul, and Verdun. In the Upper and Lower Alsace, France reached the Rhine for the first time, and she was able in the next decades to derive claims from uncertain agreements that led to further conquest, intervention, and ultimately to permanent losses for the empire. For a time the fate of Lorraine remained undecided. Sweden made the largest territorial gain: Western Pomerania, Rügen, and Wismar expanded her control of the Baltic coastline. Her acquisition of the duchies of Bremen and Verden also made it possible for Sweden to control an area on the North Sea between the mouths of the Weser and the Elbe. Brandenberg's acquisitions also brought Sweden further west: Brandenberg was given the bishoprics of Halberstadt, Minden, Cammin, and a claim to Magdeburg in exchange for abandoning her claims to western Pomerania and Rügen. These gains proved to be decisive for the later course of German history.

The religious settlement also created the basic pattern that, except for some areas later re-Catholicized, has survived unto the present. The Reformed church was recognized alongside the Lutheran Church of the Augsburg Confession at the imperial level, and the confessions were separated into the fixed division of the confessions on the basis of 1 January 1624. Certain peculiarities survived as long as the empire did, such as in the bishopric of Osnabrück where a Catholic bishop alternated with a Hanoverian Protestant prince, and in imperial cities such as Augsburg, Biberach, and Dinksbühl where confessional parity was maintained among the magistrates. The imperial estates were recognized in their rights and privileges and voted at all consultations concerning the affairs of the empire. Furthermore, they officially acquired the right to conclude treaties among themselves and with foreign powers, insofar as such treaties were not directed against the emperor and the empire.

The year 1648 marked a victory for France in the great conflict with the house of Habsburg. When the empire, thanks to Wallenstein's successes, appeared to lie at the emperor's feet in 1630, Richelieu had supported Sweden. A few years later, when Gustav Adolf had fallen and peace was concluded between the emperor and Sweden, he entered the war himself and found support among both Catholic and Protestant princes who feared Habsburg hegemony. When the Spanish danger was removed with the Peace of the Pyrenees (1659), France had a point of departure from which she would obtain political primacy in the next decades. Although the Habsburgs retained the imperial crown until the end of the empire, with the exception of the brief period after the death of Charles VI, they were never able to recover the position within the empire that had been held for a short time by Ferdinand II. Their interests thereafter lay largely outside the empire, but the imperial title was a necessary presupposition for the far-flung possessions of the Casa d'Austria. This development was at the cost of the empire, but neither the French nor the Swedes had wanted to bring it to collapse. European diplomats debated whether greater or lesser decentralization of the empire was to the advantage of their individual states, but they knew its complete dissolution would bring the European system of power completely out of joint. Even those Protestant and Catholic princes, who were concerned to protect their own liberties and distrusted Habsburg policies deeply, could not have wanted the empire's demise. As vassals of the emperor they were barely limited in their imperial territories; though they did not possess complete sovereignty, they were functionally autonomous agents in the international order due to their unrestricted right to make treaties. It was important, however, that most princes were too weak to play an independent political role and thus needed the empire for support and protection. Even those who increasingly became less dependent upon the empire – Saxony, Hanover, Brandenburg, and Prussia – never left the imperial legal association. The empire was a political power only in a passive sense after 1648, but it survived exactly in this sense as the framework for the multiplicity of German states and as an essential component in the European system of states. Still, a significant consequence of this passivity was a general stagnation of the imperial constitution until its demise in the years between 1803 and 1806.

The less political energy emanated from the empire, the more it came to reside in the individual states. In the areas of intense fragmentation the smaller imperial estates in particular repeatedly sought their fortune in larger associations, without ever being able to develop ones that were flexible and could evolve politically, however. The larger states, on the other hand, operated with alliances, their own military forces, and administratively mobilized resources within their own boundaries. It is anachronistic and misguided to regret this development from the perspective of the nation state as it first became dominant in the nineteenth century. The account must be drawn on the basis of the concrete facts of German life and on the possibilities then available. There is no "normal" path of historical development among states and nations. In Europe, furthermore, the various paths were bound together in structural analogy and individual uniqueness. We must continuously compare these developments, because the states viewed and oriented themselves comparatively; they received stimuli from each other and adjusted and defended themselves accordingly.

By the seventeenth century the developmental slope from West to East had existed for some time – for instance, in the form and speed with which the feudal system dissolved and in the share of overseas trade and colonization. Now the differences between western Europe and middle Europe became even greater, due to the confessional character of politics, the overwhelming role the state acquired in shaping social development, and the extent of decentralization and political fragmentation. Germany fell into a state of developmental backwardness with respect to western Europe, which, when men were aware of it, became a political and psychological factor within the age.

Clearly the number of states and statelike forms within the empire – the coexistence of large, small, and tiny states, of secular and clerical states, of imperial cities and the minifundia of imperial knights, of Catholic, Lutheran, and Reformed regions – contributed to the cultural pluralism and to the richness of regional and local differences that still shapes the reality of life in Germany. After the Thirty Years War, in any case, this pluralism did not express itself in terms of excessive economic energy or local and regional self-conscious pride. In this context German particularism, dynastic egotism, and corporate resistance crippled public life. This was particularly true of the urban population and the poorer part of the rural nobility. In their striving for absolute power, the territorial rulers and their governments also contributed their part to the depoliticization of the ruled.

The economic decline due to war and stagnation in the postwar era, however, forced governments to take specific actions. Their historical moment arrived as the other forces were exhausted. If we are to judge the consequences and successes of their efforts, we must not forget the context in which they occurred, how limited often was the achievement, how much never went beyond intention and attempt. Even so we must keep in mind the social costs of this development. The example of Brandenburg-Prussia is the test case for historical judgment. Whoever follows the unique rise of this state – which was not historically necessary, though consequential – cannot forget the shocking costs of this enormous, one-sided exertion and its problematical consequences.

1

ECONOMIC DEVELOPMENT

PRELIMINARY REMARKS:
STAGNATION AND RESTORATION

The economic depression after the Thirty Years War differed in intensity in the various regions of Germany and in the various sectors of the economy, but all in all it continued unabated for the next half century. The numerous measures at reconstruction had little long-range effect on the total economy, and it did not help that the economies in other European states were also stagnant. Prices of important agricultural products, most significantly of grain, declined from the second quarter of the seventeenth century until the second quarter of the eighteenth, and they remained at low levels. Though prices stabilized earliest in Germany, they were still not able to approximate prices at the beginning of the seventeenth century. Lower prices reduced living costs in the cities, but they also lowered agricultural income. In addition, agricultural wages followed these tendencies only with hesitation. Demand for agricultural products also slackened with the reduced rate of demographic growth in large parts of Europe, particularly in Spain and northern Italy, in the Netherlands and Poland. This pattern only began to change fundamentally from about 1750 when rapid and general growth set in once again. (The estimated population in Europe, including Russia, was approximately 80–85 million in 1500, 100–110 million in 1600, 110–125 million in 1710, 120–140 million in 1715, and 180–190 million in 1800. The latter growth meant that the rate doubled in the last half century.

Within a general context of European stagnation, it is clear that German suffering was not unique. The crisis in Germany, however, was deepened by the European slowdown, since exports were not stimulated to any degree and foreign capital did not seek investment. The crisis continued to persist, moreover, because no supraregional or international bodies coordinated reconstruction. This lack of direction especially affected those areas of great material and human loss that had to begin rebuilding at a very low level.

Historians have often given responsibility and credit for the reconstruction to the economic policies of the territorial states, seeing therein a typical characteristic of German development that shaped the social transition from agriculture to industry over the long term. Even with respect to agriculture, however – in the language of the day, the *Retablissement* – such active economic policies did not only occur in the German territorial states. Close ties between economy and the state were a general characteristic of the era. Governments sought to extract revenue from available sources and develop new ones, to extend their authority internally and expand state power externally; and political economists justified these efforts by measuring the power of the state in terms of the wealth and size of the population. "Mercantilist" policies stressed trade, supporting those forms of artisanal and early industrial production that would stimulate foreign trade and bring specie into the country. But England and Prussia also developed a type of agrarian mercantilism by which the state supported agriculture. The overall policies ranged, somewhat crudely stated, from armed trade wars to trading treaties, customs agreements, and subventions, to incentives for entrepreneurs in the form of monopolies and privileges, and even to entrepreneurial activity by the governments themselves. The goals were also somewhat differently accentuated, as can be seen, for instance, in Cromwell's navigation acts from 1651, Colbert's financial and industrial policy, and the "cameralist" policies of the small German states.

The preeminent role taken by the territorial states in shaping industrial and agrarian policy led within the narrow confines of Germany to a lasting practice of the state acting as guardian. Oriented completely toward a *raison d'état* defined exclusively by government, the rulers equated the well-being of their subjects with that of the state and exploited their subjects in those terms. It must be noted, however, that, with the exception of a very few cities, few options were available for economic reconstruction.

DEMOGRAPHY

Modern social historians have emphasized the fundamental importance of demography for understanding general economic, social, political, and even cultural processes. Demographic decline and growth are directly related to food supply and earning capacity. Demographic growth creates pressures for the social system, and demographic catastrophes can lead to a restructuring of property relations.

Between 1720 and 1750 the German population climbed once again to the levels at the beginning of the seventeenth century (15–17 million); but we cannot view the period as one of continuous demographic growth in spite of

the recovery. Epidemics and crises in the food supply continued to disrupt
the very gradual recovery. In many parts of Germany people returned only
very slowly to the devastated countryside and the cities. David Sabean
described this process in paradigmatic fashion for a Württemberg village.
After the war the population in the village had collapsed from 1,000 to 400
inhabitants. The herds had been decimated, the homes were often destroyed, there was no seed, the property was deeply encumbered with debt,
and taxes remained high. In this context the village recovered painfully
slowly, reaching prewar levels only by 1720. In the meantime much had
changed. Under the pressure of depression many peasants refused to accept
hereditary leaseholds (*Erbe*), because it was extremely difficult to manage
larger properties (*Höfe*). As a result, the propertyless were able to acquire
new property, largely in the form of small homesteads. Fundamentally new
property divisions were created, in other words, because of the slow
recovery of the population.

The slow recovery stemmed from complexly interrelated factors. Mortality rates had not yet dropped and life expectancy had not yet increased.
Mortality among children and adults remained high, so that average life
expectancy was barely above thirty years. In spite of a large number of
miscarriages and stillbirths and of the many women who remained unmar-
ried, there was a small population surplus in the countryside due to
relatively high birthrates, which compensated for the decline in the cities.
The rate stabilized after the war at about 3 percent. There is no need to
assume that the number of children per family was ever exceptionally high.
The problem was not the birth itself but rearing and keeping children alive.
We know from non-German sources that a marriage begun when a woman
was twenty-five years old might last fifteen years and produce four to five
children, of whom only two might survive. The rates of growth must
remain low in this situation. Other factors also affected particular cases –
for instance, lower marital ages after the war and increased numbers of
marriages after new property divisions – and clearly the lengthy economic
depression did not stimulate enthusiasm for marriage.

Wherever the governments actively supported population growth
(*Peuplierung*), they encouraged immigration and improved agricultural and
industrial production. Historians have focused somewhat one-sidedly,
though not without justification, on the highly visible immigration policy.
Religious exiles and highly motivated specialists in particular industries
were among the most prominent to be accepted. From 1699 to 1707, for
instance, a small group of French Waldensians emigrated to Württemberg.
The approximately 150,000 immigrants from Bavaria, Austria, and the
Palatinate who settled in Franconia were even more significant. German
and Czech Protestants driven out of Bohemia found acceptance in the
Lausitz and Saxony, while French Huguenots, who were forced to leave
France after the Edict of Nantes was revoked in 1685, and exiles from

Salzburg found sanctuary in large numbers in the Mark Brandenburg and East Prussia. In 1725 supposedly one-fifth of the population in Brandenburg was comprised of immigrants. Berlin was significantly transformed at the end of the seventeenth century by the addition of 6,000 Huguenots. Huguenots also migrated by way of Switzerland to northern Hesse. Economic reasons predominated for Danes and Swedes who settled in northern Germany, for Mecklenburgers and Schleswig-Holsteiners who went to the northern parts of Brandenburg, and for the Swiss who came to reside in the Palatinate. Dutch workers were also brought to the Altmark and to Havelland to build canals and drain swamps.

In addition to the immigration into Germany, there was also an external migration to the east, southeast, and overseas. From 1689 onward the government in Vienna called for new settlement in Hungary and the Carpathians. This found some resonance, particularly among Catholics from the south and southwest, and after 1743 resettled Austrian Protestants also began to follow. The first German settlers to North America came from southwestern Germany. The wars of Louis XIV forced a massive emigration from the Palatinate; more than 13,000 inhabitants left in 1709 alone. Between 1727 and 1754 some 2,000 people per year found their way via England to North America. By 1750 the number of German settlers in the English colonies is estimated to have reached 100,000.

By the middle of the eighteenth century Germany's population began to increase more rapidly and to become more geographically mobile. In 1748 Brandenburg-Prussia had 3.5 million inhabitants. By 1770 its population had already increased to 4.2 million, and the increase, though uneven, was distributed among all the provinces. Overpopulation developed in areas where a real division of property prevailed, in Württemberg, Baden, and the Palatinate, and this forced emigration. Settlers and craftsmen from the Palatinate moved into the eastern areas of Prussia and into electoral Brandenburg, where a widespread migration of artisans to the cities took place. The so-called Swabian migrations intensified, especially into the Donau and Black Sea regions. Some 100,000 people were supposed to have migrated into Habsburg domains, some 25,000 into southern Russia. The number who migrated to North America also rose dramatically: 22,000 people from southwest Germany were among those in 1754.

Population in the cities retained a slightly negative balance throughout the seventeenth and eighteenth centuries. For this reason migration into the cities from the countryside was that much more important and was supported by the governments as a means to increase taxes, particularly when they were founding new cities or expanding or redesigning princely residential cities. None of the German cities, however, ever reached the size of the great European cities. Vienna was the only city at the end of the seventeenth century with a population larger than 100,000. Hamburg and Berlin had over 60,000 people, Strasbourg, Danzig, and Breslau over

40,000. Hamburg reached the 100,000 level only a century later; by that time Berlin had grown to 150,000. Cologne, on the other hand, had been the largest German city in the fifteenth century, but by 1800 had only 40,000 inhabitants.

By the end of our period the growth in population had already stretched the production of foodstuff to its limits, making it necessary to develop new productive relations in agriculture.

AGRICULTURE

Declining prices for agricultural products after the Thirty Years War, in the midst of almost firm prices for industrial goods and wages and even rising tax burdens, generated low property and lease values. At the end of the seventeenth century noble estates in Bavaria are thought to have had less than one-half – indeed sometimes only one-third or one-quarter – of their prewar value. Land remained abandoned for long periods. By 1708 only a quarter of the abandoned farmlands in the district of Stargard in Mecklenburg had been reoccupied. Labor was costly. Noble proprietors and peasants alike complained of the high wages and the difficulty in finding and keeping laborers and maids. Decrees generally accomplished very little, since they were too conservative and did not strike at the core of the problems. Normally they supported the lords, as in the temporary ban on executing convictions against indebtedness, for instance, and in preventing peasants bound to the land from leaving. In comparison, peasant burdens were never lowered by law. Thus the traditional agrarian system remained essentially unchanged. Migration and planned colonization also had almost no impact on the structure of rural society. Within such a social and institutional system it was indeed possible to bring about some improvement in organization and technology, but it was not possible to bring about fundamental changes in agricultural production.

At this point some general comments concerning the agrarian system are necessary, for even though there was a certain structural homogeneity in Germany, rural society had taken distinct forms in the various regions. A special variation on the manorial system, that of *Gutsherrschaft,* had emerged in the colonial areas of the east, including Mecklenburg and Pomerania. The peasantry had originally been granted better property rights in the course of its eastward colonization than prevailed in the older settled areas, but since those early days their condition had altered fundamentally. As the peasant population and the number of seigneurial families had declined from the late fourteenth century, the surviving seigneurs had consolidated their titles and legal rights and had incorporated the abandoned lands into relatively large estates. They gradually limited the mobility of the peasantry, and, with the addition of new settlers, they began from the mid-fifteenth century to secure the labor force necessary to transform their estates from self-sufficient units to ones producing for export. They were stimulated by the rapid population growth that generated an increasing demand for foodstuffs. From the sixteenth century, moreover, the seigneurs began to expropriate peasant lands directly in the notorious process called *Bauernlegen*. The effect of this system was mitigated to some extent, because the peasantry was given a certain amount of land for self-cultivation in exchange for its labor.

This form of the manorial system developed even further in the seventeenth century. A noble estate *(Rittergut)* or a central farm *(Vorwerk)* normally stood at the center of the system of *Gutsherrschaft,* and the domains were administered from there. Animal husbandry formed only a small part in a system where agricultural production dominated. Large herds of sheep were maintained only on land that was otherwise too poor to cultivate. It is remarkable that the value of peasant duties and obligations was greater than the value of the land, livestock, fish, wildlife, and so forth. The manorial system in eastern Germany, in other words, was essentially rooted in the legally required labor of the serfs who populated the estates. The range and extent of these obligations differed on the individual estates, but they were substantial.

In East Prussia the seigneurs had a prior right *(Vormieterecht)* to the services of every person on the estate, and this right could be sold to others. The smaller the number of peasants on an estate, the greater the burdens. The personal obligations may not have been experienced as oppressive in good years and when there was a large number of peasant families on the estate; but it was certainly experienced otherwise in terms of crisis and dearth and when the seigneur was strict and energetic. The peasantry was taxed on its yields in addition to its personal obligations. These taxes involved certain amounts of grain, a percentage of the livestock, interest payments, and direct taxes. Wilhelm Abel estimates the total burden on peasant property on the estates to have been one-third of the gross yield, without calculating their labor obligation. And Friedrich Wilhelm Henning has determined that peasant burdens on estates in the East Prussian coastal areas to have been far higher than those on other peasants, even those who had leaseholds on royal domains.

In spite of fluctuations, *Gutsherrschaft* was profitable. Profitability depended on the average quality of the soil, agricultural technology, and the skill to manage a labor force that was not yet organized into a pure wage labor system. Social factors, however, also functioned alongside the economic ones to perpetuate the system of *Gutsherrschaft,* for it was understood to be the basis for a particular aristocratic way of life and to express concrete forms of local rule. For the serfs on the estates the system provided protection in times of crisis, but far more fundamental was the seigneur's expropriation of peasant labor and a percentage of his yield. This manorial peasantry could never rise to a level of material well-being. Certain peasants, most prominently in East and West Prussia, indeed had more extensive personal and material rights. The *Kölmer,* for instance, had personal freedom and the right to inherit property. In economic terms, however, they did not play a significant role, because their estates were smaller and not cultivated intensively, and because they were forced to pay quite substantial taxes in money and kind. Otherwise in the period of economic stagnation after the Thirty Years War, the territorial rulers thought it to be in the interest of their own political expansion not to interfere in affairs on the estates. As a consequence, the seigneurs were given a free hand to bind the peasantry more tightly in real and personal terms and to increase labor services and taxes of various kinds. In Prussia it was only in 1740, and for fiscal reasons, that the expropriation of peasant lands, or *Bauernlegen,* was abolished.

The peasantry had better property rights in the older settled regions of Germany, where the seigneurs did not run their estates themselves but lived from rents and taxes. In the areas of northwestern Germany, where the *Meierrecht* prevailed, the territorial rulers had forbidden since the sixteenth century increases in rents and the expulsion of tenants, or *Meier.* In the seventeenth century, furthermore, estates were made indivisible. That secured a certain size for the estates, but it did not prevent those who did not inherit land from living as cottagers – referred to as *Kossätten* or *Einlieger,* among other terms – on large peasant farms, or from seeking work in the cities, or from traveling as seasonal migrant laborers to the Nether-lands *(Hollandgänger).* The greater degree of social stability in northwest Germany, however, did not mean that the agricultural economy was much better. Though rents on the land had to be lowered after the Thirty Years War, the taxes paid to the territorial rulers climbed and burdens on peasant properties were never reduced. Profits from the sale of harvest surpluses were largely absorbed by farming costs and taxes paid to the seigneur and territorial ruler. In addition to these payments, there were an unimaginably diverse number of fees and payments in kind and various service obliga-tions, resulting from seigneurial monopolies such as milling, brewing, and woodburning rights. The seigneur and the territorial ruler also often had a prior right to purchase peasant products.

The seigneurial system developed its own distinct pattern in other parts of Germany as well – in the south, southwest, center, and Bavaria. The gradual loosening of the personal ties between lord and serf and their transformation into real fees had become common to all of these variations since the late Middle Ages. Though property law differed somewhat in the individual regions, the farms generally had become hereditary; they were seen as family property and often remained for a long period in the hands of a particular family. On the whole, the real burdens were quite high, but they were fixed and could not be raised arbitrarily. When they were raised after a period of laxity, they brought with them an objective worsening of conditions.

Naturally the economic situation of the peasantry was determined by a variety of individual factors – property size, soil quality, yields, cultivation patterns, and farming techniques. Though often modified, the three-field system of cultivation still prevailed in large parts of Germany, whereby inaccessible or poorer fields were given less attention. In the course of the eighteenth century the number of cultivated crops increased. Vegetables, legumes, feed grains, and oil-producing and thread-bearing plants were especially encouraged near urban areas. Other systems prevailed in certain areas – multiple-field usage, single-field cultivation with intensive manuring, pasturage, and the intensive system of crop rotation known as *Koppelwirtschaft*. Altogether the portrait is a differentiated one. There was very intensive cultivation in the Rhine-Main area, on the Lower Rhine, and in parts of Thuringia, Saxony and Silesia with their especially good soils. Land was less intensely cultivated toward the east and in the Mittelgebirge. Grain prices remained low as a consequence of the long transportation distances. Livestock was also maintained in relatively low numbers; for that reason the yield of milk, wool, and meat was also quite low. Better conditions existed only in areas with good pasture lands and in areas close to large cities where the prices were good. Smaller cities often still maintained a large livestock population within the city walls. The notable improvement in the care of livestock over the course of the eighteenth century had not yet begun to eliminate the various diseases attacking them.

Important measures to improve the land were developed in these years. Among them belonged the acquisition of new land through improving and draining the soil, cultivating the moors, and building dikes. The most important improvements occurred in the domains of Brandenburg-Prussia, in the area between the Havel, Oder, and Prietzen, and in Bavaria in the Donau moor. Along with these measures there were also various private and even state supported efforts to clear and drain land, bring abandoned fields once again under cultivation, and regulate the cutting of peat and wood rights. The division of common lands in the village also served to utilize the soil better. The first steps toward the division of common lands, and with it the joining of fields, were begun by the peasantry and not by the territorial rulers. They demonstrated thereby a capacity for cooperative action at the village level before governmental decrees began to appear. Even in Brandenburg-Prussia such efforts began slowly at the governmental level, though they found increasing support from cameralists and other writers on agronomy.

Only at the territorial level was it possible to plan to settle colonists in already existing or newly established villages. By occupying abandoned or newly claimed land they expanded agricultural production. At the same time they also increased the number of taxpayers in the countryside, since the inducement of freedom from taxation was only good for a few years. In the east there was also further settlement in the form of large-scale agricultural enterprises. Here and there seigneurs began to shift from service to cash payments and thus to create a more cost-effective class of wage laborers. Pressure exerted at the territorial level combined with seigneurial and peasant self-interest to cause gradual improvements in crop rotation and methods of cultivation. Peasants began to plant fallow lands partially in clover, thus increasing the number of livestock and the quantity of manure. The cultivation of various root and feed crops became more widespread, and the potato was introduced, though it did not become widely cultivated until the second half of the eighteenth century. Better feed and breeding increased the stock of animals, especially of sheep who were needed for their wool. In the case of farm implements, however, there was as yet almost no improvement whatsoever.

The noticeable rise in the population made possible and forced these developments. Land under cultivation grew from 1648 to 1800 by 60 percent; yields per unit increased by about 20 percent, and this was largely due to changes in the method of cultivation. In spite of this growth, the general nutritional level of the population did not improve. It worsened in the later eighteenth century, in fact, because the supply of food was not able to keep step with population growth. Moreover, wages remained behind the rise in the cost of agricultural goods, so that the wage-price differential increased once again. This fact makes us aware of the limits of the new improvements. In spite of the many stimuli from administrators and the many new impulses from the cameralist and pedagogical literature of the period, the gap was not bridged. Indeed, the enormous interest in agriculture shown by clergy, officials, scholars, and princes, and the widespread founding of "economical" and "patriotic" societies in the last third of the eighteenth century were signs of a broader awareness of a problem still seeking solutions. It was recognized that an overwhelmingly agrarian society could only be mobilized by improving agricultural productivity, by modernizing the rural social system, and by improving the cultural and material lot of the rural population. As long as the feudal system continued to exist, however, it might be opened up somewhat by the policies of absolutist rulers, but there could be no fundamental change.

THE INDUSTRIAL ECONOMY AND TRADE

The number of people involved in industrial production had declined during the Thirty Years War, as had the demand for finished goods. The postwar recovery was retarded by the destruction of the means of production, by a shortage of fluid capital and willingness to reinvest, and by the decline of trade connections and the transportation network. In spite of this, by 1700 – and in certain cities much earlier – trade and industry had overcome both phases of depression and stagnation much sooner than agriculture. The guild organization of urban industry had been preserved; the same held true for the credit system. Both were able to support the recovery that began with slow increases in demand. Here, too, the governments intervened. They sought, in connection with their population policies, to create new work; and in order to increase revenues, they sought to expand production and exports. They preferred to support those products for which there was both a highly profitable domestic and export market. For this reason luxury goods seemed of special importance. Officials sought to woo especially skilled craftsmen to their states. Once there, they were settled only to a certain extent in the old cities and were often placed in new cities and villages. In not a few cases these areas of guild-free labor attracted a stream of laborers from the established cities.

Thus the industrial policies of the states were not meant primarily to serve the older crafts. Newer crafts began to produce for new needs – for instance, standing armies and the courts – and for the supraregional and overseas export markets. This production occurred largely outside the older guild structure. Highly profitable luxury goods, such as porcelain, tapestries, and silk, were often produced in residential cities or newly established sites such as manufactories. The governments often gave subventions to these ventures in the form of housing construction, tax immunities in the first years, and special sales privileges.

The guild system largely survived within the older urban crafts. The guilds tended to become restrictive in the face of economic stagnation and surplus labor. They limited the number of masters, excluded competition, and prevented entrepreneurial and technical innovations. Masters' positions became practically hereditary and the guilds closed corporations. Strikes and revolts by journeymen in a number of places led to the so-called Imperial Handicrafts Decree of 1731, one of the last imperial laws forbidding strikes, journeymen's associations, and collective wage demands. Simultaneously, however, the guilds were required to ease admission. Nonetheless, in spite of this decree, no uniform handicrafts policy emerged. The requirement of guild membership was eased occasionally, but usually the guild system was circumvented by favoring rural industry, the putting-out system, and the manufactories. In general even absolutist governments did not attempt to abolish the guilds outright, since they saw them as a useful instrument of control and still conceived of the industrial system in terms of the guild structure. Occasionally, rural industry continued to be organized into guilds, or a factory guild might be introduced, as in the case of the cloth manufactory in Pforzheim (1729). Eliminating the guilds in favor of free market competition was outside the limited economic possibilities of the period and was simply not seriously contemplated. The situation was somewhat different in Brandenburg-Prussia, because the state additionally restricted the mobility of handicrafts for fiscal reasons. In order to preserve the different tax structures between town and country, the state suppressed almost all rural industry outside the guild system. Nevertheless, the rural handicraft industry grew over the course of the eighteenth century. This was due not so much to growing demand but to the low levels of income of the expanding rural population, which forced a growing number of people to support themselves with secondary occupations or handloom weaving at home.

Domestic spinning and weaving continued to supply the personal needs of the rural population and even a part of the urban population. Over the course of the seventeenth and eighteenth centuries, in addition, a rural weaving population, one producing for the market outside the guild system, had begun to concentrate itself in areas of surplus population and inferior soils. Researchers have recently developed the term *protoindustry* to describe this new type of industrial production. This mode of textile production was not yet industrial in a modern sense, but was rather characterized by domestic labor and the family economy. Moreover, protoindustrialization did not always become a link to industrialization; there were, in fact, many examples of deindustrialization. In spite of these qualifications, the economic, social, and even reproductive behavior of the protoindustrial population distinguished itself markedly from the surrounding agrarian population. More than the latter, they were dependent on the movement of the local and international markets, and they developed other forms of cooperation and came to value work and their labor differently. Contractors or *Verleger,* the entrepreneurs who brought the raw materials to the weavers and collected the finished products, did not have the same function everywhere. They were far more significant in isolated areas where the small producers could not easily reach market themselves.

The factory organization of spinning was especially influenced by the bleaching manufactories, which often gathered their materials from great distances. Such was the case of the bleachers in Elberfeld and Barmen in the early eighteenth century who brought their goods primarily from Silesia. Even more important to the factory system were the weaving manufactories, particularly the linen cloth weaving manufactories, whose main centers lay in the middle eastern parts of Germany, especially in the Silesian Bergland, and also in eastern and northern Westphalia (most importantly Minden-Ravenberg), Hesse and the Lower Rhine, and Swabia. In Bielefeld and Osnabrück, and later in the eighteenth century in Silesia, quality was maintained by official state inspection sites called *Legge.*

The putting-out system in cotton, wool, and silk was more widespread than either the spinning or weaving manufactories. The main centers for cotton manufacturing in the eighteenth century ranged from Swabia to Saxony. The raw material was imported from the Balkans, the Levant, and the West Indies. Wool and silk weaving occurred predominantly in the cities of middle and eastern Germany, but in the Rhineland, for instance, it occurred in the countryside near cities such as Aachen and Mondschau. Stocking production was centered in Thuringia, silk weaving in Krefeld, Berlin, and Vienna. The concentration of production or parts of the production process into so-called manufactories occurred at the earliest in the latter areas. The putting-out system was also the organizational form of other export industries: the small-scale ironworking industry in the Bergland and the Sauerland, the small arms producers in Thuringia, and the glass producers throughout Germany. There were also unique forms of production, such as among the middlemen in Nuremberg or the tailors' guilds in Brandenburg-Prussia who produced uniforms in the garrison cities by collectively buying the unfinished cloth and selling the finished goods.

The putting-out system was an early capitalist form of organizing domestic production. Merchants entered into contract with small producers. Although production remained basically decentralized, the merchant entrepreneurs centralized other areas of the process, such as the purchase of raw materials, cloth finishing (bleaching and dyeing), the distribution and sale of the finished goods. This pattern emerged from the necessity to supply growing and distant markets. Since the late Middle Ages, locally focused production methods of the urban handicrafts had already become inadequate to gauge the development of demand in extensive regions and to master the logistical problems of transporting large quantities of goods over great distances. Merchant entrepreneurs well provided with capital entered the economy at this point. They guaranteed loans against an obligation to receive the finished goods for sale and to repay the loan with a portion of the finished goods as payment in kind. In certain cases they hired craftsworkers themselves, purchased materials and occasionally also tools and machinery, such as the weaving looms, and received the finished wares at a fixed price. In other cases they stayed aloof from the production process itself, only taking the finished goods for further sale and charging a fee in cash or goods for the service. The entrepreneurs (*Verleger*) rarely constructed separate buildings; normally the producers worked in their own homes with their own tools. The so-called guild purchases, or *Zunftkauf*, occurring among linen producers, was also part of the putting-out system. In this system the entrepreneur contracted for deliveries with the guilds themselves. The system left relatively great freedom to the producers but guaranteed both that the finished products would be sold and that the guilds and magistrates would be able to control prices. The putting-out system was not exploitative in and of itself, but it could become so, especially when prices fell and the finished goods could not be sold.

The putting-out system is important because it made production for distant markets possible in isolated regions, and in many cases it preserved artisanal groups from ruin for some time. From the perspective of the entrepreneur, mercantile and industrial gains were possible that, when sustained, became important for the beginnings of industrialization. An aggregate calculation from the end of the eighteenth century indicates the significance of production in the putting-out system in terms of total industrial production: It was 43.1 percent, only slightly behind the 49.9 percent in handicrafts. Textile production accounted for 41 percent of the total industrial production. Mining, metalwork, forestry, and paper production played a very small role in comparison. Building and food production were exclusively handicrafts. The figure of 7 percent for goods produced in manufactories was astonishingly low, and most of these goods belonged to textile and other clothing industries.

Manufactories, although very few in number in the seventeenth century, increased in the eighteenth century. In form, they were centralized industrial production sites in which the labor process remained artisanal and unmechanized. They emerged especially when new production processes, such as silk production, were introduced. For instance, 2,800 people were employed at the Leyen silk manufactory in Krefeld in 1763. Manufactories were also built for producing luxury goods - porcelain, carpets - and for producing large quantities of cloth. The division of labor was soon introduced, so that skilled and unskilled, women and children could find work. The inmates of orphanages, workhouses, prisons, and asylums as well as beggars and vagabonds were often put to work in the manufactories as cheap, if especially poor, labor. The finished goods were often of such low quality that some manufactories failed. Other reasons for the difficulties and short life of many manufactories derived from poor calculation of the potential market, insufficient financial backing, and the inadequate business and technical skills of the entrepreneurs, among whom were a number of charlatans.

Certain manufactories were founded by territorial rulers, but the majority were private enterprises with state subventions. The expected profits often did not materialize. The more successful textile manufactories were organized in combination with the putting-out system as "decentralized manufactories," as was the Leyen silk manufactory. The famous "Calwer Zeughandlungskompagnie," founded in 1650, also was a decentralized enterprise. In 1787 this society of dyers and buyers gave employment to 933 woolen goods producers and 3,000–4,000 spinners and combers, though only 168 employees worked in manufactory buildings themselves. This significant Augsburg textile firm used centralized processes for only certain phases of production (bleaching, dyeing, pressing, and finishing), while the rest took place in the cottages of the workers.

The largest manufactory in the second half of the eighteenth century was most likely the Linz Wollzeugmanufaktur, which employed in 1786 over 1,000 master weavers and almost 4,000 journeymen, apprentices, and other helpers. In addition to them were approximately 30,000 spinners – most of whom lived in Bohemia – wool workers, combers, and 100 dyers and cloth finishers. This enterprise, originally in private hands, was taken over by the state in 1754. Berlin was another center of textile manufactories where private and state enterprises stood side by side. The Berlin *Lagerhaus* or Warehouse – founded in 1713 for the production of uniforms – and the Berlin manufactory for the production of gold and silver textiles were both leased out after the state had assumed ownership.

Until our own day, the name manufactory has stayed attached to porcelain manufactories. The first European porcelain manufactory was established in 1710 by the state in Meissen; other manufactories followed afterward in Vienna, Höchst, Nymphenburg, Fürstenberg, Frankenthal, and Berlin. Tobacco production was also organized in manufactories, as was sugar, and even certain breweries were organized on a large scale, as in Donaueschingen.

It is difficult to come to general conclusions regarding the success and profitability of the manufactories. Some private enterprises were apparently very successful, such as the textile firms of Schüle in Augsburg, von der Leyen in Krefeld, and the tobacco firm of Bolangro in Frankfurt. Others were notable failures. Profit margins were tighter than in the wholesale trade or in the putting-out system. The state supplied only a limited amount of the required capital. Private investors were already organizing banking houses, though stock companies only first emerged in the last third of the eighteenth century. If manufactories are still considered to be particularly interesting phenomena in spite of their small share of the total economy, it is because they were innovative in organizational form and because high expectations came with them. They were the predecessors of factorylike industrial production and labor relations to the extent that they emancipated the work process from the context of the home and transformed the laborer into a wage earner who neither owned his or her own tools nor stood within the context of seigneur or guild. The wage structure within the manufactories also anticipated the later factory system, for a relatively small middle group and a large number of badly paid unskilled workers worked alongside highly paid specialists. Women and children were even more poorly paid, and beneath them were inmates from institutions.

The manufactories and the densely concentrated rural industry produced for trade. After the Thirty Years War, foreign trade had recovered only in fits and starts, but by the eighteenth century it was vigorous once again, even though mercantilist economic policy continued to hinder expansion because of its commitment to territorialism and autarchy. Still population growth and the need for raw materials and equipment led the way to international markets; low grain prices and wages forced rural laborers to weave in order to survive, which made the German textile industry quite competitive. Leipzig, with its fairs, was the most significant trade center for eastern Europe. Hamburg was the center for overseas trade because of its links to the Elbe river traffic and its ties to the Oder by way of the Brandenburg canal system. This trade was especially directed toward England, Spain, and France. Hamburg also engaged in whaling and fishing. Bremen and the ports in the Netherlands played a significant role in the export of finished goods as well. They exported linen and agricultural products and, among other products, imported tobacco and sugar. In the middle of the eighteenth century Emden was a center for fishing and trade with Asia. Commerce in the Baltic was dominated by the grain trade. In the 1720s and 1730s Prussian merchants led the Russian trading company, exporting textiles from Stettin. Lübeck never regained its earlier eminence as a trading center, but it remained a significant port for the transit trade with the Baltic regions. The other cities on the Baltic – Rostock, Swedish Stralsund, Pillau, Königsberg, Memel – were only of limited significance. They exported grain, wood, and flax, but imports were of much greater value.

Trading companies dominated maritime trade, but in comparison to the Dutch, for instance, the volume remained small. And the attempt by the Elector of Brandenburg, Friedrich Wilhelm, to found overseas sites remained only an episode. The Brandenburg-African Trading Company, a German enterprise founded by a Dutch shipper in Pillau (1682/83) and moved in 1684 to Emden, built Fort Grossfriedrichsburg on the west African Gold Coast, but already by 1720 it had to be sold to the Dutch. Similarly, British and Dutch pressure forced the Imperial-Royal Company of India in Ostende (Kaiserliche-Königliche Indienkompagnie) to abandon its factories at the mouth of the Ganges, near Madras, and in Canton after only a few years. Germans proved incapable of economic or political penetration into the maritime trade or colonial rule of the great powers. Nor were they successful in creating their own independent spheres. Germany, consequently, remained an area that was predominantly centered on inland trade, taking part in world trade for all practical purposes only indirectly.

Regional trade inland occurred without traders, insofar as it was concerned with supplying food to the cities and selling the products of the local artisanate. Gradually, the percentage of self-sufficient trade declined and the number of small traders ("hucksters" and "materialists") increased as the need grew for special foodstuffs and luxuries, for small retail goods and ironware. The number of traders roaming the countryside also climbed. It was not especially for them but for the long-distance carrying trade and for travel that improved communications came to be of greater significance. Rivers and canals were essentially the only inexpensive means of transporting goods in quantity. In the seventeenth and eighteenth centuries small ships plied many rivers, even if only at the high-water mark, on which traffic has long since ceased. Canal construction, based on French models, began to increase in the late seventeenth century. The expanding network of canals greatly improved industry, especially in the Mark Brandenburg. Berlin was thereby made into an important industrial and trade center, simultaneously securing its future provisioning. The Elbe, Oder, and Weichsel rivers were also linked, and Bohemia and Silesia were joined to the coasts. The network of roads, on the other hand, continued to be neglected throughout Germany. An exception to this was the industrial area of southern and western Germany where highway construction began on a small but fairly intensive scale.

The generally terrible state of the communications network throughout Germany prevented the development of a unified market. So, too, did the disunified coinage system and the innumerable customs barriers, which states used to engage in economic warfare during periods of political tension. The different economic regions, as a consequence, could not achieve a sufficient balance and retained differing wage and price levels. It was only a limited advantage that improvements and market crises were often experienced only on a regional level. Entrepôts, counting houses, and fairs grew in importance with the increase in trade. Leipzig and Frankfurt am Main were the most significant trade centers, but other cities were significant. Mainz, for instance, was the most important entrepôt and center for the transit trade on the Rhine, Frankfurt an der Oder possessed exclusive shipping rights for the Oder, and Hannoversch-Münden controlled the Weser. The teamster's occupation became increasingly lucrative with the growing overland freight business. Certain mercantile families also began to scatter themselves among the various German territories and create branches, so that a network of personal connections and interests began to emerge.

England's, and especially London's, dominance in monetary matters became quite noticeable, particularly from the beginning of the eighteenth century. Interest in banking also grew in Germany, however, especially because banks began to be recognized as the best instrument for covering loans and supplying capital to states and private enterprises. The bank note system, however, did not easily recover from the horrifying example of the failure in France of John Law's Banque Générale. Still, public banks of deposit and exchange and private banks did gradually emerge. The banking system expanded beyond banks of issue to include credit institutions for agriculture and lending houses, *Hilfskassen,* for the lower orders only in the last third of the eighteenth century. The insurance system also began in these years in Germany. Frankfurt was the most important among banking cities. In southern Germany, Vienna began to dominate, though Augsburg still was able to maintain itself in the first half of the century. Other important banking centers in the north were Berlin, Hamburg, Cologne, Leipzig, Breslau, and Kassel. The banking houses not only took part in trade and industry, but they also lent to governments, acted as middlemen in loans, and earned money in times of war.

The Jewish court factors were a special phenomenon. They were a small group of families, specially protected by the territorial rulers, who were irreplaceable in the age of absolutism, because they ran the finances of the greater dynasties and their courts. Of these, Samuel Oppenheimer and Samson Wertheimer operated in Vienna, Süss Oppenheimer in Württemberg, Veitel Heine Ephraim and Daniel Itzig in Berlin, and the Rothschilds in Frankfurt. They often made exorbitant profits but took high risks. The fate of "Jud Süss" (he was hanged), however, should not be seen as characteristic, merely as symptomatic. An impression of the financial power of the court factors can be gained from the fact that the Jew in charge of the Prussian mint expended almost 29 million talers over the course of the Seven Years War.

It is still not possible to arrive at trustworthy and useful figures for the growth of the aggregate German economy during the old regime. In general, we can conclude that labor was no longer a problem in the eighteenth century and the capital was increasingly available or could be borrowed – albeit at high rates – from investors in the Netherlands. In spite of this improvement, income levels and demand for goods were comparatively very low. In this context a significant sector of private enterprise developed only slowly, making itself felt in economic terms for the first time at the end of the century, while as a dynamic social element it simply did not yet exist.

MERCANTILISM

The measures of German governments to direct and encourage economic development during the second half of the seventeenth century and throughout the eighteenth had a considerable significance, even if many handbooks and general accounts tend to emphasize those measures too one-sidedly. In judging these policies we must once again weigh the political and psychological consequences alongside the economic ones. Even as government planned and sometimes acted as entrepreneur, it continuously functioned as guardian, orienting all behavior in terms of reasons of state and thus accustoming its people to government support and economic control for fiscal reasons. The question, of course, is whether private and communal initiative was thereby stifled. In any case, a vigorous entrepreneurial spirit did develop in regions with little or no "mercantilist" intervention. The clearest examples are the duchy of Berg, parts of Saxony, the large port cities, and the trading cities that were essentially under self-rule.

Mercantilism was not only state economic policy, but also a theory of state economic administration. Its object was to improve the economic infrastructure in the service of higher state revenues. The most significant administrative measures involved increasing population size, industrial production, and exports. Mercantilist policy also sought to keep money within the borders of the state by creating export surpluses and a positive balance of payments. It was impossible to develop such a coherent policy for the entire landmass of the empire, especially one that would be approved by the imperial cities. The imperial diet attempted without success to reduce customs barriers and especially to throttle French imports. Successful mercantilist policies developed only in the individual territories, revealing certain characteristics that have allowed scholars to speak of "cameralism" as a particular German form of mercantilism.

Cameralism placed the administration of the princely estate at its center. The goal was to increase both the revenues of the chamber of accounts, or *Rechenkammer,* from the princely properties and the legal rights of the territorial prince. A comprehensive administrative theory began to be articulated at the universities for that purpose. In 1727 Friedrich Wilhelm I of Prussia founded the first two chairs of cameral studies at the universities of Halle and Frankfurt an der Oder. Comprehensive textbooks and handbooks began to handle the pertinent areas systematically, gradually treating the state as a whole. By the last third of the century a large number of cameralist journals also had been founded.

The beginnings of cameralism, however, reach much farther back into the late seventeenth century. While in the service of the Habsburgs, Johann Joachim Becher, Philipp Wilhelm von Hörnigk, and Wilhelm von Schröder had already developed certain fundamental concepts: that the state was an economic association within a corporatively structured society, that population must be increased and industrial development supported, and that the goal of the state was the common welfare and the happiness of its population. Johann Gottlob Justi was the most significant later representative of cameralism. The son of a Thuringian pastor, Justi became a professor of German rhetoric and cameralism in 1750 at the Viennese boarding school for aristocratic children, the *Ritterakadamie* "Therasianum." In 1757 he moved to Copenhagen as a colonial inspector, and in 1762 was appointed the Prussian chief inspector of mining. His two major works, *Staatswissenschaft oder systematische Abhandlung aller ökonomischen und Kameralwissenschaften (Science of the State or Systematic Treatment of All Economic and Cameral Sciences)* (1755) and *Grundsätze der Policeywissenschaft (Principles of Administrative Science)* (1756), treated the entire administration of the state. In these works Justi joined together fundamental Lutheran and Enlightenment notions; he viewed the purpose of the state to be the general happiness of the population and enjoined both the ruler and the ruled to work toward this end. Administration – in the language of the day, the "police" – had the task of reconciling the well-being of the individual with that of the whole by encouraging and directing the economic activity of everyone. In particular, administrators were directed to encourage population growth and to develop manufactories, but they were also to allow trade to develop as freely as possible and independently of state control.

If cameralism emphasized population growth more than did western European mercantilism, this was still due in part to the continuing effect of the losses in the Thirty Years War. In addition, however, cameralism had an essential inland and fiscalist orientation. It neglected foreign trade in its search to improve the standard of living, favoring instead increased labor by the individual and expanded intervention by the state. Cameralism, accordingly, placed great emphasis on improving agriculture and protecting the peasantry, because these agricultural states could not expand without increasing the taxing capacity and resistance of the rural population. Precisely in agricultural policy, however, cameralism proved basically unable to have an effect outside the private princely domains. In the area of industrial policy, on the other hand, cameralist policy was often able to eliminate production barriers created by the guilds, expand the putting-out system, and encourage the building of manufactories. In his political will of 1722 Friedrich Wilhelm I of Prussia instructed his "dear successor:"

Ergo Manufacturen im lande ein recht Bergwerck geheissen werden kan und ein rechtes gerum gerendehrum ist und die Wohlfahrt unsere[r] lender, den[n] ein landt sonder Manufactuhren ist ein Menschlicher Körper sonder lehben ergo totes landt das bestendigst Power und elendig ist und nicht zum flohr sein dage nicht gellangen kahn. (Therefore manufactories can be called a true source of treasure and a real source of life and the well-being of our territories, because a land without manufactories is like a body without life: Therefore a dead land that is constantly poor and suffering and will never be able to flourish in the fullness of its days.)

For that reason he commanded that manufactories were to be maintained and increased; furthermore, woolen goods were not to be imported, and inhabitants were only to be allowed to wear clothing domestically produced. And he mentioned other protectionist measures such as bans on imports, protective tariffs, bans on the export of raw materials, controls on quality, forced labor, and labor training.

The portrait left to us in the documents of cameralist administrators must be scrutinized for its practical consequences, because intent and result, investment and success often stood crassly opposed to each other. The economic and social costs of these policies were substantial. The striving to create a unified, integrated state economy was never realized anywhere. Corporate society could not be transformed into an economic society. But it is also true that this statist economic policy, with regional variation, did provide impulses toward modernizing economic life. Finally, mercantilist-cameralist policies were most effective in Brandenburg-Prussia, where economic development could be placed in the service of state expansion, militarism, and the social disciplining of the population. In this context such policies were also able to prepare the transition to industrialization.

2

SOCIETY

PRELIMINARY REMARKS:
ENCRUSTATION AND DYNAMIC ELEMENTS

The return to population growth, the recovery of agriculture and industry, the reconstruction of destroyed cities, the rebuilding and expansion of trade – though begun haltingly and unevenly, these represented a considerable achievement after the Thirty Years War on the part of peasant and lord, artisan and entrepreneur, magistrate and state. The achievement seems all the greater since the postwar period was in no way a time of lasting peace. The European wars of the century after 1648 no longer took place predominantly on German soil, but they did periodically reach deep into imperial territory, particularly those conflicts between France and the Habsburgs. The Palatinate was systematically laid to waste in one of those encounters during the 1690s. Other obstacles to sustained recovery and long-term socioeconomic development derived from the increased territorialization of the empire. Economic policies and recovery programs ended strictly at the borders of the particular states and were primarily fiscal in orientation. Active governments especially sought to discipline their subjects. If the motives were often benevolent and strengthened by the religious belief that humankind should be maintained within a rigid order and raised to a life of industry and work, these policies also eventually stifled individual, corporate, and local independence and accustomed society to administrative control. Even more important, the war had caused immeasurable change in the structure of the population and the patterns of property holding. These, in turn, caused social relations after the war to rigidify more than ever before. In addition, governments, aided by the long postwar period of material scarcity, sought to expand their own administrative freedom, intensify the level of exploitation, and cement the existing social system.

The encrustation of social relations in the seventeenth and eighteenth centuries was not a specifically German phenomenon; but it acquired a greater significance in Germany because of the political narrowness and economic weakness. These relations were anything but idyllic. The jealous monitoring of social differences, the emphasis placed on privilege and distance, the dense system of social controls operating in city and village – these conditions encouraged a hard, unsentimental behavioral realism and bred a high level of conformity. The narrow base of the food supply and limited economic mobility forced all people to remain within their "estate" or order, eliminate others from acquiring the same rights and privileges, and prevent as much competition and change as humanly possible. Every individual was forced to defend his or her estate and reputation, indeed to emphasize it constantly in dress, public appearances, and associations. This trait, so typical for the entire society, impressed a powerful streak of conventionality on life and made it almost impossible for social change to emerge. Servility – actual or apparent humility of the lower toward their "betters," the emphasis on the social distance of "inferiors" – was stamped deeply on the general habits and thoughts of the population. Particular anxieties existed among the various groups of commoners, in addition, concerning a loss of status due to false behavior. Connections and favors meant a great deal. Offices in the cities and seats in the church were treated as familial property; officeholders in city and countryside paid fastidious attention to the public recognition of their functions. Much more severe than the distinction between rich and poor – the rural gentry or *Landjunker* were often quite poor – was the distance between masters and dependents, noble and nonnoble, magistrates' families, and those ineligible for council elections. Master artisans held onto their privileges and prevented others from acquiring them even when they no longer had apprentices. Estatist and guild values also prevailed among jurists, scholars, and pastors.

Such attitudes were as apparent to foreign observers as the innumerable customs barriers and the large and small courts, whose pomp and display often stood in crass contrast to the size of their lands. Travelers often pointed out old and new traces of decline: the miserable condition of the roads and inns, the meager number of fields under cultivation, the provinciality of the cities, the penuriousness of the homes of the nobility, the crudity and low level of education among all orders. Certainly such travel accounts must be read with critical reserve, since they often express preformed views. In this case, however, such judgments are sustained in other sources.

If, by way of contrast, we look for those dynamic elements in German society that stimulated development, we must first eliminate the notion of a "rising" bourgeoisie or *Bürgertum*. It is not meaningful to speak of *the* bourgeoisie as a class or estate or to view it as a clearly definable part of the social system; nor can we assert that it rose as a collectivity and that its social significance increased. It is much more important to name those particular groups within the middle orders of society whose role and significance increased.

In the second half of the seventeenth century, only remnants survived from the economically and culturally potent burgher class that had shaped German industrial and trading cities in the sixteenth century. François Dreyfus has judged the "quasi-disappearance...of a true bourgeoisie" to be as profound a consequence of the war as the attendant suffering of the lower orders. A bourgeoisie – that is, an economically dynamic burgher class of both supraregional and political significance – did not reappear in Germany until far into the nineteenth century. The middling and lower elements of the burgher classes, the small merchants and artisans with their conservative and provincial mentality, remained the dominant and characteristic feature of German society. The employees and officials from the middle social orders who served the territorial rulers, the churches, and the large lords had different expectations, because they, and especially their own educated élite, constituted the most upwardly mobile group in this society. The entrepreneurs were also among the most dynamic of elements in this society, though they still functioned as individuals and not yet as a group. The ruling aristocracy and parts of the landed nobility were not themselves socially dynamic, but they helped to mobilize cultural resources. We must appreciate this fact, for if we view the nobility simply as a possessive, self-absorbed, and wasteful order, we will not be able to understand its lengthy domination in Germany. If the nobility exercised its domination in the most diverse manner, it also supplied the territorial rulers with officers, officials, councillors, and ministers of state. If the nobility thereby pursued its own interests and preserved its own privileged place, its participation also prevented it from a growing loss of function.

PRINCES AND COURTS

Absolutism – more precisely, absolute monarchy – was not simply a system of rule, but it also oriented social life from above around the ruling princes, the dynasty, and the court by forcing, more or less successfully, the entire set of courtly values upon society as a whole. For that reason it is appropriate to begin the analysis of the social system "from above." A societal network, furthermore, is not merely to be understood in quantitative terms; rather it is a qualitatively structured system, one linked by function and effect and shaped by economic and cultural factors such as property, law, political tasks, education and prestige, social habit, and power. The social system confronting us was hierarchically ordered and authoritarian far into its core. Economic, political, and cultural power was so divided that we have a greater chance of capturing reality by beginning our observations with the rulers and not "from below."

After the Peace of Westphalia the German Empire consisted of more than 250 princely territories who were represented at the imperial diet. Below them were those imperial earldoms and abbies who were only represented within a curia or college. In addition to these were the imperial knights and their innumerable territories, who attempted to maintain miniature courts when they had the wealth, even though they did not have princely status. Matters differed with respect to the ecclesiastical states. Because rule was not hereditary, the rulers were chosen by the cathedral chapters. For this reason, ruling dynasties did not exist in a legal sense; in official terms, this meant there could be no family in line to inherit, no intrigue surrounding secondary lines, no female subcourt. In practice, however, an episcopal see or an abbacy was often a matter of dynastic politics. Whenever members from the families of imperial counts or knights actually became bishops, they acquired familial ambitions, seeking to name family members as their successors or to find them lucrative clerical sinecures. Among the most successful of such families were the Franconian Schönborns, who repeatedly are found on the episcopal lists of Würzburg, Bamberg, and Speyer. Similarly, the familial also made itself felt at the ecclesiastical courts. Women were present as well. Indeed they were often no less influential there than at a secular court. Not every imperial princedom had a real court, since a number of these often came to belong to a single dynasty. In the same way, not every ecclesiastical state had a court, because, although it was not permitted in canon law, it was possible with a papal dispensation for a single individual to accumulate a number of episcopal sees. On the other hand, larger states often had a number of courts. Sometimes, for example, members within the ruling families were given their own courts to maintain; in other cases, such as that of the Austrian governor in the Netherlands, the office required that a court be maintained. A ruler who held another territory in personal union and resided mainly outside the empire – for instance, the electoral prince of Saxony in Warsaw and the electoral prince of Hanover in London – continued to maintain a nominal court at the principal residence of his native land.

Courts were distributed very unevenly throughout the empire. Large territorial states predominated in the east, northeast, and southeast; parcelization prevailed in the southwest, west, and parts of middle Germany. Worldly and ecclesiastical courts flooded Swabia, Franconia, the area of the Lower and Upper Rhine, and parts of Hesse and Thuringia. An enormous distance in political significance, wealth, and sophistication separated the imperial court in Vienna from that in Dessau, the court of the archbishop and electoral chancellor in Mainz from that of the princely Probst in Ellwagen. Including the central administration, 2,175 people were attached to the court of Emperor Charles VI (1711-40); 1,429 people in the year 1747 were at the court of electoral prince Max' III.Joseph of Bavaria (1745-77); on the other hand, only 260 individuals lived at the court of the prince bishop of Würzburg in the same year. As a last example, approximately 700 people belonged to the electoral princely court in Mannheim in the year 1723.

The size of the courts and levels of display were not primarily dependent upon the rulers themselves. The courts were political instruments, measures of the significance and reputation of the individual states. Display was therefore a form of duty, which, of course, was perceived very differently by different rulers. The difference is striking between the court of the first Prussian king Friedrich I (1701-12), that of his niggardly son Friedrich Wilhelm I (1712-40), and that of his grandson Friedrich II (1740-86), particularly in his misanthropic later years. In their differing conceptions we can see the integrating function of the court being replaced by the growing personal prestige of the monarch, his army, and administration.

There was a basic pattern to the order and composition of the court that was expanded or reduced in the individual case. At the apex were the highest court positions deriving from the traditional hereditary offices. The Protestant courts, in addition, had the office of court minister, while the Catholic courts had that of court confessor. The courts also had personal physicians, a court conductor, court theater director, court chamberlains, court master of the horse, court master of the hunt, court gardener, subordinant officeholders to the aforementioned, and finally officers of the personal bodyguard and castle guard. Added to these were court artists, architects, historiographers, gentlemen in waiting, and pages. The ruling princes, their wives, princes, and princesses each had his or her own small court with court ladies, teachers, instructors, and tutors. At any one time there were often also a substantial number of individuals with honorary titles and offices residing at court – chamberlains, pages, officers, ladies in waiting – and regular visitors who held central offices of state or military commands. Finally, there were all the necessary servants who took care of personal needs, managed the daily household, and oversaw the other personnel. Except for the merely honorary title holders, who were themselves available for material demonstrations of favor, they all received remuneration in some form and were largely cared for at court. On the other hand, the higher officeholders were often required to spend significant amounts for display. The courts were thus substantial economic factors in terms of financial need and expenditure. Trade and industry, especially in the residential cities, profitted from courts. This point was understood by mercantilist writers and by those entrepreneurs who established manufactories for the production of luxury goods, sometimes unfortunately with disappointed hopes of large profits. In general, the courts drew the landed nobility to them, but the nobility also began independently to move to the centers of power, prestige, and taste, often building their homes in the residential cities.

The general social inclination to be jealously attentive of rank and estate intensified itself at the courts. The striving for offices and honors, the concern to draw the prince's attention to oneself, the dependency of the courtiers on the ruler's moods and goodwill, the habit of intrigue, and acceptance of servile attitudes especially among the socially mobile – all these were daily features of court life. At court foreigners, artists, "project makers," mistresses, and minions could thrive and be raised into the nobility, but they could also fall into disgrace and be overthrown. Noble families could be ruined economically, and burgher families could be corrupted. The special genre of burgher tragedy from the late eighteenth century known as *Trauerspiel* most certainly exaggerated life at court, but we must appreciate these plays as reflecting both general opinion and the experiences of burghers at court, who had excruciating feelings of dependency and disregard.

Courts must be understood as special social systems, as instruments for the exercise of power, and as their own worlds. The ruling prince was at the center; at least some part of the court followed him whenever he traveled or vacationed at one of his hunting or pleasure palaces. The court ceremonies served simultaneously to represent and to discipline; they indicated one's place and function, regulated behavior, and both coerced and preoccupied. The strict Spanish ceremony at the Viennese court during the reign of Charles VI was meant to represent the imperial dignity, its universality, and its Roman Catholicity. The highly rationalized Versailles style of Louis XIV was more imitated in Germany, however, even though the material presuppositions and the ceremonial talents and energies of the sun king were largely lacking.

Courtly ceremonials extended the social distance to the population. The way of life, attitudes, cultural pretension, and language of the court belonged to another world than that of its subjects. This point was even truer for public acts of representation – military reviews, the hunt, festivals, concerts, and theater. We must not conclude, however, that the populace was as offended by these acts as they later came to be. The court was the most complete confirmation of the *theatrum mundi,* that notion brought forth in German baroque literature to answer the question of the meaning of human existence. The court was an elevated stage, on which only a few men were privileged to act and risk stumbling. If princes ruled by the grace of God, thereby representing godly force and order, the court was a model of that order. As this view dissipated, the idea survived that the court was the "wide world" and the courtier the "man of the world," who, as Johann Rist wrote in 1663, was the complete being the rest of the population could never be. But in the conditions of Germany the "world" was simultaneously socially exclusive and culturally distant from popular life. Italian opera flowered at the courts; with it came Italian singers and musicians. The courts increasingly spoke French and dressed à la mode. Foreign architects or local architects and artists educated abroad were hired to build princely palaces and decorate the residences. Italian and French influence came to dominate with the construction of Dresden, one of the most artistically significant residential cities in Germany in the early eighteenth century. Versailles had an effect on Potsdam, and the highly stylized, geometrically constructed French garden was much imitated, since it created an artificially separate space for courtly-aristocratic life in the open air.

This courtly world devoured enormous sums that can only be calculated in terms of the total income and expenditures of the individual states. In making such calculations, we must keep in mind that proper budgets did not yet exist. Still, next to military and administrative expenditures, and next to the often high cost of servicing debts, the greatest costs (with significant variations) were normally incurred in maintaining the court. It was, for example, exceptional for Germany, although characteristic for Brandenburg-Prussia, that it spent 80 percent of its regular income in 1740-1 for military purposes. More typical was the electoral Palatine court that consumed half of all income in 1719. The Hanoverian court under Ernst August used a similar percentage of all cameral sources. In any case, this corporate society of orders with courtly head skimmed off a substantial portion of the economic surplus for conspicuous consumption. Yet it is inappropriate to view this consumption simply as waste, because it was imbedded in the entire social and political system. Beyond individual whim and specific group interest, it served political purposes, most prominently the display of power. Christian Wolff wrote in 1740:

If his subjects are to recognize the majesty of the king, they must recognize that he possesses the highest authority and power. And for that purpose it is necessary that a king and sovereign (*Landes-Herr*) so constitute his court, that it occasion a recognition of his power and authority....For example,...since each should eat and drink according to his estate, [since] each should dress and live according to it, so should a king and sovereign eat and drink according to his majesty, and so dress and live. And the royal table must be set in such a manner that it surpass all others in the number and rareness of the dishes, the royal dress all other clothes in its splendor, the palace in which he lives all other buildings in its size and beauty.

The royal palace represented the nucleus of monarchical power exactly in this spirit. Palace construction in Germany, which reached a quantitative peak approximately between 1710 and 1730, manifested itself as a form of intensified monarchical self-consciousness, as in Vienna after the Turkish Wars, or as a claim to political significance, as in the Berlin of the Great Elector constructed by Andreas Schlüter.

In terms of imperial law, all ruling princes possessed common sovereignty in their territories, or *Landesherrschaft,* and status as members of the empire, or *Reichsstandschaft.* In principal, they were equal by birth but not socially equal. The distance in rank and wealth between the Habsburgs and the princes of Oettingen-Wallerstein was enormous! But, in practice, it could be narrowed through an advantageously constructed network of relatives. Indeed, both the network of relations and a careful marriage policy must be given a place of enormous political significance within the system of hereditary monarchy. It is no wonder that illegitimate and secondary ties were entered into and accepted at court, leading often to the legitimation of mistresses and their children and their elevation into the nobility. What might occur due to fate or an accident of inheritance is revealed by the accession of the house of Braunschweig-Lüneburg to the English throne (1714). Both the Habsburgs and the Wittelsbachs made successful claims to the Spanish inheritance. The Wittelsbach house of Pfalz-Zwiebrücken produced Swedish kings from 1654-1718, and after them a prince followed from the house of Hesse-Kassel. In 1762 the house of Holstein-Gottorp succeeded to the Russian crown. German princesses married into foreign ruling houses, the most successful being the Habsburg archduchesses. With its large number of ruling houses from the old peerage, Germany, in fact, presented an almost inexhaustible supply of nobility for the construction of dynastic ties. National differences played no role, since aristocratic society as a whole, and the special ruling families of Europe, was supernational in composition. Even confessional differences could be bridged.

There was no dominant type of prince, but there were a few characteristic types. In the second half of the seventeenth century until the beginning of the eighteenth, there was the figure of the baroque ruler, as represented in the persons of the Habsburg Leopold I (1651-1705) or Charles VI, the Wittelsbach Max Emmanuel (1679-1726), the Hohenzollern Friedrich Wilhelm (1640-88), the Wettine August the Strong (1694-1733), and the prince bishops from the Schönborn line. Alongside these were the Protestant "praying princes," such as Ernst the Pious from Saxony-Gotha (1605-75), and the patriarchal, pedantic administrator, as represented by Friedrich Wilhelm I of Prussia. Among them were well-intentioned, industrious patriarchs, but there were also arrogant, overbearing, and unstable wastrels, who found no satisfaction in the smallness of their lands and their limited means. There were warlike prince bishops such as Christoph Bernard von Galen (1650-78) in Münster and highly educated lovers of art such as Anton Ulrich von Braunschweig-Wolfenbüttel (1704-14). A substantial transformation occurred over the course of the eighteenth century, one that is only inadequately captured with the term *Enlightenment*. Gradually a distinction between the person of the ruler and the state evolved that led to the objectification of politics. On the one side stood Maria Theresia (1740-80), the successor to the Habsburg domains, who still belonged to the south German baroque, thought in dynastic and maternal terms, was oriented toward her people and open to reform, and was like no other in her practical sensibility and piety. On the other stood Friedrich II of Prussia (1740-86), who allied himself with the French Enlightenment, was a philosopher king, military commander-in-chief, absolute ruler, and reformer, hard worker, and increasingly solitary figure, and yet who became the model of the absolute ruler. There was really no prince who was a "totalitarian" dictator, ruling completely arbitrarily on the basis of whim.

Even the Prussian "soldier king," who broke the last political resistance of the provincial estates, was too much a pietist, acting in accordance with duty, to be more than a severe disciplinarian and become a brutal despot. And the numerous miniature editions and caricatures of these absolute rulers, whom we encounter in certain of the petty states, were usually nothing more than demanding, burdensome patriarchs.

The ruling princes, their families, and courts were also in quantitative terms a significant social element. As the heads of social hierarchies, with economic and political power, they possessed, in principle, influence without competition in the small and very small states. However, they seldom used it to shape or even to transform their communities. Most often they left the business of government to their councillors, sometimes to their favorites. If the ruling princes were vain or sought fame, they could let their states be drawn into the tempest of great politics. If they were indolent or incompetent, they might not take necessary reform measures. Yet whenever they revealed a consistent energy toward solving problems and created a capable administration, they unleashed forces within and outside their lands that increasingly attracted nobles and commoners seeking a chance to make a difference. "Aren't the myriad of princely courts," asked Leibniz in 1679, "a glorious means to allow so many people to distinguish themselves who would otherwise remain lying in the dust?"

OLD AND NEW NOBILITY

The nonruling nobility was also far from being a homogeneous estate. It had few common social characteristics and interests, except for its concern to retain its special group privileges and control the entry of parvenues. Legally, the nobility was still a feudal nobility, meaning that it was still an association built on bonds of personal fealty. This was also true of the imperial princes. The elector of Brandenburg was the vassal of the emperor not because of the Brandenburg lands, but as duke and king of Prussia, because Prussia was not part of the empire. The king of Denmark was in this same legal relationship as duke of Holstein, the king of Sweden as duke of West Pomerania and Bremen-Verden, and, from 1714, the king of England as Hanoverian elector. In the same manner, each imperial prince was the feudal lord over his resident (*landsässig*) nobility.

The significant legal difference in dependency between residency (*Landsässigkeit*) and immediacy (*Reichsunmittelbarkeit*) had no necessary relationship to property and power. Immediate, for instance, were also those members of the imperial nobility and knightly orders who often had far less property than individual families of the resident nobility. The imperial nobility had divided itself since 1557 into circles – Swabian, Franconian, and Rhenish – that were divided in turn into a total of fourteen cantons. Each circle or

Kreis had its own chancellery, each canton its own elected captain and councillors. Since 1654 the imperial knights had carried the appellation "noble and gentleborn" (*Edel- und Wohlgeboren*). The circles indicate their geographical distribution: There were no imperial knights in northern and eastern Germany or in Saxony and Bavaria. The lands of imperial knights were so concentrated in the Franconian imperial circle that territorially closed principalities could not be created. Imperial knights often had landed estates in addition to their imperial ones and were vassals of the local territorial ruler on those estates. The imperial knights were able to enlist the emperor in countering efforts by the territorial rulers to make them dependent (*landsässig*), because they supplied individials to the imperial military and administrative service and to the Habsburgs themselves. But imperial knights and their sons also entered the service of the territorial princes for income, prestige, and a chance to influence policy. Catholic families had a special interest in the benefices of the imperial church and the order of German knights and, naturally, most of all in the ecclesiastical sees of prince bishops and prince abbots. For long periods they were often able to control positions and benefices among the cathedral chapters as if they were personal property by continuously choosing younger sons for a clerical career.

Those elevated by the emperor into the estate of imperial barons – as, for instance, nonnoble jurists attached to the imperial aulic council – did not enter the estate of imperial knights. The latter was a closed corporation of the lesser nobility whose members cultivated a particular ethos of independence due to the sovereignty personal to them. Certain members of the landed nobility, however, could be superior to them in terms of rank. Thus there were families of earls in certain territorial states and, accordingly, certain provincial representative bodies had two aristocratic curia. In Austria there was a body of lords to the baronial level, who possessed sovereign lands, and an estate of knights; among the former there was a further distinction between an older and younger estate of lords. In Prussia there were separate estates for earls and knights. Lords and knights formed separate estates at the provincial diet in electoral Cologne. In Silesia and Bohemia the magnates separated themselves from the rest of the nobility. It occurred quite often in Austria, on the other hand, that individuals from the lesser and recent nobility were able to enter the high peerage.

We do not have trustworthy quantitative figures concerning ennoblement, but certainly it was granted quite often as a way to reward individuals, satisfy social ambition, and create social compromise. In certain cases it was granted because nobility was deemed necessary for the exercise of particular offices. The emperor could ennoble, as could those princes who were simultaneously sovereign rulers in lands outside of the empire. The emperor granted nobility in Bohemia and the Austrian core lands, and the Wittelsbachs began to grant it in their lands after the Thirty Years War.

Other imperial princes who could not ennoble were able to have their subjects elevated into the nobility by the emperor. If individuals were ennobled without princely nomination, the princes often bound their recognition of the new honor to special conditions or limitations. For their part, the corporately organized nobility (*Ritterschaft*) of the individual states placed a great value on distinction; it almost never granted the recently ennobled parity with the old nobility, and when it occurred in the rare case, it was usually after long delays. Even when the emperor retroactively granted nobility, the nobility (*Ritterschaft*) did not accept their lack of noble birth.

Thus the nobility was never a unified order. Difference was precisely cultivated among its members, and most important was the age of the lineage or its moment of ennoblement through patent or letter of nobility. The extent to which this was not simply a question of prestige but was bound with concrete privileges and interests is shown by the institutionalized exclusivity among the corporately organized estates of the landed nobility and the Catholic clerical nobility. Only nobles who possessed noble properties recorded in the registry of the diet and who had a lineage with at least eight noble ancestors could be accepted into the noble estate (*Ritterstand*) and thus vote in the noble curia at the diet. Nonnoble or recently ennobled owners of knight's estates thus were not eligible to appear at the diet. The aristocratic cathedral chapters required similar proofs of ancestry before a position could be made available and thereby attempted to keep closed the circle of authorized candidates. The basic tendency of the older society – distinction, concrete description of rights and privileges, sanctioning and institutionalizing positions and functions – had become even more intensified as a result of limited possibilities and as a reaction against the partial mobility unleashed by the gathering of sovereign power in the hands of the territorial princes.

Officials, officers, merchants, military suppliers, entrepreneurs, and scholars were often ennobled in spite of the resistance of the old nobility. At the moment of ennoblement it was not always proven that they each possessed landed property and lived a noble life. The obverse was also true. Wealthy officials, officers, and court suppliers purchased indebted estates that permitted them entry to the diet, and then they awaited titles of nobility. The transfer of noble estates into the hands of burghers and the recently ennobled must not have been a rare occurrence. In Bavaria from 1672 the territorial prince had to agree to the transfer, and similar restrictive measures had been passed in other states.

The social differentiation of the nobility is apparent from an administrative decree of Leopold I in 1671. The first order, set apart from other subjects, consisted of nobles possessing landed property, officials with "court posts," and doctors of medicine and the law. Those nobles without estates were placed in the second order along with administrators of seigneurial estates. If a noble wanted to live the life of a lord, in other words, he had to be a landed proprietor, for the older northern European nobility was predominantly a landed nobility. It was through the possession of landed property that *Landstandschaft* rested, meaning personal representation in the diet as a member of the noble curia or *Ritterschaft*. There was also an old urban nobility comprising those members of the patriciate from a few south German imperial cities who had earned their wealth in trade and had been elevated collectively by the emperor into the nobility. With entry into the nobility these individuals often abandoned trade and in some cases left the council. In Nuremberg and Frankfurt the patriciate was able to acquire the right to accept new members only through their collective cooperation. Thus the patriciate could prevent the emperor from forcing newly ennobled members upon themselves. Similar behavior can also be observed among the patriciate of certain older provincial cities who were functionally nobles without letters of patent.

If absolute monarchy had shown a marked tendency to use commoners in gathering power, it largely held onto the practice of dispensing to the nobility the highest offices at court, in the administration, the diplomatic service, and the military. Even difficult struggles with the provincial diets did not destroy the solidarity between the ruling and the nonruling nobility. The nobility was thus able "in diverse ways to preserve its role within the political hierarchy as the true ruling estate." To a great extent the system of absolutism had been able to eliminate the customary autonomous rights and functions of the intermediate powers, but it had preserved them "in structural terms as social and political ordering principals" (G. Birtsch). Absolutism formed political goals and not ones oriented toward social reform. It developed policies to mobilize society only in the context of increasing military strength, economic output, income, and prestige. Even enlightened absolutism was concerned to promote the well-being of each subject within his estate and thus to make him "happy" without changing the corporate order. In spite of this, however, enlightened absolutism began to comprehend and legitimate the social order as a functional order of the state; thereby it began to place in doubt the basis of legitimacy for this society of privilege.

Even then the landholding nobility remained in full control. It had an especially privileged legal status, was largely freed from taxes on its land, and retained fishing and hunting privileges. In addition, it often exercised lesser legal functions itself and controlled ecclesiastical patronage. Such privileges required that the nobles lead a life corresponding to their estate; for many petty nobles this was hardly enforceable, particularly as costs rose and higher levels of social cultivation were demanded. The educational patterns of the nobility gradually altered, partly as a result of the development of the courtly style. Aristocratic academies or *Ritterakademien* were founded, and in Catholic areas the sons of the nobility were sent to Jesuit gymnasia. Nobles hired resident teachers and tutors, and wealthier families began to send their sons in the company of educators on trips to western and southern Europe. It became more common for the sons of the nobility to enroll for short periods at universities. In addition, nobles began to pay more attention to the education of their daughters. They began to form libraries and lavish more concern on house and garden. The characteristic cultivated and active nobleman began to emerge alongside that of the courtier and cultivated burgher patriot; he was the individual who was concerned about his properties, the well-being of his subjects, and who was willing to serve the state.

Hence the German nobility of the seventeenth and eighteenth centuries was neither a declining caste nor one that was simply self-indulgent. Economic necessity, social interest, and guiding images of the behavior required of a noble station released substantial energies among the nobility. This reality helps to explain the strong and persistent leadership taken by the nobility in Germany.

CLERGY

Differences in the social physiognomy of Catholic and Protestant German states derived from the diverse position and function of the clergy. Catholic priests, monks, and nuns were, in a manner of speaking, separated from the rest of society through ordination and the sacramental commitment to celibacy; yet the often extensive property holding made it possible for the Church to provide a livelihood to an extensive clerical estate. Though whoever entered the church left the reproductive cycle, he or she was given support and work; he or she owned nothing but administered ecclesiastical property that could be neither sold nor bequeathed. The Protestant clergy-man, on the other hand, was integrated into the social order in quite a different way because of his ministerial office and because he was married in most cases.

With the exception of a few princely abbeys, archbishops, bishops, abbots, and abbesses, who were sovereign rulers, all came from the aristocracy, sometimes even from the high nobility. The same held true for the positions within the cathedral chapters. In the secular Catholic states the high clergy appeared at the diet with the first estate as representatives of clerical property. The social distance separating the aristocratic clergy from the lower clergy was enormous, since the latter were recruited predominantly from the peasant population. The village priests especially lived in humble circumstances and often had little education. Similarly, the distance was great, on the one hand, between the wealthy Benedictines in the large south German abbeys and the Jesuit confessors accustomed to living at court and, on the other, between the Franciscans and Carmelites living in the cities.

Similar deep differences did not exist among the Protestant clergy, although one cannot underestimate the gulf separating a village parson, a court preacher, a chief minister at a significant urban church, and a professor of theology at a university. And the social disparity between those with complete ministries and vicars without familial support was very depressing to the latter. The evangelical clergy were of burgher origin even in the highest offices. Furthermore, their social habitus was shaped strongly by their academic education and their function as officeholders. It was important that a significant portion of the clergy was recruited from among its own number. Since the number of clerical positions was limited, young theologians often had to survive for long periods in sometimes oppressive dependency as tutors and vicars. (Of course, the recommendations of high-placed officials could accelerate one's career.)

Where seigneurs controlled clerical patronage, the parsons, though dependent, proved to have a unique status in the countryside; they were often the only educated individuals in the village and for that reason were drawn into limited social contact with their rulers. In the cities the pastorate formed a special group among the notabilities, with whom there existed a multitude of ties through blood and marriage. Court chaplains and superintendents occasionally married daughters of the aristocracy, but to ennoble a clergyman was unusual. The evangelical clergy can be rightfully labeled an occupational order that evolved a specific social dynamic. An astounding number of poets, writers, and scholars came from the homes of evangelical clergy, and in the eighteenth century high officials and jurists as well. Indeed the clerical family became the prototype of the proper burgher family, wherein the education of the children assumed an important place. Pastors combined both spiritual and pedagogical functions in their office, but, in addition, they were required within the framework of the territorial state church system to announce administrative decrees from the pulpit and to bind the congregation to obedience to the secular authorities. For that reason the pastorate was brought into close proximity with officialdom, in their own self-estimation and in the view of others.

The spiritual element played a quantitatively different role in social life within Catholic regions, forming undoubtedly a more prominent place in daily life. Monasticism was a self-evident part of spiritual and social life. Monks often ministered to the parish; the cloisters maintained schools and cared for the poor and sick; and many cloister churches were sites of particular reverence. Cloisters often ruled over significant agricultural lands, were well-off, and managed to extend their holdings through bequests and purchases. In Bavaria, for instance, the church owned approximately a third of the land, and the secular rulers could no longer tax the land. Thus the government constantly and understandably sought to prevent further bequests to the church, the "dead hand."

In the Catholic areas the church was rooted more deeply in daily life and in the forms of popular culture and popular piety, and it increased a family's

prestige to have members in clerical orders. Clerical possession of seigneurial lands or even sovereignty at the state level was accepted without
question and in practice did not distinguish itself from secular behavior.
That it was good to live under the crozier was an adage from the late
eighteenth century when the demands placed by secular rulers on their
subjects increased greatly. Presumably, however, it held true even earlier.

The churches enjoyed enormous significance in public and private life,
not simply because of their religious functions but rather because of their
concrete existence as a social institution and their integration into the
political system. The social consequences reached from the "feudalism" of
the high Catholic clergy to the Protestant pastorate defined by officeholding and university education, to the petty bourgeois life of Catholic village
priests, and to the plebian existence of Protestant candidates of theology
who had neither office nor the means of subsistence. The literature of the
period produced many portraits of this world – especially that of the
Protestant clergy – from Grimmelshausen's portrait of conditions during
the Thirty Years War to Friedrich Nicolai's *Sebaldus Nothanker* and Johann
Heinrich Voss's *Luise.*

THE RURAL POPULATION

The peasant population accounted for the vast majority of the total population. They made their living from agriculture, but were socially varied and
diverse. Every village had its own uniqueness. The forms of cultivation and
management, inheritance laws, taxation, the concrete forms of the seigneurial system – these could differ from region to region. It is impossible
here to pursue these differences; what concerns us instead are the common
structures that we will clarify with certain examples.

It is a gross oversimplification to argue that the legal status of the
peasantry worsened dramatically after the Peasants War of 1525 and that
they were henceforth merely pawns in the flow of events. To some extent
the essential worsening of their social situation occurred only as a result of
the Thirty Years War. In this sense the free peasantry and *Kölmer* of East
Prussia retained the right to appear at the provincial diet until the second
half of the seventeenth century. Similarly, the hereditary dependence of the
peasantry both on the seigneurial estates (*Gutsherrschaften*) and the royal
domains developed fully only in this same period. At this same time in
Württemberg, on the other hand, the villages won the right to exert a
certain influence in the naming of district deputies to the diet. Even
thereafter the peasantry did not act only passively and meekly. There
occurred limited local and short-term peasant uprisings, especially in
Saxony, Silesia, and Bohemia, of which we unfortunately know very little.
The cases of peasant resistance were most likely far more numerous and

their forms far more varied than the surviving record indicates. In spite of severe seigneurial and princely intervention, village self-rule also survived in its essentials and with it the traditional internal stratification within the village.

Few things are known in detail about the real changes the war caused in the villages: What transformations in property holding occurred; how many propertyless acquired property; how many abandoned sites or *Wüstungen* were brought back under the plow by returning inhabitants, their relatives, or newcomers; whether the hierarchy in the villages altered even temporarily. In many cases new peasants found themselves in greater seigneurial dependency than before; in others they were given more advantageous rights and contracts. In general rulers paid greater attention after the war to the cultivation of the soil, to the regulation of duties and burdens, and to the legal situation of the peasantry. In electoral Bavaria in the 1660s the duties of heavy manual labor were transformed into cash payments. In the oversettled areas of southwestern Germany, where lands were divided equally at death, it became easier to be released from services in duty and kind. In northwestern Germany the principal of undivided inheritance of peasant holdings was adopted. In other areas the practice evolved whereby holdings were transferred to the heirs with princely approval, thus making the parents' situation more secure.

Naturally, structural changes in the agrarian system did not occur with these improvements. It is therefore possible to accept the threefold division of the peasantry made by F.W. Henning for the period around 1800 in connection with the work of the Prussian statistician Krug and project these divisions far back in time, extending them simultaneously beyond the boundaries of the Prussia for which they were intended. He placed in the first group those large peasant farmers who had a real income beyond their living costs and who had farms with a value of more than 10,000 talers. The second group was composed of those peasants who had a real income that permitted the life of a full-scale peasant proprietor with only the most modest of demands but did not always supply enough sustenance. The peasants in the third group were forced to engage in secondary occupations, because the soils were too meager, the indebtedness too high, or the usable agricultural land too meager as a consequence of division. This latter group was most widespread in southwestern Germany and in a few areas of the Mittelgebirge. According to this estimate, 70 to 80 percent of the peasantry had no surplus, the majority surviving at the existential minimum.

The boundary was economically fluid between the small peasantry and those strata beneath them. Two groups must be distinguished among the latter: the small property-holding cottagers who took a variety of forms and were referred to by a number of names (*Kötter, Kossäten, Gärtner, Söldner, Brinksitzer, Gütler*) and the property-poor laborers who also assumed different forms and labels (*Häusler, Büdner, Insten, Heuerleute, Einlieger, Tagelöhner*).

The members of the first group were generally forced into secondary occupations on knightly estates, on large peasant farms, or in cottage industry. They lived mostly on the edge of the villages on the commonlands or were separated from the older holdings. The second group was composed of those with very little or no property. Both groups grew over the course of the seventeenth and eighteenth centuries but did not really belong to the village commune. In 1767 only 24.2 percent of the rural population in Prussian Silesia were peasant farmers; 47.8 percent were gardeners, and 28 percent cottagers without property. Similar conditions existed in the older settled areas. We have an example from 1689 in the noble legal district of Jühnde, which belonged to the Braunschweig-Lüneburg principality of Calenberg-Grubenhagen and lay in an area of real division of the land in the region of south Hanover. Eight hundred thirty people were counted there as belonging to ninety households in six villages. Next to the district leaseholder *(Amtspächter)*, whose household comprised fifty-one people, there were twelve half-tenant farmers *(Halbmeier)*, each with a hand and a maid; everyone else was a cotter, a small cotter, or crofter; the majority possessed less than ten morgen of land (one morgen was approximately one acre) or none at all. In the same year in three other districts near Hanover, only a third of the 2,122 inhabitants in the eighty-one villages belonged to the peasantry; the rest belonged to the poorer strata beneath them, and the completely propertyless were not even counted. In an area of Fulda in the eighteenth century, only a quarter of the agricultural population was still counted as belonging to the peasantry. In general the number of the propertyless grew with the increase in population. Around 1800 one-seventh of the total population of Prussia was made up of propertyless laborers in the countryside.

Such local and regional conditions force us to conclude that the closed peasant villages of the high Middle Ages, shaped as they were by the *Hufenbauerntum,* had been transformed in their social structure almost everywhere in eastern Germany and the older settled areas over the course of the seventeenth and eighteenth centuries. "The full peasants or *Vollbauern,*" Günther Franz has written, "became in many places a minority in the village, even though they often continued to be able to maintain their political preeminence, since communal rights were still in many places connected to the holdings themselves. At the same time it is clear that, in contrast to agriculture itself or the agrarian system, the village was not able to survive through the centuries." The growing population pressure in combination with an uneven expansion of the food supply led necessarily to overpopulation and pauperization in the countryside. This in turn increased tensions – if in a mostly unspectacular manner – in the villages, particularly when it was not possible to emigrate to the cities because of the unemployment that also prevailed there. Emigration, seasonal foreign labor (as for instance the travel to Holland or *Hollandgängerei* in Westphalia), the expansion of rural industry – these brought temporary relief but no permanent improvement. The measures expanding cultivation also reached their limits in the course of the eighteenth century. For this reason the need to transform the agrarian system and free the peasant population from the inherited social and legal bonds became an ever more pressing necessity. In the last third of the eighteenth century reforms were finally begun – at first on the royal domains – under fiscalist and enlightened perspectives.

Modern social historians have let us see the older village as a complex structure in which great social differences prevailed. Peasants were concerned to exclude the lowest groups of the rural order from the formal community, the enjoyment of commonland, and marriage. Peasant sons, especially the heirs to full-holdings (*Vollerbe*), did not marry the daughters of cotters. Dowry and inheritance chances played a significant role in life, and those without an inheritance often remained single. There are examples from Württemberg and from the Westphalian region of the construction of a peasant patriciate; similar examples are known in Upper Bavaria. In such cases a few families, linked by blood and marriage, held onto the village offices. Substantial wealth could exist in these families, given favorable economic conditions and a capacity to keep the property together. We have a record of this in the substantial farms – some of which still survive – and in the peasant domestic furnishings from the eighteenth century. On the other side, the rulers' administrative measures to care for the poor in the communes and their efforts to suppress begging and the movement of vagabonds point to the distress of the propertyless part of the rural population. That concern continued to grow is witnessed by the literature and scientific writing of the eighteenth century.

RURAL ARTISANAL AND MANUFACTURING LABOR

We include among rural petty producers those groups of the rural population who produced for the market and not for their own consumption, and who thereby partly or completely furnished their living expenses. They were recruited from the peasant population but increasingly supplied new members from among their own number and began to develop their own unique traditions. Yet they remained dependent in many aspects on rural life through their place of living and their secondary labor in agriculture. In addition, they often worked a plot of land as cottagers or laborers on an estate.

There were many types of industrial activities in the countryside that could become the major occupation when the family was largely or wholly dependent on income from cottage production. In most cases these activities concerned the production of textiles. The techniques were not developed into a doctrine as among the artisanate, but were passed down from parents to children, who quite early in their lives took a place in the process in order to expand production. This use of the cheapest labor was part of the "protoindustrial" family economy, which in times of poor prices and small demand became necessarily and self-evidently a form of self-exploitation.

These petty industrial producers lived to a certain extent, as in Minden-Ravensberg, in the houses of cottagers on peasant property; in other areas they lived in their own cottages set apart from the village. If they lived in villages, they still did not belong to the village commune. There were also the so-called industrial villages, where weavers did not own their own homes but rented. In the cases where production was organized on the basis of the putting-out system and the implements and the raw materials were supplied by the factor, the status of the cottage worker approached that of the dependent wage laborer in the manufactories. It is presumed that an industrial petty producer was able to achieve a certain modest standard of living and might rise to become a supervising master within the putting-out system, but he could rarely ever rise to become a factor himself. In areas of concentrated production far from cities, this group appears to have kept largely to itself. They married among themselves and founded thereby another spinning or weaving family. Periods of crisis could not be avoided, due to the heavy dependence on the market. Crises were met with lowered consumption or with emigration because agricultural labor was not easily found nor attractive any longer. Protoindustrial production did not always link with the industrialization process of the nineteenth century either directly or indirectly by way of the decentralized system of organization.

Workers in the manufactories, especially in the early phase of production, must be clearly distinguished from petty industrial producers in the countryside. They lived predominantly in cities, their outskirts, or in the nearby countryside, although seigneurs occasionally built such sites on their lands. Due to the generally distasteful conditions, it was difficult to attract laborers to the manufactories. In individual cases, particularly in Silesia and Bohemia, seigneurs bound their serfs to such work. As already noted, prisoners and inmates of workhouses, poorhouses, and foundling homes were often forced to work in the manufactories on the basis of special lease arrangements. As a rule they were neither permitted nor financially able to found families. The value of such laborers was not great. Others coming from the propertyless rural poor did not bring skills with them and could not easily adapt to the form of work. Far more desirable were individuals with technical training; these usually came from declining crafts or cottage industry, and when found, they were given preferred positions.

Governments and enlightened publicists viewed the manufactories as effective in promoting economic progress, lessening poverty and unemployment, and preventing social degradation. Such expectations, however, were met to a limited degree within the gradual and highly costly process of industrialization and the emerging factory system. In the eighteenth century neither cottage industry nor the manufactory eliminated poverty among the lowest orders of the population. Yet it is also true that poverty would have been much greater without them both.

THE URBAN POPULATION

Seventeenth- and eighteenth-century cities were not the melting pots of preindustrial society. Urban populations remained highly differentiated in spite of their growth. The emphasis on corporate distinctions had even increased, finding a footing in the fiscal classifications of populations in the various censuses of the eighteenth century. In individual cases, naturally, the special fate of each city played an important role. Many a significant and vital city never recovered, or recovered only very slowly; others grew as residential cities, ports, or trading centers; and still others were transformed in their character into garrison or administrative cities. In many small cities gradual population growth had no effect on the social structure.

In Frankfurt am Main the sumptuary code of 1731 distinguished between five "estates." Members of the first estate were the mayor (*Schultheiss*), magistrates, the councillors of the second bench, other members of the government, syndics, doctors, and members of the urban nobility to the extent their ancestors had taken part in the city government for more than one hundred years. Belonging to the second estate were the city councillors of the third bench, noble immigrants, and ennobled and nonnoble merchants in wholesale trade and banking with a personal worth of at least 20,000 talers. The third estate comprised notaries, procurators, larger traders and artists; the fourth comprised small traders, messengers, and artisans; the fifth, day laborers and servants. The social preeminence of administrative and patrician families over often wealthier merchants is noteworthy. In other cities a similar pattern emerged where an oligarchy of magistrates emerged from the guilds and controlled the government by excluding the merchants. In Leipzig the elector forced merchants to be admitted into the magistracy, and in Breslau the Prussian government did the same. Lawyers ordinarily enjoyed high social standing in larger cities, even though they were often denied the top positions.

Court, administration, and military gave a clear stamp to the social pattern of residential cities. Even though they did not belong to the city commune and thus were not controlled by the magistracy, their presence substantially shaped the economic life of the city. This was true even for small residential cities and for those older cities to which residences were transferred. In Braunschweig in 1758, for instance, excluding the subburgher orders that made up at least 36 percent of the total population, 28 percent of the remaining population belonged to the military, and 17 percent consisted of the court, administration, church, and the arts, while 49 percent belonged to the artisanate and 6 percent to commerce.

A wealthy, self-conscious, and worldly upper class of burghers (*Grossbür-gertum*) was seldom to be found in the seventeenth and eighteenth centuries. The few truly rich merchant families who built stately and luxurious homes largely lacked the entrepreneurial energy that had characterized life in the cities during the fifteenth and sixteenth centuries. They were much more concerned with local influence and a patrician way of life than with economic expansion. Such energies were much more likely to be found among "new" families. Among the urban elites much attention was paid to family connections and marriage; these shaped reputations, influence, and the holding of offices. In smaller cities there were also notabilities that set the tone and shaped the allegiances of the middle groups.

The urban lower class of burghers (*Kleinbürgertum*), or petty bourgeoisie, consisted predominantly of artisan masters and their families, to whom belonged the journeymen and apprentices as members of the household, in a manner similar to clerks within merchant households. Not only did prosperity vary widely among the guilds, but they were also ranked differently in terms of prestige and political influence. A few of the foremost guilds often exclusively controlled membership in the town council. Often the territorial rulers economically undermined and politi- cally controlled the strict principle of guild membership by admitting masters and trades outside the guilds, but they were not able to set the guilds aside. Within urban society the guilds retained their meaning as a system of social control for a long time to come, and as such they also held signifi- cance for the traveling journeymen artisans. Finally, the small-scale peddlers also belonged to the petty bourgeoisie and as a rule belonged to guildlike organizations.

Since the nineteenth century, the terms petty bourgeoisie, petty bour- geois mentality, and petty bourgeois behavior have resonated with negative tones. Petty bourgeois was equated with philistinism and local narrowness, political anxiety, and social egotism. Recognizable attitudes of the petty bourgeoisie were thus crudely caricatured. A "middle class" (*Mittelstand*) existed in urban society, but its upper and lower boundaries were difficult to demarcate. Furthermore, group allegiance and its attendant social behav- ior cannot primarily be determined economically. Helmut Möller has quite properly labeled as borderline cases the impoverished artisan who still emulated the claims of the guild ethic, the wealthy "manufacturer" who still held onto petty bourgeois attitudes and lifestyle, the members of the lower orders who economically led a petty bourgeois life but never attained to the status of artisanal respectability, and those who indeed led the life of a member of the petty bourgeoisie but whose education took them beyond. The petty bourgeoisie was essentially composed of the master artisans, their families, and the small-scale merchants. They emphasized respectability and were much less concerned with upward mobility than with preserving their status. Their educational horizons and knowledge of the world were limited; their interests went hardly beyond their own town. They preserved an unshakable traditional religiosity, although in the lower levels in Protestant cities pietistic tendencies also made themselves felt. They accepted guild traditions as ritualized behavioral norms that gave meaning to a life of work. They valued appropriate corporate dress and speech, raising their children, and, as long as it was in any way possible, maintaining distance from the lower orders.

To these lower orders belonged those who could not establish an independent petty bourgeois household. They were the journeymen artisans who, as they became older or married, left the master's family; the domestic servants, scribes, and urban day laborers. The group of servants, *Dienstboten* or *domestique,* made up a substantial part of the population in larger cities and especially in residential cities. They were also highly differentiated among themselves, from valets to grooms and gardeners, from maids-in-waiting to housemaids. In Prussia as late as 1788, servants, like apprentices and soldiers, were still subject to the paternal power of the household. Such dependent persons did not possess rights of citizenship. Yet they did not belong to the dregs of society, but as a rule had some form of support – no matter how small and no matter how oppressive a life it was with no chance of betterment.

EXCEPTIONAL AND MARGINAL GROUPS, OUTSIDERS, LOWEST ORDERS

There were a number of exceptional and marginal groups within the social nexus of the individual German states, cities, and regions. Their situation was not necessarily always economically worse or socially lower; in many cases, in fact, they had a privileged status. Such was the case of the Huguenots in Brandenburg, Hesse-Kassel, and Franconia. Having left home because of their beliefs, they brought with them highly developed technical skills, a drive to achieve, and an awareness of their own chosen status. They also marked their special status by holding onto the French language and became, especially in Prussia, one of the most significantly upwardly mobile groups. In Saxony there were also religious fugitives of Czech origin – the "Bohemian Brethren." Individual Italian, Dutch, and French families were able to rise to wealth and prosperity in German cities and at particular courts.

Particular German religious minorities existed alongside the foreign ones. Among these were the Mennonite communities along the Weichsel, Memel, and Lower Rhine. Because the religious minorities had separated themselves from the local territorial church, they were particularly

dependent on protection by the government that had sheltered and wel-
comed them. In particular cases, such as in the duchies of Sayn-
Wittgenstein and Wied, the ruling families themselves held similar beliefs;
in others, such as in Prussia, the government practiced a type of religious
toleration. The Zinzendorfian Brethren, the movement whose origins
resided in the Hussite Moravian "Herrnhuter," to some extent left the
territorial churches against the will of their founder and in certain areas,
such as Prussia, were recognized as special religious communities. In
Saxony, on the other hand, they were recognized as related to the
upholders of the Augsburg Confession. Lutherans and Reformed Protestants
were able to join together without leaving the larger churches in the
western German communities of the Moravian Brethren, even though in
social terms the Brethren continued to be treated as exceptional groups.
Similar patterns are apparent among the pietistic communities and groups
within the Lutheran territorial churches. Finally, we should make mention
of the Calvinist court ministers in Brandenburg-Prussia, because after the
conversion of the dynasty in 1613, they formed a privileged, highly motivated, and influential minority within a state that otherwise remained
Lutheran. Finally, each of these groups stayed close together. Members
married within their own groups, and they each cultivated a distinct
religious language and an exclusionary social idiom.

Though Jews fulfilled important functions within German society, they
were utterly unintegratable. In the larger cities, they lived in ghettos, while
in other areas princely letters of protection only permitted them to remain
in small numbers. They were not permitted to own landed property, join
guilds, or become citizens. Most often they could only support themselves
through trade and financial transactions. Their letters of protection were
always issued for a fixed period of time, so their legal status was never fully
secure. On the other hand, their special status was the presupposition for
existing in a world of latent foreignness and antipathy. Not until the late
Enlightenment did the view develop that such social isolation and economic
restrictiveness produced the often criticized habits and mentality of the
Jews. There were, however, exceptional privileges for the wealthy Jewish
elite. Sephardic Jews, for instance, largely controlled Hamburg's trade
with Spain and Portugal. But it took until 1728 for special dress regulations
to disappear, even for such a wealthy and influential Jewish community as
that in Frankfurt. Until 1762 no Jews were allowed to settle in Munich; in
Saxony they were only allowed to stay in Dresden and Leipzig. In the
Prussia of Frederick II, they were excluded from owning property in the
general privilege of 1750, and, though allowed to trade and own manufactories and factories, their numbers were strictly controlled.

Pronounced social divisions existed within the Jewish community itself.
The upper stratum consisted of the court factors or *Hoffaktoren,* some of
whom were in fact elevated into the nobility. The group of specially

privileged Jews was even somewhat broader in Prussia; to their number belonged the few wealthy merchant families controlling the mints. Also among them was Moses Mendelssohn, partner in a silk company, enlightened philosopher and friend of Lessing, who proved so significant for the intellectual development and emancipation of German Jewry. The rabbis were a supraregional, interrelated intellectual elite. Beneath them was a middle stratum holding to petty bourgeois values, consisting of the small traders and rural cattle dealers. Beneath them were the poor Jewish beggars, the *Betteljuden,* who roamed the countryside and were even more despised and defenseless than the non-Jewish poor.

Artists must also be considered a special group. Actors, musicians, and singers formed a heterogeneous class that proved from place to place to be only temporarily stable. A few members found positions and income at the courts and in the larger cities; some even climbed and entered the nobility. In general, however, the social status of actors remained quite low, and the admission of women into the profession from the late seventeenth century onward only contributed to the low position. Opera singers fared better, because they were often engaged for long periods at the courts or in a large city such as Hamburg. At the lower end these people merged with the class of itinerant travelers, wandering performers, and the homeless. In contradistinction, musicians, instrument makers, plasterers, and gilders were considered to be skilled artisans, who, whether organized in guilds or not, were highly respectable members of the petty bourgeoisie. Still different was the situation of conductors, choirmasters, architects, painters, and sculptors, who, when they had secure employment, held distinguished positions at court or within the cities.

Living at the lowest edges of society were those members of "dishonorable" trades excluded from the guilds – the knackers, shepherds, tinkers, and hawkers. They were often not easily distinguishable from vagabonds but were certainly different from the totally unemployed, the beggars, the incapacitated, and the slackers. It is hardly possible to estimate their numbers, but their ranks most likely expanded after wars and in times of dearth. When we consider the low levels of health among the rural and urban poor, we must accept that a significant number could not work. Accidents, injuries, and severe wounds to soldiers brought with them permanent invalidism, especially because medical care and skill were often inadequate. Normally such individuals, like the weak and feeble-minded, were cared for by their families; but where that was not possible they had to be supported by the communes, as were poor widows without family backing. In addition, many beggars lived in the countryside without a secure residence. According to the many accounts, they must have been especially numerous in Catholic regions where the giving of alms was seen as a good deed. In the ecclesiastical states it is estimated there were 260 beggars for every 1,000 inhabitants. In the Protestant states there were continuous efforts to suppress the giving of alms, because the failure to work was viewed as a first step toward a life of sin, and laziness was a vice stemming from a sinful human nature; but even there the additional controls were not able to eliminate begging.

There were always new additions to the ranks of beggars and vagabonds. There was simply no social support or means to reintegrate the disabled soldier, released captives and prisoners, or the small peasant or cottager who lost his possessions in a fire. Failed students and discharged soldiers also often found no employment. Similarly, individuals who had escaped from seigneurial duties or from a servant's life were often unable to find new positions, and those who may have had a brush with the law did not easily establish themselves again. Poachers often faced overly severe punishments, forcing them to flee or join a gang. Bands of robbers, who appeared frequently in popular literature and were celebrated as fighters for justice, were a common reality in a society with a growing population, limited economic possibilities, and a customary legal order.

NEW URBAN ORDERS

A new group formed within the corporately ordered social system of the seventeenth and eighteenth centuries that was to have great significance and future consequence, especially for Germany. It consisted not only of state officials or *Beamte* – though they were the most important subgroup – but also of the educated who sought a place within the corporate order. Although the majority were recruited from the urban population, they cannot be termed a part of the burgher order or *Bürgertum;* and even though they called themselves burghers, they did so by applying another meaning of burgher, namely that of the citizen within the state or of the *civis* within the *societas civilis*.

As the sovereign princely state transformed itself from personal rule to a bureaucratic system, it required an increasing number of servants and functionaries to carry out the usurped and growing legal, financial, and policing tasks. These individuals needed to have particular skills and were required to have a special loyalty to superiors from whom they received their income and recognition. They were especially needed wherever the territorial rulers, in conflict with the estates, created new offices and a new officialdom to cement their unitary authority over the corporate legal system. In spite of their high positions, these officials were constantly poorly paid; they were paid partly in kind, or they had to extract their income from fees, taxes, or leased estates. In Germany profitable offices were often bought and sold – a practice that did not disappear even in Prussia until 1740. Much more widespread was the custom of *Adjunktur,* of candidacy for a future office on the basis of royal favor or the social position of one's family.

Legally trained princely councillors, hired on the basis of private contracts, had assumed high positions in the early modern state already in the sixteenth century. The title of doctor of both German and Roman law was equated with a patent of nobility, thus joining together the older tradition of ministerial service with that of personal dependence within the royal household. A new occupational estate emerged from this fusion; with it, especially in Prussia in the eighteenth century, developed a new form of technical education for higher officials in the cameral and political sciences. Normally the most prestigious and lucrative offices were still reserved for the nobility, but the upward climb of nonnobles to the office of privy councillor certainly was known to happen and usually led to ennoblement. Such nonnoble officials were tied in other ways to the territorial ruler than members of the landed nobility. Noble aspirants and officeholders, as a result, were increasingly forced to acquire similar qualifications – of course with far better chances for advancement than their nonnoble counterparts. Thus nobles and nonnobles entered into new relations at the upper levels of state service; though social differences were not eliminated, they began to blur in the world of service.

High officialdom was responsible for accelerating the introduction of uniform and rational procedures in administration and law. It also provided continuity in the functioning of government, bridging over the accidents of training and the quality of particular rulers. In spite of this, we cannot yet speak of a true "bureaucracy," one of rule by an administration and its personnel. However, the number, arena of activity, and meaning of administrative bodies steadily grew, and with that the number of individuals who were partially or completely paid by such activity. The populace thus increasingly encountered political authority in the form of administrative bodies and officials, which was an important step in objectifying and depersonalizing the state and its services.

Officials, however, still remained "servants" for quite some time to come, since there was still no developed legal code for officials that could protect them against the arbitrary decisions of their superiors. By the same token, a strict code for qualifications and career patterns only developed later with the further expansion of administration. Yet changes can be noted in the methods of choosing personnel; education, knowledge, and reliability began to be considered. Thus a "service estate" or *Dienststand* with special group interests gradually constituted itself; increasingly it sought to extend itself by acquiring special rights, occupational security, titles, and honors. A significant number of the most strongly motivated and talented members from the middle orders and the nobility entered this estate. If sons from the nobility increasingly saw a career in officialdom as an interesting option to a life in the military, it became even truer for the sons of pastors, officials, and upwardly mobile members of the petty bourgeoisie.

Other members of the educated classes – the clergy, doctors, and professoriate – should not be overlooked. Since the sixteenth century the universities had served to educate pastors and officials. Although there were as yet usually no standard curricula or final examinations, graduates still had the chance to find positions outside their homeland. It was not unusual to transfer from the service of one prince to that of another, and even confessional barriers were not unbridgeable. Admittedly, career chances remained limited. It was difficult to find a position and keep it, even as the number of people seeking an advanced education continued to grow. By the eighteenth century there were already complaints of a student surplus, especially from the lower orders without financial support, who were forced to seek free board and stipends or sing for alms in choirs. Once their studies were over they were often forced to accept positions incommensurate with their training or self-expectations. From their ranks came household tutors and teachers in the Latin schools.

The educated constituted the "public" of writers and readers and formed the substratum of an emerging public opinion that under the impress of the Enlightenment began to expand beyond narrow territorial and religious boundaries in the second half of the eighteenth century.

3

CULTURAL LIFE

Historical narratives treat simultaneous matters serially, separating the historically indivisible. Cultural life is only a partial aspect of the historical process and is inextricably woven together with economic, social, and political conditions. The real and apparent relations between humankind's material interests and its ideas, those between work, the inner meaning of work, and the stylization of the life cycle, those between power relations and the levels of education – all these are too complex to be explained in terms of a simple model of cause and effect. This is especially true for the realm of culture. Ideas and dominant images can only be understood in connection with the institutions in which people live; the patterns shaping behavior are the result of a lengthy social process of experience and learning. Formative behavior, like the sum of people's works, is the consequence of complex needs, interests, traditions, and images by which they understand their being and task.

The concepts "baroque" and "Enlightenment" are not simply derived from the different areas of art and philosophy, but they also evoke different images. Baroque leads us spontaneously to think of architecture and music, while Enlightenment leads us to philosophy, literature, and pedagogy. In the baroque era, princely residences, the opera, and courtly festivals appeared as forms of princely display, and religious architecture and the celebratory mass seemed the self-representation of an *ecclesia triumphans*. Much more characteristic in the age of the Enlightenment, on the other hand, were the novel, the realm of public opinion, secularization, and emancipation. Naturally, such associations are intellectually far too crude; so too are most efforts to see a clear temporal movement from the baroque to the Enlightenment. Balthasar Neumann, the great baroque architect, died in 1753; Georg Friedrich Händel in 1759. At this point the first German philosopher of the Enlightenment, Christian Thomasius, had been dead for more than a quarter century (1728), and Lessing's burgher drama, *Miss Sara Sampson,* had already appeared a few years earlier (1754). In spite of the chronological overlap, there were, on the whole, gradual changes within the self-consciousness and social composition of at least the dominant groups. Among other tendencies, we can see that the churches began to lose their power in controlling opinion, Catholic Germany began to fall behind the Protestant regions, and a new public and a new realm of public affairs began to emerge. A stylistic change thus began, whose significance, however, first became apparent in the period after the middle of the eighteenth century.

The baroque and Enlightenment periods were European occurrences, beginning respectively in southern Europe and in England and Holland, and from there spreading to France and finally to Germany. Here, too, we can see the characteristic lag in German developments during the seventeenth and eighteenth centuries. While Spain, the Netherlands, France, and England experienced a cultural flowering in the seventeenth century, Germany made an increasingly shabby impression in comparison. Intellectual and artistic production and religious intensity had already partially exhausted themselves from the religious struggles of the Reformation in the second half of the sixteenth century. The distance between the uneducated populace and the higher orders lengthened after the great war, and the latter became increasingly susceptible to foreign influences. Weary of religious orthodoxy and the narrowness and poverty of German conditions, the elite sought connection with the "world" by adopting predominantly French customs and culture. They discovered French Catholicism to be livelier than its German variant and western European Calvinism and Anabaptism to be much more energetic than Lutheranism. The French language, mores, and taste began to be preeminent in this period – not only in Germany, but there with particular force. Disdain for local traditions and native language and literature accompanied the act of assimilation. It was still apparent in the 1780 essay of Friedrich II, "De la Littérature Allemande," although by then such views were forcefully attacked.

In the seventeenth century, language societies came to the fore to cleanse German of the many foreign expressions and impurities and to demonstrate that German was capable of delicate expression. By the mid-eighteenth century, Gellert, Gleim, Rabener, Johann Elias Schlegel, Klopstock, and others were imbued with the desire to create a German literature. Although ultimately not free of patriotic excess and even nationalistic overtones, we must appreciate that such images in literature belong to the age-old custom of comparing character and achievements among European peoples. It is much more important to understand how significant the cultural and literary revival of the second half of the eighteenth century was to the formation of a national consciousness among the Germans.

CONFESSIONAL COEXISTENCE

In imperial law the Peace of Westphalia was primarily a religious settlement. Yet confessional conflict continued to present the greatest danger to
the peace and existence of the empire because potentially it could paralyze
the imperial institutions and provoke military intervention. This situation
continued after the peace, even though the evolution from a unitary church
to a pluralistic confessional system was largely completed. If the Peace of
Augsburg in 1555 had known only two confessions, the "old religion" and
the Augsburg Confession, then the Westphalian settlement expressly recognized the Reformed faith as well. Legal parity, however, did not mean
toleration, since other faiths and movements continued to be excluded or
suppressed, among them Anabaptism, Mystical Spiritualism, and Socinian-
ism. Except in the very few imperial cities with religious parity, the faiths
rarely comingled but were separated by territorial boundaries. Members of
particular faiths normally stayed among themselves, regarding home
regions of other faiths as foreign territory in more than one sense.

A heightened confessional consciousness developed as a result of the long conflict
and the educational efforts of the authorities; it was filled with defensiveness,
hatred, mistrust, bitterness and misperception of the dictated relationship of the
churches among themselves. The unhappy consequence of the hundred years of
religious conflict was to constrict religious life and place it under a respressive
regimentation by the state (E.W. Zeeden).

Luther's teachings had triumphed with the aid of the territorial rulers
and the magistrates in the imperial cities. In addition, the formation of the
territorial churches and the episcopal system not only derived from Lutheran ecclesiastical theory but from the German constitutional and political
situation. Proof of this emerges from the analogous pattern in the Catholic
states, for there, too, the territorial rulers took control of the churches. The
rulers also recognized that confessional uniformity was a political affair,
that support of and by the church strengthened princely sovereignty. For
this reason, they were largely responsible for implementing the Tridentine
decrees of the Counter-Reformation. Both evangelical and Catholic princes,
in other words, used the church similarly to influence belief and discipline
their populations politically. It is thus significant that the territorial
churches and the sovereign power of the territorial authorities developed
simultaneously.

It would be ahistorical simply to regret the particularism of German
political life and complain of the religious confessionalism. Until the end of
the old order, the Westphalian Peace was celebrated as a document of
imperial liberties and as the foundation for a political system that constitutionally both prohibited the exercise of unlimited political and clerical
authority and allowed various confessions to coexist. In fact, religious
coexistence not only preserved peace within the empire, but it also served

as the basis for German cultural life unto our own day. The cost of peace, however, was dear. The substance of Christian teaching was not in itself jeopardized; but the churches' power to shape and control life was eventually harmed by involvement in political struggles and by allowing the secular authorities to become the ultimate adjudicator of religious conflict. In any event, it was precisely the combination of the confessional with the territorial principle that stamped itself lastingly on the thoughts and habits of the German people.

The peace treaties of Osnabrück and Münster had confirmed the Augsburg settlement of 1555 with numerous dilutions and compromises. Subjects practicing a different faith than their territorial lord were allowed to emigrate but could not be forced to do so. If they remained, they were permitted the private exercise of their faith. The basic proposition "cuius regio, eius religio" was set aside: The religious status quo was based on the year 1624 and could not be altered even when individual princes or entire dynasties converted. In this way the religious power of the territorial ruler over the *ius reformandi* was limited considerably and, in practice, became increasingly less significant. Henceforth the conversion of individual princes or dynasties no longer altered the confessional status of their lands. When elector August (the Strong) converted to Catholicism (1697), Saxony retained its Lutheran character. He remained the titular first bishop but actually delegated institutional authority to the general consistory. A number of other converts to Catholicism – Duke Christian August von Holstein (1705), Duke Anton Ulrich von Braunschweig-Lüneburg, and Duke Alexander von Württemberg – also left the religious faith of their populations intact. Life at court did alter, however, once Catholic services were held, and confessors and tutors arrived. In the case of Württemberg, for example, the conversion of the duke strengthened the political estates, who, as in Saxony, now saw themselves as defenders of the Protestant character of their state. The Württemberg estates even managed to enlist in their defense the great Protestant powers of Prussia, Denmark, and England.

After 1648 the imperial diet continued to be occupied with large numbers of religious gravamens; it was also forced now and then to deal with actual religious oppression. In the Palatinate, for instance, French occupation brought complaint, and later in the Treaty of Ryswick (1697) the diet had to resolve a treaty clause that sought to preserve a reinstituted Catholicism lands returned by the French on the right bank of the Rhine. On the whole, however, confessional struggles were not as significant as they had been in the previous century. The confessional status of the individual states or regions was expressed less in political terms and more through culture, in the thought and attitudes of the inhabitants, in schools and the system of poor relief, and, finally, in the reception of the secular movements of enlightenment and sensibility.

It is a fact of enormous general significance for Germany that multiple Christian confessions have been legally and politically recognized since the seventeenth century. The three confessions, supported by the secular authorities, created a body of teaching that fostered doctrinal distinctiveness, distrust, and misunderstanding instead of the sense of a common Christian community. The broad populace often accepted only its own rituals and festivals, while seeing the others as filled with heresy and superstition. Protestants thought the cult of Mary and the saints idolatrous, while Catholics saw Protestant rejection of most of the sacraments as blasphemous. The effort to convert was thus abandoned in favor of theological, educational, and political separation.

Northeastern and middle Germany had been and remained Protestant, the southeast and the Rhineland Catholic. The distribution was on a smaller scale in other parts of the empire. Upper Silesia was Catholic, Lower Silesia Protestant; the county of Mark, Protestant; Jülich, Berg, and the duchy of Westphalia, Catholic. Vienna, in many ways a truly international city, had an elementary Catholic character. The church, closely tied to the court, shaped the face of the city, and the religious orders played an important role for the aristocracy as well as the common people. Nuremberg and Ulm, on the other hand, were completely Protestant cities, as were Leipzig, Hamburg, and Berlin. In Protestant lands many of the Catholic holidays were unknown; pilgrimages and church anniversary celebrations did not occur; the number of clergy was significantly less; the church controlled much less property; and religious rituals and religious life were soberer, often stricter, and much more focused on teaching and obligation.

In Catholic Germany the Counter-Reformation had strengthened the common ground between church and state, stressing the affinities between the hieratic church and baroque absolutist sovereignty. *Ecclesia triumphans* and absolute monarchy were tightly joined together. The Counter-Reformation church developed the same tendencies toward displaying its power as did the monarchy. The high clergy exercised authority and the distance between them and the lower clergy grew. Spanish late scholasticism gradually triumphed in academic theology under the influence of the Jesuits. With it came its special form of logical argumentation and teaching and the veneration of the supernatural and the sacraments in ritual and sermon. Painting, music, and architecture represented the majesty of God and the church in sensual and ecstatic form to demonstrate religious and ecclesiastical security and provide religious discipline. These modes of representation permitted mystical inwardness and a popular style of preaching, but they were also a source of superficiality and led to a neglect of the village communes and of the general cultivation of souls. Only in the eighteenth century under the influence of the Enlightenment, and much later than in France, did the German Catholic church begin to emphasize the religious service, elementary and seminary education, and an active caritas. Indeed even then the reformers were more likely to be enlightened princes than the church itself.

In Protestant Germany the territorial rulers, in their function as first bishop, reestablished religious institutions wherever necessary after the Thirty Years War. There is much evidence that this required as much effort in sorely stricken areas as the general recovery itself. The pastorate, often living in collapsed and decayed housing, shared the wretched life of the population and waged a heroic struggle against need, brutality, illiteracy, and injustice. In this way they were often more goaded than given practical help by the territorial lords, consistories, and general superintendents. Through inspections, the latter intervened in the inner life of the church, controlling church attendance, teaching of the catechism, parish mores, the condition of buildings, the collection of money, and even the activities of the pastors themselves. All of this weakened the church's inner vitality and contributed to its appearance as an arm of the state. The rigidification of learned Protestant theology into a new orthodoxy had a similar effect. In addition, the struggles between Lutheran and Reformed theologians for a pure doctrine were by no means over. Both insisted dogmatically on the literal truth of scripture as the only source of salvation; both equated religious belief with ecclesiology, mistrusting every pietistic tendency and effort toward subjective religious certainty.

A scholastic component existed in seventeenth-century Lutheran theology alongside the learned humanistic teaching founded by Melanchthon. Lutheran scholastics accepted Aristotelian metaphysics and intensified the study of the church fathers. They assimilated the methods of Spanish late scholasticism in order to repudiate both Catholic and Reformed teachings. These theologians transformed the church into a teaching body concerned with a narrow range of private, familial, and communal questions; they lost almost all interest in political ethics and politics and even in the larger notion that the group was a communal body living in the grace of God. Instead, they stressed the sinful nature of humankind, thereby justifying religious and secular discipline and eliminating much of the emancipatory effect of justification by faith and individual salvation by the grace of God alone.

General interest in dogmatic conflict waned after the beginning of the eighteenth century. Even before the Enlightenment began to affect theology, theologians started to appreciate the demand for individual happiness and, within limits, to accept a subjective and optimistic view of life. Already in the late seventeenth century certain groups began to read the Bible together and to practice greater individual piety. Often led by the laiety, these *collegia pietas* were not manifestations of a protest movement, but still they were an index for unfulfilled religious needs and therefore challenged the "official" church. The pietists usually did not leave the regular parishes when they were allowed to continue their group practices.

Those groups or sects who did separate could not expect recognition as an independent confession, and they most often did not receive it. The community of brethren of Count Nikolaus Ludwig von Zinzendorf was the single group with a pietistic character that achieved a certain organizational independence. They were founded in 1722 in Herrnhut in Saxony in order to shelter the Moravian Brethren driven from Bohemia. Gradually German pietists and separatists of diverse social backgrounds joined their number. Externally, these communities remained part of the Lutheran church in Saxony; they were organized in synods, governed by elders, and remained, in theological terms, thoroughly christocentric. An intense religious life unfolded in these communes. Bound together by an emotional belief in Christ that despised all rationalism, they expressed themselves in devotional speeches and songs, confessions, and prayers. They were carriers of the first spontaneous missionary movement within German Protestantism. By the time of Zinzendorf's death in 1760, the Moravian Brethren had sent 226 missionaries to various parts of the world. Zinzendorf sponsored new communities and created new friendship circles within Germany as well. This new impulse within Protestant religious life found particular expression in church hymns and continued to influence even the young Herder and Goethe.

It had become evident in the era of religious warfare that Christian unity could not be regained through the suppression and reconversion of "heretics" or through a forced Reformation. Only irenic, selfless, and conciliatory efforts had any chance in bringing this goal closer to realization. Both theologians and politicians did make such efforts; they were all directed toward reunification on the basis of certain concessions from the Catholic church. From 1673 onward the cleric Spinola conducted numerous negotiations at Protestant courts with the support of the emperor and indirectly with that of the pope. His trips were as unsuccessful as Leibniz's vision of a universal church, one that would include all existing churches, smooth confessional controversies, and secure a common core of Christian doctrine. These plans for union were supported by Emperor Leopold I and the electoral archbishop Johann Philipp von Schönborn, in an effort to form a common front against both the Turks and the incursions of Louis XIV. Toward the end of the seventeenth century there were also irenic and conciliatory theologians among the Lutherans and the Reformed. Leibniz developed his plans for union, for instance, with both the Lutheran Gerard Molanus and the Reformed minister at the Berlin court, Jablonsky. Even though they remained marginal, there were a significant number of converts who were weary of Protestant orthodoxy.

Theological differences and competing political interests stood in the way of reunification. If the confessional barriers could no longer be set aside, it remained important to go beyond them.

RELIGIOUS AND SECULAR BAROQUE,
COURTLY CULTURE

With justice the baroque has been termed the art of the Counter-Reformation and of monarchical absolutism. It was stimulated and promoted by both, even as both church and monarchy found in the baroque the proper expression of their will toward self-display. Architecture, sculpture, painting, music, theater, and literature – all unfolded within the church and the courts but had an impact outside those domains. Baroque art essentially extended the formal elements of the Renaissance while bringing forth a new creative spirit. The static harmony of the Renaissance became dynamic; artists supplemented the ideal of natural beauty with a desire to represent the splendor of the supernatural by exalting forms, gestures, and color and by intensifying the symbolic. It was characteristic, especially in architecture, to create a tension between the geometrical spirit on the one hand – the strict rationality of the plan and the grounds – and, on the other, the suggestion of the infinite, by setting the strict lines in motion, shifting proportions, and exalting the decorative. Artists and architects paid greater attention to the visual dimension as well. They employed views, perspectives, light, and color to awaken the subjective impression of the infinite. The striving to create a total work of art was also characteristic. These artisans tried to make all the arts work together in order to create a total impression; space was thus shaped differently, and even the natural world of the garden was artificially reshaped and integrated into the design. If it was practically impossible to abolish spatial boundaries, artists and architects still sought to create the illusion of the infinite in order to experience the unity of the transcendentally ordered world. They shortened the perspective on ceiling paintings in order to create the impression of infinite space; they extended perspectives with staircases, lattice-work, and pathways; they intensified sensual reality in sculpture and painting. The representative creations of baroque art were the actual palace grounds with gardens and squares and church buildings with their surrounding lands.

Baroque palaces, gardens, theaters, and allées constituted extended spaces for the processions and receptions of courtly aristocratic society; they served the self-display of sovereign authority as its symbols and decorations. Similarly, baroque churches were sites for the presence of God and represented the power of the church. The congregations were to be filled with ecstasy by the wondrous representation of the supernatural. The opera also expressed baroque artistry and the unfolding patterns of social pleasure and display. In the opera all the arts were joined in the pursuit of festive pleasure. Its analogue in religious life was the grand celebration of high mass.

Baroque art was concentrated essentially in Austria, Bavaria, Upper

Swabia, Franconia, and the Rhineland. There was almost no religious baroque architecture in Protestant Germany, except for the construction of new court and palace churches, for instance, in Dresden, Wolfenbüttel, and Bückeburg. In Catholic Germany we must distinguish between new buildings and baroque renovation and refurbishment of older churches. The Jesuits, and particularly the Benedictines, built significant new monasteries. Princes and members of the wealthy nobility were even more substantial patrons – especially in Austria, Franconia, along the Rhine, and in Dresden and Berlin. They continued to build far into the eighteenth century, though German architects gradually replaced the Italians. Unimportant princes and members of the provincial nobility became involved, and in northern Germany baroque elements even appeared in the construction of burgher houses. In northern Germany as well, burghers cultivated baroque music, both religious and secular, and baroque literature. A lively music culture developed in Leipzig, where Johann Sebastian Bach was active as choirmaster at the Thomas church (1723-50), and in Hamburg, where Georg Friedrich Telemann was active for a time. Hamburg even cultivated the Italian opera that dominated at German courts, such as those in Vienna, Munich, Dresden, Berlin, Wolfenbüttel, and Mannheim. Every attempt to found an independent German opera failed, although there were permanent companies in Hamburg from 1678 to 1738 and in Leipzig from 1693 to 1729. The urban German public simply could not be persuaded to accept the mostly mythological themes of the great Italian operas and the German operas that were largely written in Italian.

The concert and spiritual music flowering in Protestant Germany shared with architecture and the visual arts the characteristic of tight logical construction alongside color and sensual elaboration. Orchestral works with pompous instrumentation and artistic solos served at moments of entertainment, festive pageants, courtly ceremonies, and religious rites. Need and taste often made them into slick commodities, but, especially in the Protestant hymn, cantata, and oratorio, they could also achieve deep inwardness and thereby enrich the expression of the emotions. Baroque art had its broadest social effect through this music, even if in Germany there was no national equivalent to the impact in England of Händel's *Messiah* and his *Judas Maccabaeus*.

The culture of baroque music brought with it a decisive expansion of musical technology through the improvement of instruments, the system of notation, and the printing of music. Builders developed new instruments and composers discovered new forms of instrumentation. The number of musicians and singers climbed substantially, and so did their social prestige.

Baroque art developed later in Germany than it had in southern and western Europe, and it only slowly achieved the same quality and independent significance. The first significant architects were Johann Bernhard Fischers von Erlach and Lukas von Hildebrandt, who from the 1690s were both active in Austria, and particularly in Vienna. The first is known for Schloss Schönbrunn, the second for Schloss Belvedere. The Dientzenhofers, father and son, were active in Prague; in Dresden, Daniel Pöppelmann and Georg Bähr. Already in 1688, Andreas Schlüter began to construct the palace in Berlin, and Balthasar Neumann started construction on the palace in Würzburg in 1720. Religious architecture in Bavaria and Upper Silesia flowered with the activities of the Asam brothers, Dominikus Zimmermann, and Johann Ulrich Fischer. The buildings, squares, and gardens of this era bear witness to the high artistic imagination and technical skill. Though money was "squandered," construction nevertheless created work and supported artists and artisans. Creative talents were tapped according to the extent and size of the tasks. We must remember that the buildings of this period remain among the most significant architectural structures unto our own day; in some sense they were without descendents. Among such surviving sites we need only think of Mannheim and Karlsruhe, Herrenhausen near Hanover and Kassel-Wilhelmshöhe, Bruchsal, Brühl, Donaueschingen, Pommersfelden, Nymphenburg, Potsdam, and Breslau.

In the second third of the eighteenth century, the baroque style was gradually transformed into the rococo. The transition, at first in the construction of interiors, did not simply mark a fall into the ornate and the purely artistic, but also meant a rejection of the solemn, a greater intimacy, expansion in the wealth of forms, and, in the best examples, an incomparable union of intellectuality and sensuality, humanity and perfection. The rococo palace already symbolized the break with the solemnity of a strict monarchical absolutism, and the rococo church no longer represented the *Ecclesia triumphans* but a much more "humane" and less strict church, in which both sensuous fervor and superficiality appeared side by side.

Baroque sculpture was subordinated to architecture, with few exceptions (for example, the famous equestrian statue of the great elector by Andreas Schlüter). In the rococo, however, sculpture had a special flowering in porcelain art. German painting was at its best in architectural ornamentation and wall painting, but panel painting remained behind the levels of the Italian and Dutch masters. Music, on the other hand, gradually emancipated itself from its Italian and Dutch models over the course of the eighteenth century. Händel, the sons of Bach, and the Mannheim school were all influential outside Germany, and they laid the groundwork for the great flowering of Viennese classicism at the end of the eighteenth century.

Although Spanish protocol continued to dominate at the Viennese court at least until the death of Charles VI (1740), the model of the French court and French courtly manners came to shape other parts of Germany. The French style was characteristically dominated by the garden as the setting for a closed society, where it could be preoccupied with its own display and entertainment. Constructed in a strictly geometrical pattern, the French garden extended the rational architectural style into the open, created a formal nature from the natural setting, which then served as part of the architecture. The rococo contributed a playful and exotic tone to the garden, adding rare trees and animals, pagodas and teahouses. Social gatherings at court or in the garden, at festivals or the hunt also became works of art. Codes of hierarchy and dress regulated such gatherings and daily life; they made life at court costly. The normal and the habitual were constantly staged anew, redecorated, varied, and elaborated. Life at court was subordinated to the pressure of fashion, ritual, and an elaborate social style. Religious services were also integrated into the way of life, and those chosen for life at court were educated to its demands.

Courtly culture lacked a popular dimension and was far removed from the life of commoners in the cities. The use of French at court and contempt for the inelegance of the German language intensified the distance. Nonetheless, attempts had been made already in the seventeenth century to reintroduce German – the "Fruchbringende Gesellschaft" (1617) and Martin Opitz's *Buch von der deutschen Poeterey* (1624) as famous examples – and a number of smaller courts began to recultivate the use of the German language and literature even before the Enlightenment began to have an impact. There also was an indigenous courtly literature in the seventeenth century. Novels of politics and individual heroism by Zeesen, Lohenstein, and Anton Ulrich von Braunschweig were extensive compendia of knowledge and courtly life, and these continued to have influence far into the eighteenth century.

Although baroque art and literature remained intensely formal and rule-bound, they were able to express suffering, doubt, resignation concerning the illusory nature of the world, and even mystical ardor. This occurred, however, in the dictated and customary style codified by art theory, rhetoric, and poetics, whereby each emotion had a particular mode of representation. The categories mirrored, according to the aesthetics of the era, the order of things. Preserving and using such categories was the need of men who had experienced the greatest shocks to their sense of order and security.

SCIENCE, CULTURE, EDUCATION

The seventeenth century was one of the great epochs in the history of the sciences. The eighteenth century largely built upon and transformed into practice the inventions, discoveries and intellectual formulations of the seventeenth century. These developments certainly cannot be followed within the confines of a particular region or nation, for political and even confessional differences did not constitute an insuperable barrier. In general, however, the Protestant states gradually became preeminent –

especially Geneva, England, and the Netherlands. If the German contribution remained relatively slight, it was due to the lengthy dominance of religious questions in the sixteenth century, the economic and cultural collapse as a result of the Thirty Years War, the lack or relative insignificance of overseas shipping and trade, weak domestic markets, and encrusted social relationships. The awkward style of late humanist erudition long continued to dominate, while the spirit and methods of experimental natural science found resonance only with the greatest difficulty.

Mathematics was basic to scientific thought in the seventeenth century. Its development largely began in the service of astronomy with the publication of Copernicus's *De revolutionibus orbium coelestium* (final version, 1543), and followed from Kepler's calculations of planetary movements at the beginning of the seventeenth century, to Isaac Newton's gravitational theory and infinitesimal calculus (1660s) and Leibniz's development of differential calculus. Developments in optics (Galileo, Newton, Huyghens) and mechanics (Torricelli, Boyle, Guericke) were closely linked to those in mathematics and astronomy. Harvey's discovery of the circulation of the blood and Leeuwenhoeck's studies in microbiology had, by the first half of the seventeenth century, prepared the ground for modern biology, physiology, and medicine.

Scientific thought emancipated itself from the primacy of theology in this process, even if individual scientists often thought the search for better understanding was not in real conflict with the truths of a revealed Christianity. Did not the lawful, calculable, and measurable movement of the planets, resting as it did on gravitation, prove that God had created an ordered universe? Were not men's innate ideas a pure demonstration of mathematical laws? Were not the mathematical structure and the mechanical movement practically proofs for the existence of God? René Descartes made such thoughts the basis for methodical "scientific" thought – the search for distinct knowledge by using doubt systematically and by bracketing metaphysical explanations. Cartesianism spread rapidly throughout Europe in the second half of the seventeenth century, though it did not appear in Germany until the eighteenth. By then countermovements had already begun. The new experimental method, promoted especially by Newton, was among those movements; it stressed careful observation and thought based on inductions from individual cases to general explanations.

Experimental scientists were not completely lacking in Germany, however. Otto von Guericke, mayor of Magdeburg, learned jurist and diplomat, used his sizable wealth in the service of science. Typically, his discovery of the vacuum stemmed from cosmological concerns that finally had practical consequences. In his famous demonstration of his discovery before the imperial diet in Regensburg (1654), he had sixteen horses on each side attempt to pull apart two half-spheres held together by a vaccuum; this, of course, was basically an example of scientific propaganda.

Gottfried Wilhelm Leibniz (1646-1716) was the towering scientific figure in Germany during these years and one of the most significant thinkers between the medieval and modern periods. He was a doctor of law, a diplomat in the service of the electorate of Mainz, and a scholar in contact with the leading scientists and scholars of his day. He concerned himself with philosophy, mathematics, mechanics, physics, physiology, and chemistry. In 1685 he entered Hanoverian service as court councillor and librarian and began to support Hanoverian political claims on the basis of a broadly conceived history of the Guelf dynasty. He was simultaneously an organizer and promoter of science on a large scale; he also drafted recommendations for securing a lasting peace and for reunifying the Christian churches on the basis of a natural theology. In 1700 he was named the first president of a society of sciences that, largely modeled on his own plans, became the subsequent Royal Prussian Academy of Sciences in Berlin. Similar societies were established in Vienna, Dresden, and Petersburg based on his recommendations. As a universal thinker, one who still had a pansophic ideal of the unity of the sciences in terms of a "mathesis universalis," he was an important transitional figure in transforming scientific inquiry into practice and into a form of knowledge that shaped the eighteenth century. He remained a philosopher and his cosmology stayed metaphysical: God is not the first cause but rather the sufficient reason for causes, the prime monad; the world functions mechanistically but cannot be explained mechanistically; it is the best of all possible worlds because its preestablished harmony is the necessary expression of the order of all monads in time and space. His impact predated the emergence of individual scientific disciplines, but he pointed the way even there. Convinced that science encompasses all areas of human thought, activity, and behavior, and that the state must be its supporter, he believed – along with Newton and most of the principle thinkers of the seventeenth century – that scientific method was unified.

Leibniz represented in exemplary fashion the dynamic tendency and independence of scientific thought in Europe. Historians have spoken not improperly of a scientific revolution that preceded the economic and social revolutions of the next period. The conflict between the "ancients" and the "moderns" in all areas of knowledge, behavior, and practice was one of the symbols of the age. The moderns supported change according to rational principles based on experimentally proven truths, and they rejected learned opinions that could not withstand methodological doubt and systematic examination. Progress became a goal that necessarily stretched far into the future because the majority of humankind was not yet ready for it. Even among those who took the step toward recognizing modern natural science were some who hesitated to adapt these notions to social and political life. But even here modern science could not be stopped. Thomas Hobbes adapted the Cartesian method to the study of society, Spinoza developed a rational ethics; Christian Thomasius expanded natural rights theory in connection with Pufendorf, Leibniz, and Hobbes; and Christian Wolff, who joined together traditional Aristotelianism with the Leibnizian drive toward system, evolved a closed and logically consequential rational system linking nature, society, and religion. He became one of the great inspirations for systematic compilations of knowledge, as in Zedler's great *Universallexikon,* and the law, as in the great legal codifications of the late eighteenth century. If Christian Wolff's works are to a certain extent a throwback to the universal interests of the baroque era, they also anticipate the Enlightenment in their rational structure and practical focus.

The development of scientific thought and practice in the European republic of letters was spurred onward by the growing interest of the public in scientific research; in turn, this stimulated a rapidly expanding publications network. Scholars involved themselves increasingly in the topics and results of scientific discussions and research. Natural science, in particular, became a fashionable object of discussion in courtly society, even as the same scientific discovery was being rejected at the older universities. If the liberal arts had only a preparatory status and the natural sciences as yet had no place, traditional teaching at the universities continued to be disseminated in the other faculties of theology, law, and medicine. Professors continued for quite some time to lecture in Latin, and students continued to write in Latin; the entire university life, in fact, was stamped by a corporate, erudite style. Change began only with the founding of Halle (1694) and Göttingen (1737). Even at these universities, however, there was at first no place for the natural sciences; but in Halle the cameral sciences began to be taught from an early date, and in Göttingen natural scientific training occurred within a philosophical faculty who quickly achieved parity with the other traditional faculties. The academies proved to be a much more important form of organization for the natural sciences. They first appeared in Italy during the Renaissance but flowered in France and England. In Germany the first academy of natural scientists was founded in 1652 in Schweinfürt, due to the private initiative of a few medical doctors, and was named the Leopoldina in honor of the emperor who granted the privileges. The Berlin Academy was founded in 1700, the Göttingen Academy of Sciences in 1751, and the Bavarian Academy of Sciences in 1759.

The experimental investigation of science was developed by individuals and small groups in their studies and in early laboratories that were no longer alchemical kitchens or astrological chambers. Princes and wealthy members of the nobility and burgher class often sponsored the research. They developed an interest in foreign lands, peoples, religions, customs, and constitutions simultaneously with their interest in natural phenomena. Similar impulses stimulated the scientific interest in economy, geography, and political science – fields that were to be called statistics in the later eighteenth century.

In the eighteenth century chemistry, geology, biology, and anthropology gradually came to the fore. Physicists occupied themselves with problems of electricity, in mechanics with steam power, and in metallurgy with the use of coal to extract iron ore. The tendency toward comprehensive systemizing and classifying, which reached a peak in Carl von Linne's *Systema Naturae* (1735), was soon surpassed by the developmental view of Buffon in his *Histoire naturelle* (1749). In a parallel manner the eighteenth century began to use a concept of development to understand both culture and human society. Within church and legal history the first steps were taken to examine the historical roots of the present and to collect documents systematically; in spite of this beginning, however, history did not yet become a scientific discipline.

The number of works published in the vernacular clearly climbed from the second half of the seventeenth century, even though we only have secure statistics for a later period. In 1714, for example, 628 new works were published in Germany; by 1800 the number had climbed to 3,900! In Leipzig (1682) the first scholarly periodical, the *Acta Eruditorum,* was published, and already a few years later (1688) Christian Thomasius edited the first German language journal. Over the course of the following century the publication of general, popular, and specialized journals increased greatly, and by the last third of the eighteenth century they reached astounding numbers. Again in Leipzig the first newspaper began to appear thrice weekly by 1660. By the eighteenth century newspapers began to separate into those dealing in commentary, so-called intelligencers, and those that dealt more strictly in reporting events. These trends reveal the growth and formation of a reading public within the nobility and the urban burgher classes, who had increasingly broader intellectual interests and who required a specialized academic education for their professional activities.

The seventeenth century was as innovative in educational theory as it had been in philosophy and natural science. Indeed the attitudes toward education altered with the new philosophical understanding of nature, with its changing view of humankind's purpose and place in the cosmos. In the beginning of the century, education was still meant to prepare the individual to recognize and follow God's intentions, but it became reorganized around a more secular self-realization. Educational theory became ethically didactic, teaching the individual to avoid evil and seek the good in the service of self-knowledge. For this reason the seventeenth century has often been called a didactical age, even though it took until the eighteenth for true teaching methods to develop.

Educational theory is bounded at both ends by the great figures of Johann Amos Comenius and Johann Heinrich Pestalozzi. Comenius wanted to improve both humankind and the world through the dissemination of knowledge; moreover, he attempted to codify all existing knowledge in one large encyclopedic work that also linked together God and Reason

(Pansophia). In his *Didactica Magna* he sketched a model of education structured around the development of understanding in the pupil that stretched, in stages, from infancy to the twenty-fourth year. Comenius brought new assumptions to bear concerning knowledge and the nature of the individual; he conceived humankind as comprising morally responsible creatures, whose wills enabled them to acquire particular knowledge in the pursuit of individual goals. Comenius's teaching could have led to a one-sided emphasis on rote learning and could have reduced teaching to a mere conveying of information. But he resisted this by emphasizing self-knowledge and demanding that humans place all knowledge in relation to themselves. Comenius thus placed the teaching of the will at the center of his theory; the task was to seek the perfection of man as man, that is, humanity itself.

Although the educators of the period believed in schooling, they did not attempt to alter social relations. Individuals were still raised within their particular estate and educated to fulfill their appointed social roles. There were few efforts to educate the broad population, but among the upper strata the educational ideal remained that of the gentleman, the courtier, and the learned scholar. Schools for the aristocracy or *Ritterakademien* were created alongside the Latin schools; and, in the eighteenth century, as aristocrats increasingly began to study at universities, other specialized schools were established to teach courtly behavior, dancing, fencing, and riding. The *gymnasia illustria* deserve special emphasis in the context of early schools. Larger Latin schools were transformed into educational institutions for higher servants of the state. These schools scorned the "pedantic" school system of their own day. The dominant perspective in these *gymnasia illustria,* and in the aristocratic schools as well, was to develop useful knowledge in an aristocratic world increasingly politically rationalized and dominated by the courts. They emphasized modern languages, especially French, over the study of classical languages; the practical study of political geography and politics gained in significance as well.

As much as these schools distanced themselves from the older theological-humanistic system, they were by no means completely secularized. In Catholic Germany, for instance, the Jesuits knew how to join religious training with the new curriculum, and in Protestant Germany as well there were interesting and effective syntheses of the new educational ideal with the new religious ideals of pietism.

The political significance of education and schooling was recognized early. Among the seventeenth-century cameralists, for example, Johann Joachim Becher wrote in his *Methodus didactica* (1668) that nothing better could be recommended to the sovereign and regent than the "proper education of the young," because that is the "foundation and noblest maxim of the state." In fact, princes and governments increasingly concerned themselves with schooling. It was among the most important

duties of the territorial princes within the Protestant states to see that
ministers were well educated and that the catechism, the hymnal, and Bible
reading were spread throughout the population. Compulsory schooling
was introduced as early as 1598 in Strasbourg's ecclesiastical code. In the
seventeenth century – Weimar in 1619, Gotha in 1642 – required schooling
became a more regular part of school codes. Although it was some time
later that compulsory elementary education emerged, the movement in
that direction can certainly be recognized. Protestant states led the way,
especially the smaller ones, such as Saxony-Gotha under Duke Ernst the
Pious. There and even more so in Brandenburg-Prussia, where Friedrich
Wilhelm I introduced compulsory education in 1716/17, religious and
educational motivations were tightly linked to the economic interests of the
state. The Prussian school code of 1763 required attendance from the fifth to
the thirteenth or fourteenth year.

The Enlightenment and pietism contributed other newer impulses to the
expansion of public schooling. Both were actually pedagogical movements.
Under their influence, notions of the individual, the citizen, and the patriot
became educational ideals.

The actual state of the schools in the eighteenth century remained far
behind the legislation. Regular school attendance was never achieved in the
countryside. The usual curriculum consisted largely of religious instruction,
with some reading, writing, singing, and simple arithmetic. There were
insufficient numbers of schools and teachers; the latter were often poorly
educated themselves and even more poorly paid. In the cities and large
villages the sextons and choirmasters often doubled as the teachers.
Teachers were usually so poorly paid that they supplemented their income
through some handicraft. Parental poverty and indifference was often
matched by seigneurial selfishness and indifference and by the failure of the
state in rural areas to put its decrees into practice. Essentially, it was left to
pastors to concern themselves with the choice and education of the teachers
and with the curriculum itself. In Catholic areas many a monastery was
responsible for popular education. In the cities numerous private schools
existed alongside the elite Latin schools. These "street corner schools" or
Winkelschulen often had large numbers of students, uneducated teachers, and
inadequate quarters; but for the lower orders they were often the only
source of education outside the family, and their significance should not be
underestimated. More established poor schools or elementary schools were
fairly rare until late in the eighteenth century. Then middle schools or
Realschulen also emerged. These were established alongside the Latin and
classical schools to educate the lower and middling orders of the urban
burgher classes. They originated in Halle, where mathematical, natural
scientific, mechanical, and artisanal courses had been given since early in
the eighteenth century. Johann Julius Hecker came from the Francke
educational institution in Halle, becoming at first the inspector of the royal

poorhouse in Potsdam (1735) and then minister in Berlin (1747) where he founded the first economic-mathematical *Realschule,* a vocational school that also educated future teachers. Hecker was also the author of the Prussian school code of 1763.

The beginnings of practical and political education also can be traced back to the second half of the seventeenth century. Veit Ludwig von Seckendorff, the author of the famous book, *Vom Teutschen Fürstenstaat* or *Concerning the German Princely State* (1665), believed that every "future housefather, burgher and inhabitant of the land" in every estate should acquire the practical knowledge required concerning the "natural and intelligent matters...of the government." The Gotha school code recognized civics as a subject, and gradually handbooks of the state, officeholding, and particular occupations were also written. Christian Weise, the director of the Zittau humanistic secondary school or *Gymnasium,* wrote books (1675 and 1688) about the intelligent steward and the political orator. In them he developed a theory of political behavior as the guide for governmental and administrative practice and for the individual at court and the officeholder as well. Eventually Weise introduced his *Politica* in the secondary curriculum, because he thought the knowledge of political matters to be useful and interesting. The Prussian general school code of 1763 planned to instruct future teachers in silkworm raising; thus we can still note at the end of our period the interpenetration of economic and political motives that was articulated in the parallel developments of the modern state and universal public education.

PIETISM

The same impulses transforming the sciences are apparent in the recommendations, plans, and measures toward improving education. These were decisive in secularizing thought and gradually rationalizing social life. Additionally, they had an impact on religious and ecclesiastical life that was even more profound than the direct reaction to the confessional era. Orthodoxy and the pastoral church lost influence within Protestantism, especially over the educated classes. They began to seek new avenues of intellectual and emotional piety, seeing reason as the capacity to comprehend the wisdom of God, and the truth of revelation and love or emotion as the capacity to grasp the love of God. Although contemporaries and especially later interpreters often viewed rationalism and pietism, Enlightenment and sensibility as opposites, they were closely joined. Both emancipated and empowered the individual to independent thought and feeling. For pietists and members of the Enlightenment, there was harmony with, and not conscious opposition to, Christian revealed religion. Both groups entered the established churches and produced their own theologians. Evangelical clergymen and educated theologians belonged to the spokesmen of the German Enlightenment; and pietism produced ferment both within the established churches and in the cultural life of the period.

Pietism was an educational movement as well as a religious one, and it exerted a powerful influence on the educational system. Emerging from Lutheranism, pietism strove to rekindle the Reformation. Religious life was to supplant a rigidified dogma, and spirit was to infuse the sense of office. Belief was to be more than "correct" and become a practical, living belief affirmed in love. A theology of self-justification was to be replaced by one emphasizing spiritual rebirth through belief. One could find in Luther's writings the individual struggle for correct beliefs and security in belief experienced as the grace of God. Also important were traditions of mystical spiritualism that had been bitterly resisted by orthodox Lutherans: the early seventeenth-century works of Jakob Böhme, Johann Arndt, and Johann Valentin Andreae. In the eighteenth century, furthermore, pietists assimilated the writings of English Puritans, French mystics, and French quietists. Philipp Jakob Spener and August Hermann Francke thought highly of Puritan devotional literature. The French influenced Gottfried Arnold and Francke in emphasizing a selfless, silent love of God that gave the individual, in opposition to the world, a sovereign inner freedom.

The beginnings of pietism can be traced to the movement of piety by Johann Arndt, whose devotional writings were widely read. Philipp Jakob Spener, the true founder of pietism, wrote the foreword, the "Pia Desideria," to Arndt's breviary in 1675. The fallen state of the church, he was convinced, was caused by the loss of living belief; for that reason he believed rebirth was necessary, particularly among the pastorate. For this to occur, in turn, the clergy had to be better educated and trained and special focus needed to be placed on reading the Bible. Spener's enormous correspondence in combination with his students spread pietism as far as Switzerland and Scandinavia. Pietists also deeply affected the new university of Halle. There and elsewhere – in Leipzig, Erfurt, Hamburg, and Gotha – pietists and the orthodox began from the 1690s to engage in severe controversies.

In the midst of these controversies Francke's activities in Halle gave a new accent to pietism. In 1695 he began the construction of the so-called orphanage or *Waisenhaus*. With state support, private gifts, and money from his own economic activities, he was able to expand its facilities into a comprehensive set of school institutions, whose effects reached socially far into the nobility, and geographically as far distant as Russia, England, North America, southern Africa, and India. Halle became the starting point for the domestic and foreign missionary movement; the Bible was printed there in cheap editions, completely according to entrepreneurial principles. Francke's seminary for future teachers became the model for teaching seminaries throughout Prussia. Many of the theologians, jurists, and cameralists later trained at the university were stamped by the practical spirit of Halle pietism. In its practical direction this strand of pietism was a social reform movement, not one, however, that sought to alter the social system as much as to improve society by bettering the individuals in their preappointed orders. Practical piety or the *praxis pietatis* went hand in hand with occupational training: The Christian was "trained and fitted out for all good works," so the world would recognize there were no more useful individuals than those who "committed themselves to Jesus Christ." Francke had a significant religious and pedagogical impact in the eighteenth century; his teachings kept alive both the work of Ratichius and Comenius. He emphasized that children needed strict oversight and constant work, and he organized burgher schools around a practical curriculum. He stood close to the Enlightenment both in these attitudes and in his religious ecumenicalism. Thus Francke contributed in many ways to supplanting Lutheran orthodoxy, activating religious life, tying that life closer to profane pursuits, and interpreting that life more optimistically.

In Württemberg pietism took another no less significant form. There pietism found its beginnings in Arndt and Andrae and in the eighteenth century retained a speculative biblical dimension in spite of its home-baked educational character. Johann Albrecht Bengel, its most important representative, united a strict philological method of textual criticism with a speculative belief in revelation; he calculated the exact date for the return of Christ and the beginning of the thousand-year reign on earth as the year 1836. His original student, Friedrich Christoph Oetinger, discovered in the concept of "life" the transcendence of spirit and matter. In arguing against Cartesian rationalism, Oetinger brought together the writings of Jakob Böhme, the pansophy of the seventeenth century, and the new natural scientific speculation, creating a sacred philosophy or *philosophia sacra* that recognized God in worldly appearances. His struggles against enlightened rationalism had far-reaching consequences. His ideas were transmitted through the Tübingen Seminary to Schelling, Hegel, and Hölderlin, and through their writings they entered into philosophical idealism. Pietism deeply affected religious life and the views of broad segments within the Württemberg church.

Pietism had a more diffuse impact in other regions and areas of culture. The movement, for instance, did not have the same significance within the Reformed parts of Germany, and where it managed to sink roots – in Bremen or Mülheim a.d. Ruhr – it had a mystical and quietistic dimension. On the other hand, pietism exerted a strong influence on religious hymns and sermons. It also contributed significantly to the examination and description of individual development to the point of spiritual conversion. Heinrich Jung-Stilling's autobiography was written in the pietistic spirit; and without pietism, neither Karl Philipp Moritz's psychological novel *Anton Reiser* nor Goethe's *Wilhelm Meister* or *Poetry and Truth* are thinkable.

It is possible that the spread of pietism into worldly affairs in the decades from 1740 to 1750 onward was not less significant than its effect on religious and church life. It is equally possible that pietism furthered secularization by emphasizing the devout life of the individual and by abandoning the official church in favor of gatherings of small groups of the like-minded. Did not the interest in the new individual in the new group cause interest in God to be suppressed and bring with it the conclusion that the traditional church was a failure? At the same time, however, pietism intensified and activated religious feelings; it developed a greater interest in the individual and his or her spiritual development; and it brought forth a new willingness to care for others. All of these notions spread beyond the inner pietistic circles by way of prayer, devotional tracts, and literature, which significantly enriched the language and altered social sensibilities. Pietism was not a reaction to the Enlightenment but a parallel movement. Both contributed to secularizing thought and behavior and to a sense of individual certainty by emboldening the individual to independent thought and feeling. Both movements expanded individual self-awareness and expressiveness. Pietism unmistakably influenced patriotic language and early nationalism as well, especially in forming a secularized language for the political community from concepts of faith and personal piety.

Certainly not all the irrationalism and emotionalism of the eighteenth century can be attributed to pietism. These strands were European-wide in scope, having begun first in England. At the turn of the century, Shaftesbury had formulated feeling and sensibility as basic categories of moral and aesthetic perception and education. He also attributed to the creative individual, the artistic genius, the right to make his or her own creative rules. The continental reader discovered in English literature a hitherto unknown free language of the emotions – discussions of mourning, pain, and a yearning for death. Melancholy and cults of friendship sprang up everywhere; people gave themselves over to moods in order to experience themselves and the world anew. Such feelings were often linked to a critique of contemporary life, or to irony and a real or mannered sense of cultural despair. From Arthur Young and Thomas Gray to Samuel Richardson, Oliver Goldsmith, and Lawrence Sterne, numerous works explored the world of the emotions and formed a new moral and aesthetic sense of judgment. These works were especially important for the Germans, since through them they experienced for the first time the free intellectual and cultural world of the educated gentleman and lesser noble. Their importance was only matched later by the writings of Jean Jacques Rousseau, who explored the inner world of the passions with even more directness.

If the movement of sensibility in Germany had pietistic and quietistic strands, so too did the Enlightenment have a conservative religious dimension. Both movements unfolded within the traditional order shaped by the church, state, and society. Members of the Enlightenment had no desire to break free, but through proper action they sought to change and reform their world slowly from within.

ENLIGHTENMENT

The so-called Enlightenment or *Aufklärung* emerged later in Germany than in England, the Netherlands, or France. Among the factors for its emergence within Europe were the formation of a capitalist market system, the gradual expansion of the nonnoble, urban classes, the development of the natural sciences and beginnings of a historical textual criticism, the emergence of philosophical rationalism, and the rational politics of the sovereign states. Bacon, Descartes, Hobbes, Spinoza, Leibniz, and Thomasius paved the way, and the Enlightenment transformed their thoughts into a general pattern of thought, a program of action that was to affect all areas of social and cultural life.

The Enlightenment came to dominate in Germany, or at least to become the motive force, only after 1763. Naturally, however, it originated much farther back in time and had its own independent contours in relation to the broader European movement. Leibniz was a crucial German figure. His universalism, interpretation of the world as a theodicy, and optimism all shaped German Enlightenment thought. Certain of his convictions proved especially significant: that this world is the best of all possible worlds, that everything strives toward completion, and that the true progress of humanity lies in the advancement of knowledge. These ideas, in fact, survived the Enlightenment and continued to influence the worldview of classicism and the great systematic efforts of philosophical idealism.

Although Leibniz saw himself as a metaphysician, the Enlightenment excluded metaphysics from the domain of intelligent understanding. It sought to explain the world rationally and wanted the practical actions of humankind to be shaped by rationality. Philosophy acquired a practical imperative in this way. Perception became the basis for practical knowledge, psychology became more important than formal logic. Samuel Pufendorf, Christian Thomasius, and the most influential of them all, Christian Wolff in Halle, were the chief figures in the early phase of German Enlightenment philosophy. Using mathematics as the foundation, Wolff sought to make philosophy into a useful and certain science by constructing clear concepts and proofs. He created a rationalistic system, a system of the sciences whose subdisciplines encompassed the knowledge of the world. Philosophy should only be concerned with possible matters insofar as they are logically free from contradiction; it must join together a science of facts with true relationships. Religious revelation cannot contradict this system of reason; if necessary, it must transcend it. Similarly, religion might well crown ethics, but it cannot be its foundation.

Insofar as religion is an object of knowledge, in sum, it must be conceived rationally.

Wolff's system dominated in German academic philosophy until Kant's great critiques appeared and shattered the bases of dogmatic rationalism. Wolff's students did little to extend it farther, but they did apply it to practical philosophy and psychology. From these areas his influence spread into the legal thought of the eighteenth century. Another movement of "popular philosophy" also spread broadly throughout the population. The popular philosophers concerned themselves with happiness and utility, with realistic questions concerning morality and emotional life, with, in other words, the practical and theoretical difficulties in coping with life. In Germany they dissolved the boundary between philosophy as a strict science and as a general philosophical literature, creating both a philosophically shaped, analytical, and reflective language and new literary genre – small treatises, descriptions, tracts, dialogues – that reached an ever-growing audience.

Growing book production, increases in the number of writers, and an expanded reading public were basic factors to the spread of the Enlightenment. An enlightened society of readers and writers developed a loose consensus of assumptions and beliefs, a certain shared attitude and concern for problems of practical life, a common sensibility for psychological, moral, aesthetic, and political questions. Indeed this consensus went beyond the boundaries of particular states, nationalities, and even religious beliefs. The age of the Enlightenment engaged in a common activity of reading and writing, reasoning, reviewing, and criticizing. The number of books and journals grew to an extraordinary extent. Printers and booksellers, translators and reviewers shaped literary life and patterns of journalism that have largely survived to our day. Although German literary life lagged behind developments in France and England, it still achieved an overriding importance in the last third of the eighteenth century. Enlightened literature reshaped Germans' knowledge of the world, their social consciousness, and their educational patterns.

In the first third of the eighteenth century, moral weeklies were characteristic journals for transmitting enlightened values. The *"Vernünfftler"* was among the first journals of this kind, appearing in Hamburg (1713/14) essentially as extracts from the English *Tatler* and *Spectator*. The number of these mostly short-lived journals grew dramatically. Their titles were meant to be suggestive: *Der Bürger (The Citizen), Der Patriot, Der Menschenfreund (The Friend of Humanity), Der Weltbürger (The Cosmopolitan), Der Freygeist (The Free Spirit), Der Einsiedler (The Hermit), Der Redliche (The Candid One), Der Träumer (The Dreamer), Briefe (Letters), Anmerkungen (Notes)*. The weeklies spoke directly to the reader; they were not concerned with current affairs but with moral instruction and conversation that fostered human happiness. They were read by sectors of the nobility but predominantly by burghers who found their own self-worth confirmed in the "message of virtue" or *Botschaft der Tugend* (W. Martens). Women and children were also frequently addressed in the weeklies, and they, too, became a significant segment of the readership. Indeed, the weeklies seem to have created this audience. For women and children, especially, the weeklies expanded their life experience and made them indirect participants in discussing issues directly facing them: virtuous behavior in home and society, children's education, the use and advantages of education for girls and women.

The Enlightenment was an educational movement at its core, seeking to emancipate the individual from senseless authority, to foster learning and autonomous thought and action. It stressed process and self-education; but, in the view of its writers, the process needed strengthening by establishing adequate social and political institutions. Government and administration also needed to become enlightened, in order to comprehend that proper education rests in the nature of humankind and society. The social and political order, in turn, must become identical with a rational legal order that promotes the individual as citizen and patriot, as rational thinker and actor. Such an individual will act with insight within the social order and community; he will make himself useful and will help others to become independent and useful individuals. Such an education did not attempt to eliminate social differences, but it did seek to interpret those differences functionally; in so doing it could awaken enormous energies and social expectations for the future. German political and social reality, however, prevented such expectations from being fulfilled. So, too, did actual enlightened educational practice, because it merely sought to prepare the individual to fulfill a useful function within society. There was indeed a certain dictatorial quality to enlightened pedagogy particularly insofar as the Enlightenment believed that the individual must be encouraged and even forced to pursue his well-being and happiness. This attitude was also shared by enlightened regimes who saw themselves as benevolent guardians and educators of their people. In any event, the practical consequences of enlightened educational theory were first felt in the last third of the eighteenth century. The so-called philanthropy movement began with a work by Basedow, one that bore the characteristic title *Vorstellung an Menschenfreunde und vermögende Männer über Schulen, Studien und ihren Einfluss auf die öffentliche Wohlfahrt* (*Thoughts to Friends of Humanity and Men of Means Concerning Schools, Studies and Their Influence on the Public Welfare*) (1768).

The Enlightenment focused on political and social questions in all their dimensions: the form of the state, the legal order, the judicial system, criminal punishment, social welfare and hence communal government or *Policey*, the economy, the relations between the social orders, and public morality. Typically these issues were first discussed in scholarly and moral tones in learned books and journals. In Germany this is one more sign that the Enlightenment basically was carried by scholars and the educated classes who saw politics and ethics as inseparable aspects of practical philosophy. In the later eighteenth century, however, particularly as the discussions became more concentrated and interwoven, practical reform issues increasingly became more significant. Indeed, as the demand for reform became greater, these discussions became more overtly political.

Enlightened thinkers reinterpreted the existing world with ever increasing certainty. Substantial differences between Germany and western Europe emerged in this regard. Not only had enlightened social and political thought developed later in Germany, but it remained more derivative. There was no independent political, social, and economic theory. Practical philosophy, traditional jurisprudence, and cameralism, long under the influence of Wolff, continued to dominate discussions of state, economy, and society. It is symptomatic that Johann Heinrich von Justi, a Thuringian pastor's son, developed his theory of the state and society in the mid-eighteenth century in books dealing with political economy and social welfare or *Polizeiwissenschaft*. Similarly, contemporary political life and its history was treated in legal histories dealing with the empire and the individual states and territories. The most famous of these was Johann Jakob Moser's fifty-one volume *Teutscher Staatsrecht (German Constitutional Law)* that began appearing from 1737 onward. Germany did not produce distinguished political theorists with the intellectual independence and social prestige of Locke or Montesquieu. Friedrich II of Prussia was a particular exception. He viewed politics as the active domain of the absolute ruler, even though he no longer based his rule on divine right but on a social contract between ruler and ruled.

The Enlightenment did not generate any profound changes in social and political reality before the end of our period, but it did cause attitudes to alter. There must be cultural consequences once people begin to conceive of humanity as comprising individuals born free in nature, who established a common authority in order to preserve their security and freedom. Authority was thus not an end in itself but a means to achieve individual and general well-being. Government and administration, accordingly, were instruments to achieve this goal, and legislation gave it shape. Consequences also necessarily followed once the image of the ruler became that of a benevolent, enlightened officeholder who administered the state in trust – even though there were as yet no practical or institutional limits placed on that rule. Finally, there were also consequences once rule was no longer discussed exclusively in terms of individual rulers but focused more broadly on public morals and the social system itself, the nature of authority, the characteristics of a good prince, the responsibilities of ministers, councillors, and officials, the duties and rights of individuals, and justice and oppression.

These comments still require restrictions. No well-educated and free realm of public opinion – a consequence of the Enlightenment – existed as yet in Germany. The general exercise of censorship, especially in religious matters, was questioned, however, and to some extent suspended. Professors at the newly founded University of Göttingen, for instance, were granted freedom of expression. As another example, Gerard van Swieten influenced intellectual life in the Habsburg domains from about 1760 onward by allowing Jansenist writings and enlightened literature to enter there. Obviously the public need for information grew, causing a corresponding reaction in book and journal production. The circle of themes expanded from devotional and ethical literature to the practical, and thence to the political and critical. It is estimated that devotional writings still constituted 19 percent of the total book production in Germany in 1740, while literary works made up only 5.8 percent. By 1800 the percentages had more than reversed. The custom of reading grew, capturing the spirit of burgher women and even penetrating into the petty bourgeoisie. This happened not so much because of better schooling but because people had a growing interest in information, education, and knowledge of other peoples and the world. Reading was an important substitute in a society where there were few chances to gather practical experiences.

The Enlightenment was an educational movement in literary philosophical form throughout Europe, and this was even more exclusively the case in Germany. Its spokesmen were convinced of the need for constant learning and free public discussion of significant issues. Widespread publicity, freedom of the press, and abolition of censorship became a continuous and loudly stated demand from the 1760s onward. An intensive, critical public discussion of social and political problems, in fact, did develop in these years. Such discussion, of course, joined with earlier literary and journalistic discussions of belief and education and of ethics and useful behavior that also had had a political and emancipatory dimension.

It is characteristic of the German Enlightenment that its members believed change and improvement were part of a long-term process. They hoped that publicity and education eventually would create an independent political consciousness within the population, one that would affect the behavior of both rulers and ruled. Such an assumption was justified, they believed, because numerous princes and governments had already proven themselves sympathetic to enlightened language and had begun reforms in the name of enlightenment. In the process enlightened publicists supported and praised, often uncritically, the reform efforts. By accepting enlightened ideas and reform proposals, in turn, the monarchies in Germany – especially in their absolutist form – were able to gather political prestige about themselves at the very moment the French monarchy entered into a period of irreversible decline. In particular, the energetic activities of the rulers in the two great states – Friedrich II in Prussia and Maria Theresia and Joseph II in Austria – brought about increasing rationality in the affairs of state, and their efforts to promote administrative reform awakened the impression that social and political developments were once again in flux after the long period of stagnation.

THE WORLDVIEW AND VALUES OF THE
BURGHER CLASS

As an educational movement of burghers, the Enlightenment has often been set in opposition to the aristocratic and courtly movement of the baroque. This social explanation is only superficially meaningful, because the ruling and nonruling aristocracy continued to dominate political and cultural life in the eighteenth century. Wealthy burghers in the larger cities were as yet hardly competitive as patrons and sponsors. Moreover, in individual cases the aristocracy continued to contribute to the educational and literary movement. Yet the emphasis indeed shifted as the number of bourgeois scholars, writers, artists, and educators increased. They constituted the core of a new subgroup of educated or *Gebildeten,* who permanently came to enlarge ranks of those concerned with personal culture and education.

This group of the educated was characterized more by a burgher mentality, worldview, and life-style, than by a special social status. Within the Enlightenment the concept of citizen or *Bürger* was tied to two complexes of meaning: one stemmed from the notion of the citizen within the city state *(polites, cives)* and one derived from natural rights doctrines wherein the citizen was an equal member of civil society. This concept, in other words, intersected both the older conception of the urban burgher and the newer and modern class notion of the bourgeois. The basic element of the burgher worldview was the emphasis on personality. One's value and position was not determined by birth or membership in a particular estate or association but was derived from an inalienable human dignity. The degree of human dignity, in turn, was shaped by service, achievement, and thus by the extent of an individual's realization of his or her potential within society. Such a personality could only develop free from domination by others, proving itself in contests for prestige and profit but being grounded in self-worth. But such development was only possible when the individual was propertied or gifted. The social relations among people thus became rationalized and functionalized, moralized and sentimentalized. These relations no longer were accepted as given but as a task of formation in terms of the particular individual. These notions did not eliminate a social order based on birth, but increasingly such an order was no longer accepted as corresponding to the nature of humankind. Society was accepted as the natural form of human association, but it was a purposive association for satisfying human needs and a communicative association in which humans realized their varied potentials.

Attitudes must develop in such a "civil society" that are independent of estate or class. Nonetheless it was the educated burghers who formulated this vision and who were most interested in extending it. They thought, however, that they were speaking for all of humanity. Burgher consciousness was in this sense not confined to a particular estate; nobles also accepted it and by the last third of the century it entered the courts, especially the smaller ones. Gradually the ideal of the courtier was displaced by that of the enlightened citizen and patriot. The latter was to be active for the commonweal and participate in the intellectual, political, and economic life of the times. The enlightened citizen was concerned to become ever more enlightened and contribute to the enlightenment of others. Of course, the chances to put such ideals into practice were severely constricted by conditions in Germany.

New social groupings and forms of sociability grew within the corporate and monarchical system as a manifestation of the new burgher consciousness. Among them were the freemasonic lodges, the first of which, following English models, was founded in Hamburg in 1737. Though freemasonry was not strictly a consequence of the Enlightenment, it became tightly linked to its spread. Freemasonry penetrated both the world of the courts and that of the educated and propertied burgher classes. The members all came to share a beneficient, cosmopolitan attitude, one that expected an improvement in humanity.

Naturally, the new values and worldview expanded slowly. Often the changes were barely noticeable, since they took place within a largely stable social system. The Enlightenment – with its demand that reason should prevail in all spheres of life and that individual rights must be recognized – was still not able to triumph over corporatist status consciousness and social prejudice. As a response to the upward striving of the burgher classes, aristocratic self-awareness even intensified over the course of the eighteenth century. A similar sense of distance increased between the educated and the illiterate and between the upper strata of the burgher classes and the petty bourgeoisie and peasantry. If the educated turned toward the peasantry, it was only to educate them – to tear away the veils of ignorance and bring them useful knowledge. In addition, we must be aware that the burgher classes were not yet able to develop a socially independent position. Conditions were still not changeable enough, and the burgher classes in their entirety were still not wealthy enough to assert themselves. Thus the essential function of the new burgher values was to provide moral and cultural self-assuredness. The emphasis on order, regularity, thrift, industry, politeness, and probity gave self-worth to the individual. Yet we must also admit that it could bring with it a certain stiffness, a moralizing correctness, a false propriety and sense of gravity; such attributes emphasized the distance to one's inferiors and, it was hoped, would bring recognition by one's betters. Other values were more meaningful, especially the pietistic emotional ones that stressed individual development and communion in private circles of the like-minded. All these values contributed essential features to the formation of a burgher mentality and burgher consciousness that became increasingly political.

4

POLITICAL ORGANIZATION

PRELIMINARY REMARKS: THE ESTATES
SYSTEM AND ABSOLUTE MONARCHY

The estates and absolute monarchy are two of the structural elements in the older European political system. The *estates system* does not refer to the general division of society into social estates but presumes it; the term instead encompasses the institutional network of local and regional self-government and signifies the participation of the ruled in government. In Germany the imperial and territorial diets come first to mind; these made up the upper stratum of corporate institutions, in the same manner that the emperor and the territorial lords made up the upper stratum of sovereign authority. The individual members of the imperial estates, however, were also themselves territorial lords, the members of the territorial estates seigneurial lords. The difference between the right to appear in the diets *(Standschaft)* and sovereign authority itself *(Herrschaft)* cannot easily be derived from different communal and sovereign principles. The territorial lord did not have a monopoly over sovereign authority within his own lands that might have made the ruled into subjects; but neither did the territorial diets actually represent the entire population.

Estatist institutions, notions, and practices shaped social life in old Europe in the most diverse ways. It was in the nature of the estatist world that sovereign lords had a claim to political offices, that substantial local and regional functions in administration, law, and finance were controlled by resident lords, that the territorial lords were limited in their choice of officeholders, and, as a special case, that similar limits were placed on urban government. The estatist system was formed by privileges – in other words, by a system of specially graduated rights. These privileges assumed special regional forms in the historically evolved contours of legal and property titles and in the division of power between the diets and the territorial lords. Even when a "country" or *Land* acquired a new ruler on the basis of

87

inheritance, conquest, or treaty, it normally retained its estatist rights and often its own administration. Estatist deputations often survived the assimilation of their areas into larger territories, so that a particular territorial lord might face a number of provincial diets. These diets, by the way, did not have any institutional links among themselves. In electoral Hanover, for instance, there were at least six different territorial diets in the eighteenth century. The house of Austria has been characterized as a monarchical union of estatist states *(Ständestaaten)*. Since the seventeenth century the territorial diets became responsible for preserving the confessional allegiance whenever the territorial lord changed his faith. Finally, there were cases where the territorial diets attempted to retain – usually without long-term success – the sense of a unified country even when the lands were divided hereditarily, as in Jülich-Cleves-Berg, Hesse, and Mecklenburg. Institutions of an estatist character also developed at the regional or local level where no territorial diets had emerged or where they had disappeared. Their survival was always viewed as a presupposition of freedom – namely the freedoms of the country or the estates. In fact, they did limit the power of the territorial lords with varying degrees of effectiveness, especially where there were functioning diets whose deputies could negotiate binding agreements with the territorial lord.

The provincial diets doubtless marked a historical phase in the evolution of the modern parliamentary, representative system. Yet the differences are important, because diets were not actually representative. Members were not legitimated by elections; rather they possessed the right to represent themselves on the basis of their property. They did not represent the country but *were* the country in their collective entirety. Their powers often differed greatly in detail; but in every case they faced the territorial lords claiming an independent, and not delegated, right to advise and assent to all governmental matters affecting them, their subjects, and indeed the entire country's traditional social and political order. For their part the territorial lords did not reject every aspect of this claim. Agreement, not open conflict, usually determined the relations between the territorial lords and their estates. This was even true where princes strove to achieve absolute authority. "Absolutism" was not a clear form of rule as the sloganlike term might have us believe.

Absolutism, like the system of estates, assumed numerous forms within the empire and the multiplicity of German states. If absolutism means the unlimited exercise of authority at will by a sovereign territorial lord, then absolutism did not exist in legal terms within the imperial community. But it also did not exist practically either, because the unlimited exercise of authority was restrained by local and estatist rights and by an inadequate administrative apparatus. Absolutism can more precisely be understood as a system of rule in which the sovereign acted as legislator and supreme judge and possessed military and supreme administrative authority. In this system the sovereign exercised authority without the consent of other institutions and groups, but he did observe the rights of his subjects. Such a system was prominent in Germany. In numerous places, though certainly not everywhere, monarchs extended their power and thereby limited or excluded the political estates; but they were not able to eliminate estatist institutions completely. Elimination was both unnecessary and impossible, because the monarchies lacked the tools and manpower to assume the varied administrative and judicial functions, both regional and local. And the territorial lords lost the conflicts in not a few cases. The chances for success, of course, depended on the prince's finances and the unity or discord among the estates; they depended, in other words, on the energy, vanity, wealth, and foreign connections of a particular dynasty and the obstinacy or political will of the estates.

In the many small states the pattern varied greatly. In some states without diets an absolutist patriarchalism often prevailed; in others a narrow bureaucratism predominated in spite of the existence of a diet; and in still others the estates proved a powerful hindrance to well-intentioned reforms by the territorial ruler. In general, however, the territorial princes and their administrations increasingly determined the pace of development. They were the most significant initiators of reforms that ranged from repopulation to economic development. They intruded increasingly upon the collective life of their populations with new policing regulations. They demanded ever more personnel for their armies and administration and stimulated the rationalization of social life. In the process monarchical rule became state power, princely servants the bureaucracy. Those ruled were increasingly drawn into a comprehensive process of social discipline. The provincial estates were able to slow the process but were certainly not part of a "democratic" resistance to absolute authority. In Germany there was indeed a continuous line from the old estatist system, to the estatist constitutional order of the early nineteenth century, and to the representative system of the later period. But these changes did not begin before the great disturbances to the political system around 1800.

In our period of the late seventeenth and eighteenth centuries, the territorial princes proved, on the whole, to be more powerful than the estates. Yet the significance of the system of estates must not be underestimated, as can easily happen when the political institutions of the era are viewed only from above. Further, absolute monarchy cannot be conceived as a completely effective system. It was much more a political framework in which a great deal survived, but gradually acquired a new valuation. Seen in historical perspective, monarchical absolutism contributed fundamentally to the erosion of estatist freedoms and the privileged orders, thus paving the way for the process of democratization.

EMPEROR AND EMPIRE

The terms *emperor* and *empire* were originally identical. The emperor was the individual head of the empire conceived as a catholic and permanent organization. By the fifteenth century at the latest, however, an opposition developed between the elected king and emperor, who followed his own interests as a territorial lord, and the empire "as the totality of the estates without the emperor" (Fritz Hartung). The latter or imperial estates were empowered to appear at the imperial diet, and the emperor, in turn, was one of their number. This dualism, sanctioned by the Westphalian settlement, did not always manifest itself in crude opposition and did not exclude the possibility that dynastic and imperial politics could partially coincide.

The Peace of Westphalia, the *Instrumenta Pacis Osnabrugense et Monasteriense,* functioned as the basic law of the empire until its end in 1804-6. The imperial constitution thus acquired no new impulse to change. The political organization of the empire was not altered or even reformed but rather put to rest. The imperial estates acquired the right to conclude alliances among themselves and with foreign powers, as long as they were not directed against the emperor and the empire; this meant the legal recognition of far-reaching autonomy, if not complete external sovereignty. At the same time they had confirmed extensive internal sovereignty over their subjects. Thus they had recognized as imperial law the principle of territorial sovereignty, the *ius territorii et superioritatis* that had emerged since the thirteenth century. The emperor's powers were tied to the consent of the estates meeting in the imperial diet. As a territorial ruler, moreover, he shared an interest in the autonomy of the other imperial estates. In addition, he was involved in almost every European power struggle so long as he both came from the house of Habsburg and was accepted among the imperial estates as leader of the Catholic party.

Unresolved constitutional questions had been left to the next imperial diet in the instruments of peace that were actually formal treaties with Sweden and France. In practical terms they remained largely unresolved because the emperor and the imperial estates – and the estates among themselves – simply could not come to an agreement. The so-called Recent Imperial Recess *(recessus imperii novissimus)* of 17 May 1654 left open basic problems, such as the reform of the imperial tax system, the constitution of the imperial circles or districts, and the election of the emperor. The few laws passed to improve the imperial legal and judicial system quickly proved insufficient. The imperial estates managed to require that the territorial estates pay the imperial military contributions and pay to maintain the territorial fortresses. This represented an effort of imperial law to support at the territorial level the expansion of standing armies so critical in economic, financial, and political terms to the emergence of absolute monarchies. The emperor retained certain rights or "reservata" *(Reservat-*

rechte) that he exercised partly alone and partly in consultation with the imperial diet, for instance, the right of ennoblement, pardon, exemption from the jurisdiction of the imperial courts, certification of notaries, legitimation of individuals, and the conferring of privileges. He was unable to strengthen imperial power by using his personal powers of enfiefment as the supreme overlord, because he could not refuse to invest when the succession was clear, nor could he claim vacant fiefs and dispense them of his own accord. Whether he proved able to force the imperial estates to maintain the peace and respect imperial laws depended more on the particular constellation of power than on his legal competence as emperor.

Much was written about the constitution of the empire in the seventeenth and eighteenth centuries. Officially still called the Holy Roman Empire of the German Nation, the empire was a subject of commentary because it did not fit within the traditional Aristotelian political forms. Monarchical and aristocratic elements were intertwined, and even democratic elements appeared in the imperial cities. For this reason Samuel von Pufendorf had characterized it as an "irregular and monster-like body" ("irregulare aliquod corpus et monstro simile") in a famous phrase from his treatise *De statu imperii Germanici (The Constitution of the German Empire)* (1667). By this phrase Pufendorf had wanted to emphasize the uniqueness of the empire's political form and not its inability to survive. The empire was neither a federation nor a confederation. Certain elements of each were present, others were missing. There was no government and only a few imperial offices. An imperial taxation system had developed only rudimentarily. There was no imperial financial administration. The imperial courts were among the most significant of imperial institutions, but there was no imperial police force. Then, too, an imperial army could only be called together for defensive purposes on the basis of special monetary contributions granted by the imperial estates. Indeed the empire was not much of a "state;" it was more a public legal system that did not include all Germans but did include many non-Germans. For the imperial cities, knights, counts, and ecclesiastical princes, it was a negative defensive organization (Gerhard Oestreich) that guaranteed their existence against the expansionist tendencies of the greater imperial estates. Finally, it was also a bulwark for the estatist system and for the rights of the subjects of territorial rulers, insofar as their access to the imperial courts was not cut off by the princes under the privilege *iura de non evocando et appellando.*

Although sovereignty in the territorial estates – with the exception of the ecclesiastical principalities – was hereditary, the office and majesty of the emperor was tied constitutionally to an election by the electoral princes. In political reality, however, the Habsburg family held the crown from 1438 until the end of the empire, with the single exception of the reign of the Wittelsbach Emperor Charles VII (1742-5). Its dispersed domains and European interests made it an issue of state for the Habsburgs to hold onto the imperial crown with its high prestige. From the other side, the empire could not let the Habsburgs withdraw. In addition, since the majority within the electoral college would only permit a Catholic prince to become emperor, the Habsburgs had no competitors under normal circumstances. Only the unique political constellation in 1740 – the death of Charles VI without male heir and the exclusion of the husband of his heir Maria Theresia – made it possible for the Wittelsbach king to be elected.

Imperial power was substantially limited, not by the act of election itself, but by the process beforehand. Since 1519 elections occurred only after the candidate agreed in a capitulation to a catalogue of concessions submitted by the electoral princes. Such election capitulations, though tied to their predecessors, were prepared anew for every prospective emperor until 1711 when a permanent capitulation (*capitulatio perpetua*) was formulated. The number of electoral princes had remained fixed at seven since the Golden Bull of 1356. In 1648 an eighth vote was added for the Palatinate, since the original Palatine vote had been transferred to the Bavarian Wittelsbach dynasty. In 1692 the house of Braunschweig-Lüneburg received the ninth vote. Finally, the Bohemian electorate, completely under the control of the Habsburgs, reacquired its full rights in 1708.

The college of electoral princes constituted the first estate at the imperial diet. The diet was a gathering of ruling princes and magistrates from imperial cities. After 1663 it became known as the eternal diet when it began to meet permanently in Regensburg, becoming thereby a congress of ambassadors. Membership in the imperial diet (*Reichsstandschaft*) was limited to those territories immediate to the emperor. (For this reason families raised to the rank of imperial princes could vote in the imperial diet only after they had acquired such imperial territories.) Immediate to the emperor (*reichsunmittelbar*) were the electoral principalities, princely states, imperial abbeys, and imperial counties. Votes were not doubled in the case of property division. Similarly, when a territory passed to a new ruler, its vote also transferred intact under his control. Thus many princes had a number of votes at the imperial diet. The elector of Brandenburg, for instance, controlled the votes of Magdeburg, Halberstadt, and Minden, even though as duke of Prussia he did not belong to the empire. The elector of Hanover, as another example, controlled the votes of Calenberg, Grubenhagen, and Celle.

After 1648 new members were also added to the imperial council of princes. The exact number of members fluctuated continuously. The precise figures at the end of the empire in 1803 were as follows: The college of princes had eight votes, since the Bavarian and Palatine votes were united in 1777. The imperial council of princes had one hundred votes; of these thirty-seven were held by clerical states and sixty-three by secular states. Included among them were two clerical and four secular curiate votes, because the imperial abbots formed the Swabian and Rhenish bench of prelates, and the imperial counts formed the Wetterau, Swabian, Franconian, and Westphalian college of imperial counts. Each of these representatives had one vote apiece. In addition, the imperial cities also possessed the right to membership in the imperial diet. Along with the Rhenish and Swabian bench of cities, they made up the college of imperial cities and acquired a full vote in 1648. In 1803 there were fifty-one cities in the college, and they voted together as a curia. The votes of the small college of electoral princes, the large council of imperial princes, and the weak college of cities each had the same weight. In case of conflict between the imperial and the electoral princes, the vote of the cities was then contested. Consultations occurred separately in the individual curiae; their conclusions (*conclusia*) were written in the form of an imperial memorandum of advice (*consultum imperii*), and after ratification by the emperor they were issued as imperial decrees (*conclusum imperii*). The emperor appeared as infrequently at the eternal diet as the imperial princes, being content to conduct affairs through commissioners. The small imperial estates often avoided paying the costs of their emissaries; for this reason individual envoys and local lawyers regularly represented a number of interests.

The legal competence of the imperial diet was unlimited. The diet could consider all matters pertaining to the empire. After 1663 it no longer was even bound to consider matters in the order submitted by the emperor. Private individuals as well as imperial estates could petition for advice from the diet. The process, however, was complicated and painfully slow. The imperial emissaries, strictly bound by their instructions, could not make individual decisions and this, of course, delayed every matter. Furthermore, imperial decrees could only become law if the three curiae and the emperor together agreed. That occurred all too rarely after 1648. Two pieces of imperial legislation were passed: an imperial code regulating handicrafts (1731) and an imperial coinage decree (1737). Of the two, the supraregional control of handicrafts had been especially pressing, because journeymen traveled from area to area.

The imperial diet was a gathering of states and did not, of course, represent the German population. The college of imperial cities also did not represent the interests of the burgher class, but rather those of the oligarchical magistracies. Concrete social and economic issues almost never made it to the imperial level; and insofar as they were recognized, they were treated as issues of the territorial states. Yet the empire was not completely functionless. The emperor, imperial diet, and the few existing imperial institutions prevented all disagreements from becoming violent confrontations and protected somewhat the many small territories.

The imperial chancellery became the least significant of imperial institutions. The imperial chancellor, the archbishop of Mainz and himself an electoral prince, acted as the spokesman for the rights of the imperial estates, but his functions and the daily business within the chancellery were assumed increasingly by the resident imperial vice-chancellor. Moreover, the Austrian court chancellery in Vienna acquired increasing weight since imperial and Austrian matters were often handled there without distinction. The imperial aulic council *(Reichshofrat)* handled feudal matters and issues of privilege and competed with the imperial cameral tribunal *(Reichskammergericht)* as a court of last appeal in matters pending before the emperor. The imperial cameral tribunal, on the other hand, was the emperor's actual court, but its appointments were shaped by the estates. Unlike the cameral tribunal, the emperor chose the personnel for the imperial aulic council himself, and the court by its decisions supported the emperor's policies without becoming politicized. The imperial aulic council was particularly successful in the eighteenth century, and it acquired even more significance because conflicts among the imperial estates hindered and even periodically paralyzed the imperial cameral tribunal in its work.

Still, the imperial cameral tribunal did perform important functions. It met in Speyer until 1688 and then thereafter in Wetzlar. It consisted of a president *(Kammerrichter)* and associate judges. The former, named by the emperor, had to come from the imperial nobility; half of the associate judges, on the other hand, were trained jurists and together they represented the electoral princes and the imperial circles. The court was the original jurisdiction for those immediate *(reichsunmittelbar)* to the emperor and court of appeal for subjects appealing decisions of the territorial courts – except where the territorial rulers possessed the privilege of appeal. There was much complaint and ridicule over the financial, technical, and organizational struggles of the court. The numbers of judges were never raised to the levels approved in 1654, so that the number of legal cases unresolved over the decades grew steadily. An imperial deputation to accelerate the handling of cases, approved in 1654, began working for the first time more than 120 years later!

The troubles of the imperial cameral tribunal resulted from the completely inadequate funding of the empire. The so-called chamber marker *(Kammerzieler)*, the single imperial tax for funding the tribunal, had been instituted in 1495, but it never arrived regularly or in the full amount. The "Roman month" *(Römermonat)*, a tax to mobilize and maintain an imperial army, was levied only after a special decision of the imperial diet and paid according to a special distribution scheme in the imperial membership roll of 1521. This tax could be doubled or quadrupled, was collected by the imperial estates or imperial circles, and was given to the imperial paymaster *(Reichspfenningmeister)*. There were enormous outstanding debts in this area, too, and lengthy negotiations often were required before the sides could agree on the tax bill.

Imperial organizations proved to be even more inadequate in the intermediate area between the empire and the imperial estates, on the one hand,

and the individual regional institutions charged with carrying out the decrees of the emperor and the courts on the other. This intermediate area was the domain of the imperial institutions. The imperial circles were conceived as institutions of self-rule, empowered with administrative competence in matters dealing with the military, social welfare, coinage, and execution of the imperial court decrees. The ten circles were managed by a directory that, in turn, was dominated by the most illustrious imperial prince. If this prince was a cleric, then a secular prince was chosen as convener and commander of the district contingent of troops. Either he or the district directors, who were aided by a chancellery, represented the imperial circle and called the estates of the circle to the district diet. These diets were concerned with executing the laws, legal decisions, and other decrees of the imperial diet and courts, supporting the circle's contingent to the imperial army, distributing and collecting the imperial taxes, and maintaining the local peace by adjudicating conflicts among the estates in the circle.

Given the large number of responsibilities, it is illuminating that the imperial circles could function only where the territories were so divided that the individual territorial rulers could carry out only a small portion of their sovereign responsibilities and thus clearly understood the need for supralocal legislation. The large imperial estates that, in the main, led the district directories, rarely could be forced into particular activities or hindered in using the circles to their own advantage. The circles of Franconia, Swabia, the Upper Rhine, and the electoral Rhine came closest to fulfilling their constitutional functions in the last phase of the empire; this stemmed from the enormous French pressure on the western border areas at the end of the seventeenth century. The division into many small states, or *Kleinstaaterei* as it was called, was most advanced there as well, and it fostered a profound attachment to the empire and its institutions.

The Westphalian settlement had expressly committed the parties to the reintegration (*redintegratio*) of the imperial circles, because the war had made manifest that weak institutions could neither defend the states nor maintain the domestic peace. The roads and traffic in goods were, indeed, improved and better protected in the Franconian and Swabian circles. Numerous decrees were also promulgated and enforced in the domain of police activities. The circles actually did assume state functions in these areas. If we keep in mind that the Swabian circle consisted of forty ecclesiastical states, sixty-eight secular territories, and forty imperial cities, and that the Franconian circle was hardly different, we can see the members understood the importance of functioning intermediate organizations. These circles were in marked distinction to those comprising Habsburg dynastic lands, for in the Habsburg areas no district diets continued to meet. The Westphalian circle was somewhat different, but there, too, confessional differences and political conflict largely brought about institutional paralysis. Similarly, all efforts to form standing armies failed within the most politically splintered circles, because the estates feared the costs and the loss of their political "liberties."

The inadequacies of the imperial system were not solved in spite of the experiences of the Thirty Years War, and we must suppose that reform lay beyond the power of the existing system. The emperor's capacity to induce fundamental reform was narrowly circumscribed by a need for consent from the imperial diet. He could not even easily expect support from the Catholic estates. For this reason he could only act where he himself was the territorial lord or where he might count upon a strong imperial party. The mistrust of Habsburg expansion and imperial despotism survived the first phase of the great war and was nurtured by French and Swedish policies and by confessional fears in evangelical areas. No state was more allergic to Habsburg claims to leadership, however, than Catholic Bavaria, which itself pursued an expansionist foreign policy from the days of Maximilian I (1595-1651) until finally it led to open warfare with Austria in 1740.

Other imperial institutions also proved incapable of launching reform within the empire. The imperial cities proved inadequate because confessional and political opposition, the fear of the small for the large, and the divergent interests of the great, even in times of extreme external threat to the empire, all prevented common action. The case was somewhat different with the limited associations formed among the imperial estates. Such groupings were not forbidden by imperial law, and they did provide a chance for partial reforms. In fact, the movement to form *Assoziationen* grew dramatically in significance in the period between 1648 and the end of the empire. In the period around and after 1650 a number of somewhat unstable estatist defense leagues emerged particularly along the Rhine and in northwest Germany in response to the French–Habsburg antagonism. The Rhenish League of 1658 allied itself with the French because it lacked the power to engage in an independent foreign policy and feared the Habsburgs were the greater threat to corporate "liberties." The league was not simply an instrument of French policies. Its members did not place themselves against the empire; they supported the election of Leopold I as emperor against the will of Mazarin, and they fulfilled their imperial responsibilities in the struggle against the Turks. The league dissolved itself when Louis XIV openly attacked the empire.

Johann Philipp von Schönborn, the archbishop of Mainz and imperial chancellor, began the next initiative from the side of the imperial estates. He envisioned a league – for which Leibniz wrote a famous memorandum on the security of the empire (1670) – that would remain neutral between the Habsburg and French camps. It would, however, raise an army and create a common treasury for its support. Even the emperor, as territorial ruler over his German core lands and Bohemia, would be able to join. After this project had no success, the depressing results of the empire in its wars against France provided a new occasion. An imperial army had failed to materialize; armed and unarmed estates had been unable to overcome their mutual distrust, and the latter had resisted the quartering of imperial troops; the emperor had followed his own foreign policy goals even as the Turkish threat grew. In this crisis the imperial diet passed a decree (1681) for the defense of the empire. The imperial circles were to function as the carriers of the imperial army from that moment onward. They were to be given certain contingents that they were to raise, equip, and pay. Their strength was to be set at a basic total of 40,000 men, and this number could be quadrupled. The estates were to be redistributed within the circles according to a new order. The new defensive system actually came to function only within the Swabian and the Franconian circles. Elsewhere the large estates that had their own armies refused to place their troops under the command of the circles. Thus the opposition between the armed and the unarmed estates grew, and this became an essential negative feature of the imperial constitution after 1648.

Still the new military system was of considerable importance to the western imperial circles. Under the pressure of French advances, with the loss of Strasbourg, and in the midst of fundamental disunity within the empire, they committed themselves in the Frankfurt associational decree to fielding a unified army. This army then played a defensive role in holding the Rhine line. Although the army never rose to its projected levels of manpower, it did survive after 1715; it was integrated into the imperial army in the Seven Years War – an imperial war against Brandenburg-Prussia – only to be destroyed in battle at Rossbach.

The southwestern and western portions of the empire remained committed to reform of the imperial order. These were the areas that were referred to simply as "the empire" in the eighteenth century. Such attitudes became even stronger in the later part of the century when it was hoped, falsely as it turned out, that Joseph II would devote himself to the cause of imperial reform. After the collapse of these hopes they grew once again when a new league of princes was founded in 1785. But then, too, the new league was unable to achieve anything significant in the midst of the Austro–Prussian dualism.

PRINCES AND TERRITORIAL ESTATES

Johann Stephan Pütter, the famous Göttingen jurist, wrote that in the spirit of the original German constitution "most German princes treated their territorial diets in just about the same way as the emperor the imperial diet" (1786). He was careful to warn, however, that the comparison could not be carried too far, because the power of the territorial rulers was in the ascendancy even as that of the emperor was in decline. The imperial domains had long been distributed among the territorial rulers, weakening the emperor's authority. Indeed, Pütter was correct. The territorial rulers often disposed of extensive crown lands and domains either that were beyond the control of the territorial estates or that could be touched only indirectly. Even the territorial ruler most constrained by his estates could react more independently than the emperor in the empire. Though we can speak of a double estate system or note that the ecclesiastical princes were elected by a tight circle of electors, as was the emperor, such formal analogies between the empire and the territorial level do little to illuminate German constitutional life. Although the empire was a bulwark for the territorial estates, the empire was simply not strong enough to hinder the absolutist policies of active dynasties.

Since the twelfth century the process of state formation had shifted to the territories with varying results. State structures with quite different manifestations of sovereignty and estatist institutions had arisen. I can only indicate something of the multiplicity of forms, since it is practically impossible to describe the variations in detail. There were, first, differences in size, ranging from the lands of the Habsburgs, electoral Saxony, and the principality of Salm, to the imperial county of Bentheim, the archbishopric of Mainz, the imperial abbey of St. Blasien, the imperial city of Nuremberg, and the imperial village of Zell am Harmersbach. There were, second, differences in power and prestige, from the electors of Brandenburg, who were simultaneously kings of Prussia, to the princes of Anhalt. There were, in addition, fundamental practical differences in the degree of internal sovereignty and in dynastic connections, ranging again from the extensive power and connections of the electors of Bavaria to the far less significant imperial barons who occupied the episcopal see of Paderborn. Many small principalities were without significant cities. Many ecclesiastical and secular states were not enclosed units but were built of various pieces of noncontiguous land. When viewed precisely, many sovereign territories were simply loose parcels of land, titles, and sovereign legal rights. For this reason it is difficult to view many of the imperial estate owners as ruling princes or to call them monarchs. Similarly it is difficult to give to many of the imperial territories the qualities of a state. Legal parity among the imperial estates was a political fiction.

The survival of the small states, states predominantly without any military might, was due to their membership in the empire and the large states who jealously controlled their neighbors' strength. It would have been very dangerous for the small imperial estates had the emperor arranged with the large estates and the European powers to partition and absorb lands within the empire. No such agreement ever came to pass, however, and from 1740 onward the Austro–Prussian dualism made it impossible.

The empire provided institutional safeguards for the external existence of the states and for their internal political order as well. In the Westphalian settlement the territorial princes had been given the right to the free exercise of sovereign authority in all secular and religious matters. Thereafter they attempted to use imperial law to pressure their territorial estates into guaranteeing them all the necessary funds for military purposes. The majority of princes agreed to such a memorandum at the imperial diet in 1670, and, although the emperor at first refused to support these plans, he could not sustain his veto. The imperial courts, however, were much more effective in defending the rights of the territorial estates against their rulers. Complaints by the territorial estates were not rare, and they were often successful. Still, in most cases the conflicts between princes and their estates were settled in lengthy and tenacious negotiations. In the event a legal process was instituted, it, too, was most often resolved in an out-of-court settlement. In the eighteenth century it was the opinion of the princes and their governments that the imperial Aulic Council was benevolently disposed toward the complaints of their "obstinate vassalls and subjects."

In the eighteenth century the imperial Aulic Council played a decisive role in the two most spectacular cases of successful resistance by the estates. In Mecklenburg the estates obtained special prominence on the basis of the *Old Union of 1523,* a document that had remained in force in spite of all territorial divisions, and after they assumed the burden of ducal indebtedness. They turned to the Aulic Council in 1672 when the dukes forcibly levied a contribution for the maintenance of fortresses and garrisons. It took years before the impaneled commission could effect a compromise. At the beginning of the eighteenth century Duke Friedrich Wilhelm von Mecklenburg-Swerin (1692–1713) attempted to appropriate the tax administration of the estates, and once again the estates appealed to the Aulic Council and this time simultaneously to the government in Hanover. Duke Friedrich Wilhelm's successor, Duke Karl Leopold (1713–28) intensified the pressure, entered the Northern War, married the niece of the czar, and admitted Russian troops into his lands. By then the emperor issued an imperial warrant, charging troops from Hanover and Braunschweig to occupy the lands. Karl Leopold was replaced by his brother, Christian Ludwig (1728–56), and the latter eventually (1755) agreed to a hereditary constitutional compromise *(Landesgrundgesetzlicher Erebvergleich)* with the nobility and the estates *(Ritter- und Landschaft).* The estates had their rights and liberties guaranteed. They also acquired the right of consent in all measures tangential to their interests. For all unresolved complaints, in addition, they retained the right of appeal to the imperial courts. This contract prevented the development of absolute rule in Mecklenburg and remained the basis of its constitution until 1918. But it also produced constitutional and political deadlock. An attitude of special privilege and rigidity intensified within the noble estate *(Ritterschaft)* to the extent that the estates increasingly became a barrier to necessary reform and a chief cause of Mecklenburg's growing material backwardness.

Württemberg was the other case. The officeholders within the Württemberg diet came to dominate political life after the nobility had elevated itself to the imperial nobility in the sixteenth century. The evangelical prelates of burgher origin sitting on the ecclesiastical bench also played a significant role that often overlapped with the interests of the burgher notables. The estates stubbornly defended constitutional rights detailed in the Tübingen Contract of 1514. In exchange for assuming princely debts, the right of consent to taxation was among the guaranteed rights. In addition, the estates were called together after the Thirty Years War for regular meetings of the diet and came to exercise a form of corule that lasted for more than two decades. This situation changed fundamentally when the dukes began to extend their power and particularly sought to maintain a standing army. The territorial diet was not called together in its entirety for almost forty years after 1699. When complaints to the imperial Aulic Council at first met with no success, the large committee of the diet approved a permanent contribution for the upkeep of the military. The estates were strengthened when their princes, beginning with Karl Alexander (1733–7), converted to Catholicism, and they were able to get England, Denmark, and Prussia to guarantee the Lutheran religious character of their lands. This external support soon proved necessary when under Duke Karl Eugen (1737–93) the latent conflict over finances broke out into open warfare. At the end of the Seven Years War he attempted to burden his lands with supporting a standing army that until then had been paid for with foreign subsidies. The standing committee of the diet then demanded that the whole diet be called. This diet convened in 1763 and met continuously for the next seven years under the careful scrutiny of German public opinion. Already before convening, the estates had appealed to the emperor and the three guarantor powers. The latter indeed helped the estates to victory but in doing so Württemberg's internal conflicts became entangled in the larger struggle between Austria and Prussia. In the end, the Aulic Council decided in favor of the estates, and the emperor mediated an out-of-court settlement that ended in the hereditary compromise of 1770.

Both examples are certainly unrepresentative of the relations between princes and estates, but they do show that the estates in the eighteenth century had not become completely negligible, especially when they were united and prepared to resist. Usually, however, the parties arrived at a working agreement. Whenever the estates were forced to give ground, they emphasized they were not abandoning their rights and liberties, or they had them explicitly guaranteed. On the whole, the estates were gradually put on the defensive; they began to be perceived as selfish defenders of privilege even as the rulers and their governments became the more successful advocates of the common good and the interests of the entire state. In spite of this shift, the estates continued to carry out significant local and regional functions. Governments were more or less dependent on them as hereditary holders of offices, since, with the exception of the domains, they had only a limited control over these offices. From the other side, there were no laws requiring regular consultation with the estates even where there were functioning diets. As long as the princes solved their financial needs or were not placed in difficulty by war or a vainglorious foreign policy, they could often rule alone without calling the estates together. Ordinarily the princes attempted to circumvent corule with the estates and to extend an area of "state" income that was beyond the competence of the estates.

The maintenance of standing armies in a time of peace remained the most important and intensely contested issue. This was the main reason for the estatist struggles of the seventeenth and eighteenth century. Events in Brandenburg-Prussia provide the most consequential example. Elector Friedrich Wilhelm understood from the experiences of the Thirty Years War the need to strengthen central authority and raise a standing army. This army was not meant to defend the state, since the state consisted of a patchwork of widely separated lands; rather the army was meant to give the state political prestige and greater military weight. In 1653 the diet of the electoral mark of Brandenburg agreed to a military tax or "contribution" *(Kontribution)* for a period of six years. The nobility did not approve this decree without substantial concessions from the elector, so much so in fact that they thought the new contract was a victory for the aristocracy. They themselves remained free from the contribution, and they had seigneurial rights expressly recognized that perpetuated peasant serfdom *(bäuerliche Leibeigenschaft)* on their lands. In actuality, the contribution remained as a permanent tax. However, it proved much more difficult for the electors to assert control in the external areas of Prussia and Cleves-Mark. Under Polish sovereignty the Prussian estates had received complete control of the territorial administration. But after the tie of fealty between Prussia and Poland was dissolved in 1660, elector Friedrich Wilhelm forced the military contribution on his Prussian estates meeting in Königsberg (1661–3) by intervening militarily and arresting the leader of the opposition, Julius Roth, the mayor *(Schöppenmeister)* of Königsberg. The elector never kept his promise to call regular meetings of the diet. Opposition had grown in Cleves from the beginning of the seventeenth century when it had passed to the Brandenburg Hohenzollerns from a unified Jülich-Cleves-Berg inheritance. The estates refused to recognize the property division, and they finally approved laws in 1649 that recognized constitutional rule by the diet and the rights of residents to hold all offices *(Indigenat)*. After lengthy discussions, employing great pressure and threatening military invasion, the elector withdrew the right to reject taxes (1661), set aside the requirement that officials swear an oath to the territorial constitution, and declared his right as ruler to maintain a standing army. In spite of this the estates still managed to retain the right to approve taxes and meet with prior announcement. The estatist dimension managed to remain far more vigorous in Cleves than in the other Prussian lands. Partly this was due to a native strength, partly to the proximity to the Netherlands, and partly to the disinterest of the elector and his successors in this marginal province.

Once the contribution and, within the cities, the excise tax or *Akzise* was collected regularly, Prussian state finances became independent of the estates. The state largely came to control whatever share in the tax administration the estates retained. The estates were never completely eliminated but their political influence shrank substantially. As a next step Friedrich Wilhelm I then bound the aristocracy more tightly to the monarchical state. He forced the Prussian aristocracy to pay certain taxes in the course of regulating the so-called *Generalhufenschoss,* a tax on land to support the army. In other provinces the aristocracy remained free from taxation but was forced to make a yearly payment for every fief horse on allodial lands attached by an oath of fealty to the royal house. The electors and later kings did not intrude in the seigneurial system of *Gutsherrschaft* or in the private liberties of the nobility. But they did force the nobility into military service – and this often brought forth extensive resistance, even to the point that the Magdeburg nobility appealed to the Aulic Council. Gradually, however, the new social system prevailed. The sons of the nobility typically came to be educated in special schools for cadets; these boarding schools educated them to their future military calling and prepared them to serve the military–monarchical state.

Organized resistance by the estates eventually disappeared. Since the majority of the nobility were not wealthy, they remained interested in the positions dispensed by their rulers. Indeed, they were granted almost unlimited authority at the district and seigneurial level. In exchange for such power Prussia's kings demanded loyalty and service to them. Once this problematical and consequential alliance was forged, Friedrich II began to favor the nobility once again. The symbol of this relationship came to be the district councillor (*Landrat*), who assumed an intermediate position between aristocratic, estatist self-rule and royal state administration.

It is somewhat exaggerated but on the whole correct to argue that Prussian state administration was formed to maintain the army. Indeed the entire state served to maintain the disproportionately large army. From the second half of the seventeenth century, Brandenburg-Prussia had become a military state. Relatively small, with its territories dispersed, small in population, with naturally poor agricultural lands, it was brought together by the dynasty and raised to political significance by its army. By the middle of the eighteenth century the dynasty had managed to raise the state to the ranks of the European great powers due to its military successes and consequential policies freed from checks and balances by the estates.

Developments in Austria took a different course. The Thirty Years War had been decisive in forming this state that was actually a union of estatist states *(Ständestaaten)*. In the course of the Counter-Reformation and the defeat of the Bohemian rebels, the largely Protestant nobility of Bohemia and Austria came to be excluded from power. Since then estatist opposition no longer played a role at the center, though the estates did retain extensive provincial power, ranging from the tax system, to the administration and the common defense. Estatist colleges thus held onto significant administrative power at the provincial level, while absolutist tendencies came to dominate in the central administration. These were supported by the military and political rise of Austria around 1700 that is associated with the name of Prince Eugene of Savoy. Later these tendencies were reinforced by the negative experiences of the Austrian War of Succession and the first two Silesian wars; they then triggered the administrative reforms of 1749.

We can distinguish between states in which absolute rule emerged on the basis of excluding the estates from the central government and those in which the diets and parliaments survived. But we must be careful not to draw too sharp a line between the two constitutional systems. Central administrations could remain active in states organized on the basis of diets, as for example in electoral Saxony. States without parliamentary estates could also be ruled in a predominantly traditional, patriarchal, and inactive manner. The continuous absence of a ruling dynasty in states such as Hanover and Holstein created a pronouncedly aristocratic government. On the whole, however, we must emphasize that government was thought to be the responsibility of the princes, while the estates were predominantly charged with preserving legal rights and privileges. The estates could be brought to resist or challenge corule by the expanded activity of princely government or by its weakness and incompetence. The rulers normally retained the initiative, and over time this shaped the distribution of both prestige and power.

IMPERIAL CHURCH, CITIES, AND NOBILITY

The "official" end of the empire occurred on 6 August 1806 with the final decree of the imperial deputation. A number of acts of dissolution, however, had preceded this event. In 1803 the ecclesiastical states had been placed under secular authority and almost all free imperial cities had been mediated, that is, placed under the authority of a territorial ruler. Between 1803 and the Rhenish confederation of 1805 the lands of imperial counts and knights had also been mediated. The empire could not exist without these independent entities; after their disappearance the empire no longer possessed the areas closely linked to it and in which the idea of emperor and empire were political reality.

Imperial religious territories – ecclesiastical states – were areas tying together the offices of spiritual shepherd and territorial ruler. The canonic election to bishop, abbot, or abbess brought with it elevation into the estate of imperial princes. Ecclesiastical cathedral or monastic chapters functioned as a secular electoral college. Only those were to be chosen as territorial rulers who met the spiritual requirements for election. Dynastic succession was impossible, although it did happen that one bishopric was held by election in the same family with little or no interruptions. Those elected did not need to be members of the electing chapters, but the chapters did require that candidates meet the requirements for election to a chapter and conferral of a benefice. This meant in practice that the candidate was required to have a certain number of noble ancestors, usually eight or sixteen, but sometimes even thirty-two. In other cases the candidate's family needed to possess the capacity to be members in a provincial diet (*Landstandschaft*). A few cathedral chapters demanded that candidates come from imperial princely families; others that they come from families of imperial counts or knights. Understandably, such tests of exclusivity derived from efforts by the ecclesiastical nobility to restrict access to the lucrative benefices and even elevation into the ranks of imperial princes. Thus in areas where there were no members of the imperial nobility, the so-called monastic nobility or *Stiftsadel* separated themselves as a more privileged stratum from the local nobility; and families who were able to produce one or more prince bishops demanded extraordinary prestige for that fact. Certain aristocratic families particularly come to mind in this regard: of the imperial nobility, the Dalbergs, Seinsheims, Erthals; of the monastic nobility, the Fürstenbergs, Plettenbergs, Spiegels. But great dynasties also acquired episcopal sees for their younger sons – for instance, the Wittelsbachs and the Habsburgs – thereby transforming episcopal elections into explosive political events.

The cathedral chapters sought to bind the candidates to election capitulations as the electoral princes bound the emperor. The capitulations preserved the rights and privileges of the chapter and tied the candidate to particular policies. The pope forbade such documents in his Innocentiana of 1695, and the emperor supported the papal decree. Yet election capitulations were still formed in the eighteenth century, and even if they did not hinder active and wealthy princes to any significant degree, the capitulations did tend to influence other less powerful princes to let everything run its habitual course. That these offices were electoral and not hereditary also contributed to princely inactivity. Still certain princes did exhibit absolutist attitudes and practices in the ecclesiastical states after the Thirty Years War. Absolutism prevailed, for instance, in Würzburg and Bamberg. Such behavior led to struggles with the cathedral chapters and the estates, although there was rarely conflict over standing armies, since these were quite rare in the ecclesiastical states. Christoph Bernhard von Galen, bishop of Münster (1650–78), was one of the few princes to maintain such troops, and he found it possible only with foreign subsidies.

Ecclesiastical principalities were not secularized in the period between the Westphalian settlement and the final recess of the imperial deputation in 1806. The prince bishopric of Osnabrück was a curious partial exception, one legally recognized within the imperial system. Osnabrück had an alternating Catholic–Protestant succession. When Protestant the bishopric fell to an evangelical prince from the house of Braunschweig-Lüneburg; when Catholic it was led by a Catholic bishop elected by the cathedral chapter. Otherwise there were unrealized Hanoverian and Prussian plans during the Seven Years War to secularize the bishoprics of northwestern Germany; but had they been effected, it would have been a deep wound to the imperial system. We can appreciate their historical claims to independence from the lengthy debate over the constitution and future of the ecclesiastical states that occurred in the last third of the eighteenth century; in that debate no one recommended they become the booty of the large secular states.

The imperial cities in the later seventeenth and eighteenth centuries still counted among their number some of the significant cities of the empire, for instance, Frankfurt, Nuremberg, and Augsburg. But they no longer held the pride of place they had in the sixteenth century as cities such as Leipzig, Vienna, and Berlin began to supplant them. New princely capital cities began to grow rapidly, even as many old imperial cities never regained their earlier population figures. Hamburg fought long and hard for its status as an imperial city, first receiving a seat and a vote in the college of imperial cities in 1770. But its legal status did not seem to affect its economic and cultural development. Indeed, we should not overestimate the significance of imperial immediacy (*Reichsunmittelbarkeit*) in our period. It could even be a burden if a city's territorial neighbors sought to squeeze it economically or if the internal balance of power produced political and economic stagnation, as occurred in Cologne. Many territorial cities also had a "democratic" constitution, although these were often oligarchically rigidified; some, such as Hildesheim, Erfurt, Münster, and Rostock, were practically independent. In any event most of the imperial cities in the eighteenth century were no longer viewed as among the most internally alive. There was some element of defensiveness in the speeches of pride for the imperial autonomy of their cities that burghers uttered yearly on the day of oath taking.

Imperial cities paid direct taxes to the empire and were placed high on the imperial and district rolls due to their former financial strength. The elected magistrates in the imperial cities exercised political sovereignty, although sovereignty over the courts differed from city to city. Sovereignty over military affairs came to have little meaning in the seventeenth and eighteenth centuries, except in terms of the internal structure of the cities themselves. Cities could still be distinguished according to whether power was in the hands of an older patriciate or, as was more usual, the guilds. In practical terms only members from the more prestigious guilds held the important offices, and often they came from interrelated families.

Naturally not every inhabitant was a citizen within the imperial cities. In Augsburg during the eighteenth century, for example, there seem to have been only 6,000 citizens out of a population of 33,000. Citizenship could be purchased, and the magistrates often attempted to increase the number of citizens, even as there were economic limits to such efforts. The internal structure of the cities was based on the church parishes or the corporations and guilds. Town meetings rarely still took place or had much power; instead the cities were run by committees, and much struggle often occurred over committee membership. The major zone of friction in the larger cities lay between those who directly participated in urban government and those beneath who were excluded from the council and the magistracy. The merchant patriciate had achieved noble status in a few of the upper German imperial cities and thus had largely abandoned trade. In Ulm, for example, these families left the city proper to reside in the surrounding territory controlled by the city. There they were able to live a noble life-style without completely abandoning their political influence.

The political system in most imperial cities was threatened by ossification in the seventeenth and eighteenth centuries. The cities where the guilds prevailed – Cologne and Aachen, for instance – were especially resistant to reform. The guilds fought entrepreneurial initiative that went outside the guild system, and they continued to exclude religious minorities from citizenship. In cities of religious parity, such as Augsburg and Biberach, double officeholding paralyzed government and led to a jealous oversight over daily life. Many cities were encumbered by heavy indebtedness; in a few cases imperial regulatory commissions had to be put in place. Yet the imperial cities, especially the larger ones, did retain something of the older spirit of burgher independence and responsibility that was stifled elsewhere by princely power and administration. Elections to the council recalled past greatness and kept alive the notion that government was to be run by men who had been charged by others. Furthermore, a commitment to the commonweal clearly survived in the imperial cities. The problem was that the room for maneuvering was small and that the activities of the citizenry depended less on the particular constitution and more on a city's economic well-being.

The imperial nobility formed a peculiar corporation within the empire. Members were only subordinate to the emperor and were not represented in either the imperial or the provincial diets. They paid no imperial or district taxes; rather they granted a *subsidium caritativum* to the emperor from a common treasury. This sum was granted only periodically to stress its voluntary nature. The imperial knights thought it so important they should not be listed in the rolls of the empire and the circles that they occasionally attempted to enter the ranks of sovereign estates *(Reichsstandschaft)*.

Their autonomy within the empire rested not on sovereignty per se but on rights attached to a particular property that was listed in the rolls of the imperial nobility and that granted to the owner of said property membership in the community of immediate and free imperial nobles. The nobility, divided into circles and cantons, was served by a general directory that alternatingly passed from one circle of knights to the next. The directory had no administrative power; the competence of its three directors was limited to solving issues of common interest. The cantons were more significant. They were communities constituted to assert knightly rights and fulfill obligations beyond the financial and political capacities of the individual knight.

Imperial knights possessed sovereign powers within the lands entered in the rolls of the imperial knights but not within additional lands they might possess. In the individual case their authority to control the courts might even be limited within their own lands. Often neighboring princes attempted to transform the imperial knights into subjects. It was, however, a loss for the corporation of imperial knights when such estates passed by way of inheritance to princely families, when a knight entered the estate of counts, or when the estates of imperial knights were sold to nonimperial knights. Thus the knights had received special protective legislation from the emperor in order to preserve their lands and family lines. The estates of imperial knights were supposed to be sold only to other imperial knights; when sold to others the lands were available at a just price for repurchase. Even more important was prior right *(Retraktrecht)*. Notice of an intent to sell had to be given to the directory and the lands first offered to other imperial knights and, finally, even to the entire corporation itself; they were given three years to purchase, and such purchase could not be refused. With these and other measures it was hoped that the number of imperial knights might be maintained.

What was the significance of these legal and political curiosities in the seventeenth and eighteenth centuries? Political critics of the later eighteenth century often asserted that the territories of imperial knights could be recognized by the extent of the populations' poverty, backwardness, and ruin. It is difficult to qualify such a broad generalization. But in many cases the knights clearly lacked the means to make improvements and aid their populations. In the best examples they practiced a form of benevolent patriarchalism; in the worst they neglected their lands and subjects. Due to their narrow scope for activity, many imperial knights left the confines of their lands and corporation, and entered the church or, more likely, served with the empire and the emperor. For this reason, the imperial knights did not belong merely to the social substratum of the empire. Their political significance was, on the whole, far greater than their numbers or holdings would indicate.

The contours of the German territorial states had already been formed in the late fifteenth and sixteenth centuries. The "early modern state" (Gerhard Oestreich) continuously expanded its regulating powers into new areas of communal life – as peacekeeper, source of impartial justice, and supplier of basic foodstuffs. The state, in addition, was concerned to regulate correct religious doctrine, control daily church life, and unify a disparate legal system. Yet the state still largely lacked the personnel and institutions to transform its decrees into practice. Of course, administrative bodies did exist. Serving this early modern state were colleges of court councillors, court judicial bodies with administrative and legal powers, princely financial administrations with an exchequer and revenue collectors, and privy councillors as the chief administrative officers. In this process the lower administrative bodies emerged much more slowly. With these new institutions the need for officials and princely servants grew, of course, and in this formative period nonnobles predominantly filled the offices. Princely councillors were often highly educated members of the urban patriciate. But from the seventeenth century onward the nobility began to be more strongly represented.

The Thirty Years War and its consequences generated new governmental and administrative activity that primarily resulted in strengthening central institutions. In its practice absolutism involved centralizing state power, in order to tap and exploit national resources, eliminate domestic resistance, and protect the state from external threats. Absolutism often, in fact, hardly went beyond monopolizing force and centralizing the system of government and administration. Significant sums, however, were necessary to extend and systematize the delegation of bureaucratic power and support the necessary body of trained officials. For this reason, administration developed quite unevenly in the German states, and in most cases it never went beyond the most modest of beginnings. The most noted development of administration, that in Brandenburg-Prussia, was exceptional for the energy expended and the success achieved. For this reason developments there were examplary only insofar as they served in the eighteenth century as a model for other states. Of most enduring significance, Prussia demonstrated that the state could organize from above the rise to external power and internal order.

The increased financial costs for army, administration, and officialdom was one of the strongest impulses of absolutist policies. Cause and effect is complexly textured in this area. Since the finances raised through court Jews and subsidies could only maintain miniature courts and toy soldiering, the princes both sought to extract more from their subjects and to make themselves financially sounder. In Brandenburg-Prussia the state increased revenues, first, through a careful escalation of income from the royal domains; second, it raised new taxes partly by transforming exceptional levies into permanent taxes; and, third, it established new manufactories. The state also attempted to make the taxing system independent of the estates in those areas where the monarch was not seigneur by exploiting indebtedness and internal struggles among the estates to bring the estates' administrations under state control.

In Brandenburg-Prussia the standing army became a professional army recruited from inside and outside its own borders. Friedrich Wilhelm I gave the army a specific shape through the canton system of 1733 that created special districts and recruitment quotas for the regiments. Nobles, prominent burghers, officials, and students were freed from enrollment. Free recruitment continued to exist alongside the canton system, and this often led to the brutal methods in the countryside and far beyond Prussia's borders that gave the country such a bad reputation. Some sense of the domestic consequences can be gleaned from the remarks of Friedrich II in his political testament (1752), requesting that the companies only be half-filled with natives for the sake of preserving local agriculture.

Prussia's modern administration emerged from the military financial apparatus developed in this period. It took its beginnings from the new institute of the commissariat, as "an exceptional body of state power" (Otto Hintze). Its uniqueness stemmed from the personal contract between individuals and ruler that was engaged without the cooperation or consultation of the estates. The war commissaries became permanent officials with the appearance of the standing army. From 1660 onward a general commissariat was created for the entire state; shortly thereafter it acquired control of the military war chest filled from the income of the contribution. The administrators within the commissariat also became responsible for developing the finances and the economy needed to maintain the great army; in this way the commissariat became an important agent in formulating Prussian economic policies. This military financial institution collided on many fronts with the older financial administration tied to the estates, forcing Friedrich Wilhelm I eventually (1723) to create an umbrella financial body or general directory with the full title of *General-Ober-Finanz-Kriegs- und Domänendirektorium*. It became the most important institution within the entire domestic administration and also shaped economic policies. It was subdivided into four departments that still revealed the earlier autonomy of the various parts of the Prussian state. When Silesia became

Prussian, it, too, acquired a special provincial ministry within the general directory. Each of these provincial departments functioned at the same time as a thematically specialized department for the entire state. This coexistence of two administrative principles was a stage in the development of the centralized state. After 1740 additional specialized departments were formed, and they received some of the responsibilities of the provincial departments. An independent cabinet ministry for foreign affairs, consisting of two or three ministers working together, was created to handle affairs once within the domain of the privy council. The older privy council retained competence over judicial and ecclesiastical matters; gradually these, too, were given to specialized departments and unified (1737) under a Lord High Chancellor (*Grosskanzler*).

The monarch personally controlled the three important administrative bodies. Under Friedrich II such personal rule acquired the special form of cabinet government. The king withdrew from his highest officials, communicating with them only in writing. After reading the direct ministerial reports, he made decisions in the form of cabinet orders prepared by secretaries on the basis of his oral remarks or from marginal comments in the ministerial reports. The king controlled all the strands of government, making individual decisions in all areas. He was truly an autocrat. It is easy to see that this system required industrious and capable rulers if it were not to become corrupted; at the same time it also proved crippling to independent administrators.

The significance of the governmental bodies within the former states faded with the increased power of the central administration. They practically only retained judicial decision-making at the provincial level, becoming courts of appeal for urban and patrimonial courts and primary courts for the privileged. At the same time, the war and domain boards became more significant at the provincial level. They exercised a wide-ranging administrative legal competence that allowed the interests of the revenue gatherers (*Fiskus*) to come to the fore. Local administration was in the hands of the urban councillors, manorial lords, or officials of the royal domains. The district director, after 1701 the provincial councillor (*Landrat*), was the intermediate official at the district level between the provincial administration and the rural local administration on the manors. For a number of cities there was the analogous figure of the tax councillor; but unlike the provincial councillor, the tax councillor was purely a state official who controlled the collection of the excise and gradually the entire urban administration.

Prussian administration in the eighteenth century was a model for the transition from a system built on stemming injustice, immorality, and harm to the general good, to one that took an active role in social and economic development. The state produced officials and a bureaucracy stamped with an authoritarian character. It was by no means yet a unified system. After

1740 nobles received distinct preference, but there was still not a sharp line drawn between the higher and lower positions. Many noncommissioned officers were given posts at the lower levels, particularly in administering the excise. Officials were held to their duties by often the most rabid of means and filled with the consciousness of working for the king of Prussia (*travailler pour le roi de Prusse*). The custom of disbursing offices in return for payments to the recruitment chest – a form of venality of office – was eliminated after 1740, and remarkably little corruption continued to survive among Prussian officials. Even though they did not always follow the interests of the state, they became a strictly controlled and disciplined group capable of high achievements. In the process they became enormously important to the state, developing with their authority a tendency to become the permanent guardians of the population.

Prussian officialdom and administration constituted a special case, but one that allows the historian to recognize certain features of the general development. The older system of officialdom, the one shaped by the estates and the territories, was not simply abolished; either it was subordinated to the expanding central authorities or new institutional bodies with special competences were created alongside. The responsibilities of the new centralized, princely officeholders grew, and their collective "policing" functions began to shape internal social and economic policies.

The Austrian rulers also had had a privy council since the sixteenth century. A smaller body had emerged from it – called after 1709 the Standing Conference (*Ständige Konferenz*) – without becoming a true central bureaucracy. The Austrian court chancellery had adopted a collegial form from 1655 onward and was responsible for foreign policy, domestic administration, and justice, but not for finances or the army. Other independent court chancelleries also existed in Vienna for Bohemia and Hungary, and later for Italy and the Netherlands. The court treasury (*Hofkammer*) for finances and the war council (*Hofkriegsrat*) were also organized separately for Austria, Bohemia, and Hungary. In addition, government and administration in the individual states and provinces was still largely controlled by the estates; they administered, for example, the payment of direct taxes. In this way the local administration was insulated from direct intervention by the rulers, except in the Austrian core lands where they retained seigneurial and judicial rights as overlord. It took wars – the new wars against the Turks and the war of Spanish succession – to integrate the conglomerate of Habsburg lands more tightly.

When Charles, the second son of Leopold I, went to Spain in order to renew the extinguished Spanish Habsburg line, Leopold I, fearful of the Spanish example, negotiated a *pactum mutuae successionis* (1703) in order to prevent the disintegration of Habsburg lands at a point of uncertain succession. It was agreed that male primogeniture was to prevail in both branches. In the event that the male line should die out in either branch, the male line in the other branch should succeed; and in the event that both male lines were extinguished, then the oldest daughter of the last living male should succeed and thereafter her male issue. When Joseph I (1705–11) died in 1711, he was succeeded by his "Spanish" brother. While still childless, Charles VI created a testament to regulate his own succession. If there were no legitimate sons at his death and only daughters, then his eldest daughter should succeed him to the throne. In 1713, after having already declared Habsburg lands to be indivisible, he proclaimed the so-called Pragmatic Sanction, which established the order of succession as dynastic law. When his only son died in 1716, thereby making his eldest daughter Maria Theresia his successor, Charles forced the estates in all the hereditary lands, including Milan, to agree to intervene in support of the Pragmatic Sanction if the expected international complications actually came to pass. With these actions Charles raised the Pragmatic Sanction to the level of the first and only law binding all the Habsburg lands. It became the fundamental law guaranteeing the unity of the monarchy. On this basis, then, Maria Theresia and Joseph II sought to transform this union of states into one state and expand the competence of the central administration. The standing army and its maintenance became the occasion for various agreements with the estates and then for other institutional changes.

In 1749 fundamental administrative reforms were carried out in the Austrian and Bohemian hereditary lands. Count Friedrich Wilhelm von Haugwitz was the chief architect, partly basing himself on the teachings of the Austrian cameralists and partly on the example of Prussia. Remarkably he began the reform at the middle institutional level. He created so-called representations (*Repräsentationen*) for financial, military, and economic matters; these consisted of officials who now bound themselves to the queen and no longer to the estates. Officials in district offices (*Kreisämter*) were beneath them. Unlike in Prussia, they were pure state officials. Although responsible for the countryside and the cities, they functioned primarily to protect the peasantry for the military system, since Austria also shifted in these years to a recruiting system similar to the Prussian canton system. The so-called Theresian land registration established the basis for direct taxation of even the nobility. At the central level, the Austrian and Bohemian court chancelleries were unified under a new name, *directorium in publicis et cameralibus*. A supreme office of justice (*Oberste Justizstelle*) was established at the same time, but it did not completely manage to separate justice from administration, functioning both as a ministry and as a supreme court. The general war commissariat and court commercial commission were drawn into the directory in a manner analogous to the Prussian general directory. But this solution was not long-lived. Under the influence of Count Kaunitz the financial administration was removed and reestablished at the provincial level in a number of offices with limited powers, called "gubernia." At the head of this system was a council of state without executive functions. Such decentralization did not signify a return to the old dualism between ruler and estates or *Ständestaat,* but rather a bureaucratic division of jurisdictions. Maria Theresia neither desired nor was capable of creating the personal system of rule exercised by Friedrich in Prussia. For this reason the estates in the lands of the "Austrian house" retained far greater influence than in Prussia; similarly, Austria still lacked the personnel and the institutional infrastructure to create a functioning bureaucratic absolutism.

ABSOLUTISM AND ENLIGHTENED ABSOLUTISM

Absolute monarchy and enlightened monarchical government were European-wide phenomena. Still, if we see the reign of Louis XIV as the paradigm of absolutist rule, there was nothing comparable in Germany. Absolutism, however, did not take simply one form. Louis XIV's elevated style of monarchical rule was not an essential dimension and neither was the colorless, prosaic, arbitrary, and pious absolutism of Friedrich Wilhelm I's rule in Prussia. Both were extreme manifestations of a form of rule that was more often striven for than realized, more asserted than practiced, and one that remained most often at the highest levels of the state and did not extend into the daily world of the rural population. In theory such rule resided in the undivided and unlimited authority of an individual, who, as legislator, was not bound by the laws, who was independent of all control, and who exercised sovereignty without consulting any groups or institutions except those created by himself. But this was theory only.

Absolute monarchy was aided and even politically justified in the seventeenth century by the real need to constitute an authority that could prevent civil war; secure order, property, and the food supply; and reconstruct and improve living conditions. To the extent that absolute monarchy was successful in establishing domestic and confessional peace, preventing where possible arbitrary seigneurial actions, encouraging economic development, and creating at least the beginnings of a centralized administration, it represented a significant phase in the emergence of the modern state.

Absolute authority is sovereign authority, the *summa perpetuaque potestas,* as Jean Bodin had defined it. Against the background of particular historical sovereignties, absolute monarchy created both the idea and the instruments of a uniform state authority; simultaneously, it developed as the arena for its activity the notion of and legal arrangements for a unified and enclosed state; and, finally, it established itself as the carrier of that authority within the state. Such definitions also eliminated competition and resistance both conceptually and juridically. Equally, it eliminated the idea of a higher political and legal order, as well as participation by the estates in rule by the state. Absolute monarchy was only able to understand the functions and privileges of the estates as matters that had been ceded, authorized, and delegated to them.

Various elements made up the self-understanding of absolute rulers. Divine rights theory could be linked to a principally rational theory of sovereignty, but each could also remain independent of the other. Then, too, natural rights theory could be conjoined, whereby sovereignty was founded and then exercised on the basis of an original social contract. Such enlightened theories could also be attached to a benevolent paternalism. Absolutistic policies seem to have been justified in almost all cases in various combinations of these ideas. Even "enlightened absolutism" remained a form of absolutism. It also excluded the participation of the ruled in the system of government. In many ways enlightened governments were even more expressly founded on the unlimited exercise of authority, and they used this authority against the traditions and habits of their subjects, in order to institute political and social changes that followed the dictates of reason. Absolute governments saw themselves in this sense as custodians, guardians, and educators of the future.

The older Protestant understanding of office also continued to survive in absolutist theory: Authority was linked to the paternalism of the well-ordered police state. This authoritarian paternalism was bound together, in turn, with the enlightened conviction that government must guide humankind to think and act rationally, and eventually to become enlightened and mature citizens. Enlightened government should be sovereign rule *for* the people, but not based on majority rule *by* the people, because the Enlightenment first had to create the presuppositions for popular government. Enlightened governments believed, of course, that they could already count on agreement by the few enlightened members of the population. These enlightened few, furthermore, were expected to act within the system as the carriers of enlightened ideas; they were to be society's educators and critics. As critics they would, of course, be well-intentioned, since the goals of enlightened governments had to be identical with enlightened criticism itself.

Enlightenment government was fundamentally justified insofar as it extended the sovereign's capacity to overcome backward social relations and political institutions, but, to the extent that Enlightenment and political consciousness developed throughout the population, it was equally necessary that enlightened policies overcome their own absolutist elements. There is, however, no historical evidence of such a pattern in Germany during our period. Until the end of the Seven Years War enlightened absolutism was and could be nothing more than rule by a monarch who no longer founded his power on divine right but on the nature of man, social necessity, and history. He was able to see the state as a rational institution and politics as rational action, and could attempt to transform "enlightened" thought into reforms. Yet such a monarch could not dissolve the existing social and political system but only adapt it to modern demands and needs.

Friedrich II of Prussia was of decisive significance for the expectations placed on such enlightened governments. Already as crown prince he had opened himself to ideas of the European Enlightenment. As king, he sought to consolidate and expand the power of the state in conjunction with demands for the material well-being and education of his inhabitants. His reputation as a philosopher-king was enhanced because he occupied himself with contemporary philosophy, consorted with philosophers, and wrote philosophical works. Victories in battle also increased his prestige. In addition, he developed a style of rule and instituted policies in his first years that intensified expectations. He developed tolerant religious policies, especially in recently conquered Silesia; he reformed the courts; and he began the lengthy process of codifying the laws for the entire state. In so doing, however, Friedrich did not lessen the severity of the military and administrative state, and he ruled as autocratically as had his father. Still, by his presence and actions, he created in the awakened political consciousness of Germans the example of a monarch who by better policies could generate substantial improvements in public and private life. Such hopes, as well as the actual activities of the governments, however, also caused German political thought to be more strongly fixated on the state.

5

WARS, CRISES,
AND CONFLICTS

———— · ————

The Westphalian Peace in 1648 was much more a European event than earlier peace settlements had been. Delegates from almost every European power took part in negotiations that became the first of the peace conferences typical of future European diplomacy. Although the signatories assured that the peace was to be "Christian, universal, and eternal," this proved not to be the case. There were indeed no further internal German wars until 1740, but German dynasties were continually involved in new wars. This was especially true for the Habsburgs with interests and lands spread throughout Europe and overseas. Still Germany was no longer the main staging area for war. More than ever before and for more than a century to come, the important political decisions were not made in central Europe. At no other time were the policies of the German states so determined by those of the great European powers. This fact had direct, though contradictory, consequences for German domestic policies. In one case a ruler's efforts to win prestige or additional territory might cause him to link himself to the great powers; the alliance might thereby unleash intense struggles with the estates, causing foreign policy in the end to trigger an expansion of central authority. On the other hand, the conflicts might remain unresolved or the prince might be defeated, thus generating turmoil and even disaster. It is no accident that autocratic absolutism emerged in a number of German states in this period of the greatest political dependency and most obvious national egoism.

We should not, however, evaluate this historical problem from the perspective of the nation state. In particular, we should not condemn the imperial estates in some blanket manner for a lack of national commitment. There were waves of imperial patriotism and national anger, for example, when the French occupied Strasbourg in 1681, and the memory of a great

116

past and the awareness of a national culture did continue to grow over the course of the eighteenth century. Yet it still lay beyond German political reality to draw political conclusions in terms of national interests or shape foreign policy in terms of national goals. Within the empire the imperial estates were committed to decentralization and far-reaching political independence: This preserved their "German liberty" (*teutsche Libertät*). Importantly, the great powers agreed, since any substantial change within the empire, at least before 1740, would have resulted from an expansion of Habsburg power and unhinged the European political order. Habsburg expansion, in addition, would have awakened concerns about a new wave of Counter-Reformation.

Therefore European diplomats were committed to preserving the *Corps Germanique*. The political literature of the eighteenth century also emphasized how important the empire was for maintaining peace in Europe. Jean-Jacques Rousseau wrote in his "Excerpt from the Plan for Perpetual Peace by Abbe de Saint-Pierre":

In reality the European system of states is mainly held together, to the extent it is, by the negotiations themselves; but this system has yet another more effective support: namely the German Empire, which is held in check in the heart of Europe by all the other powers and which perhaps serves the security of the others more than its own. By its size and the number and bravery of its peoples, it is an imposing empire whose constitution is useful to all. It limits the means and the will to conquer, even as it simultaneously causes any conquerer to founder. In spite of the errors in this imperial system, it is certain that the European balance of power will not be disturbed as long as the empire continues to exist, that no ruler need fear being dethroned by another, and that the Westphalian Peace settlement may permanently remain the basis of our collective political system. The public law studied so thoroughly by the Germans is thus far more important than they believe, because it is not simply German public law, but in a certain sense that of Europe itself.

This quotation was, of course, not an adequate analysis of the imperial constitution and the political role of the empire in Europe or even an accurate prognosis; but it is a remarkably positive evaluation of the empire as the guarantor of the European system and as the model of a supranational, federal order. As a citizen of Geneva, Rousseau certainly thought that a federal system comprising small principalities was the political form that best preserved the greatest freedom. But even pragmatic diplomats were aware that the European balance of power (the term first becomes common in the eighteenth century) depended on preserving the empire.

In the second half of the seventeenth century and even farther into the future, religious affinities and conflicts continued to play a role in German and European politics, but that role was clearly reduced. Interconfessional alliances were no longer something exceptional. Neither were alliances between imperial estates and external powers, especially against the Habsburgs. Naturally, such alliances were never thought to be directed against the emperor and the empire. From the perspective of the Habsburgs, it also became less possible for the emperors to turn their wars into imperial wars. In fact, the empire as a body rarely engaged in war, though individual imperial estates were often partners in alliances, or were drawn into struggles because of dynastic interests, or engaged themselves as independent actors in the political struggles of the period. In this era of hereditary power, there was nowhere else where so many ruling houses were drawn into high politics because of family connections and questions of dynastic succession. Indeed, the century after 1648 demonstrated to what extent succession struggles could unleash political crises and conflicts: The Spanish, Polish, and Austrian successions led to European wars.

These wars, like the others in which the German states participated, were not in their entirety part of German history, and thus they do not need to be treated here in great detail. But we must discover in what ways the wars, crises, and conflicts of Europe influenced German historical development.

THE PREEMINENCE OF FRANCE AND
THE RISE OF THE HOUSE OF AUSTRIA

When Austrian hegemony in Central Europe was delineated in the Peace of Prague (1635), France entered the war on the side of Sweden, even though the Spanish and Austrian Habsburgs threatened her on a broad front. By 1648 the tables had been turned. The Westphalian Peace documented a difficult defeat for Habsburg policies and the Peace of the Pyrenees in 1659 underscored its European extent. After crushing the internal opposition of the Fronde, France now became the dominant figure in the great struggle between the Habsburgs and herself that had been a basic feature of the European international system since the fifteenth century. It must have been expected that France would attempt to extend her borders farther northward and eastward. The marriage between Louis XIV and the infanta Maria Theresia negotiated in the Peace of the Pyrenees opened an even more threatening prospect for the European states system, that of Bourbon sovereignty over the Spanish domains. The other possibility was also threatening, namely the reestablishment of unified Habsburg rule through the transfer of the lands of the Spanish line to the Austrian branch. The marriage of the emperor Leopold I with the second daughter of Philipp IV, the infanta Margarete Theresia, would also have shifted the balance. The question of the Spanish "succession," as a consequence, came increasingly to overshadow the great foreign policy issues of the late seventeenth century.

Louis not only prepared himself diplomatically, but he tried to shape future political facts before the events themselves. The following decades were filled with French attacks against Flanders and the Rhine. His efforts to control the imperial elections failed in 1658, but they were not a total loss since Leopold was forced to renounce Spanish support in his election capitulation and the Rhenish League fell under French control after its admission. Thus the league that had been led by Mainz was not able to play the role of a third force between France and the empire, as Johann Philipp von Schönborn had originally conceived. Already in 1665, the death of Philipp IV – who left an enfeebled son as heir – had been the occasion for French armies to invade Flanders and the Spanish bailiwick of Burgundy using a dubious appeal to the old Brabantine private law regarding "devolution." Spain, the emperor, and the imperial estates offered no resistance. The emperor was even prepared to enter with Louis into a secret agreement to partition, and the Rhenish princes denied Austrian and Spanish troops passage through their lands. It was finally the maritime powers England and Holland, who, with the later addition of Sweden, forced France into the Peace of Aachen (1668). The French agreed to leave the France Comté but retained twelve Flemish fortresses as outposts for further action and kept open the Spanish succession.

Although this peace was simply a temporary military truce and otherwise a French success, it did clarify the configuration of forces for the future. When faced with the threat of hegemony by a single power, the others, following the lead of the maritime powers, were able temporarily to put aside their differences. The "universal monarchy" of Louis XIV was not merely the effective propaganda slogan promulgated especially by the Austrian diplomat Franz von Lisola, but it was a real danger. How much so was demonstrated by Louis' attack on the Netherlands (1672), the one country that most consequentially resisted French aspirations and sought to divide the Spanish inheritance.

The renewed warfare was first preceded by a French diplomatic offensive and the abrupt exchange of allies that characterized the international order in this period. The Triple Alliance dissolved; the English king and Sweden joined France, who also concluded treaties with the Rhenish princes, Bavaria, and Hanover. The Palatine elector married his sister Liselotte to the brother of Louis XIV, the duke of Orléans; Bavaria prepared itself to take Austrian territories and even the imperial crown itself once Louis had worn it; and the Wittelsbach archbishop of Cologne opened his borders to French troops. A French army invaded Lorraine in 1670, expelling Duke Charles IV for a second time. French military pressure and money prevented common action or even any resistance by the German princes, who in any case were under the influence of French political power and culture. In 1671 the emperor even managed to conclude a treaty of neutrality with his great opponent.

The French armies were superiorly outfitted and brilliantly led; yet their attack on Holland remained unsuccessful in spite of military victories and simultaneous Dutch involvement in a third war at sea with England. On the one hand, internal changes within Holland proved more important than opening the floodgates against the invaders. These were, first, the revolts against patrician rule and, then, the appointment of William (III), prince of Orange, as stadtholder of the province of Holland. On the other hand, the international balance of power also changed. Already by 1673 a peace congress had gathered in Cologne as the pressure of public opinion forced the English government to come to terms with Holland, and the emperor with Spain, Lorraine, and Holland. At the same time, Denmark and Brandenburg entered the anti-French coalition, and an imperial war was declared, even though Hanover and Bavaria remained aloof. France had only Sweden, Poland, and Turkey as allies with which to face this great coalition. In spite of this, she proved to have the better armies, the better diplomats, and the more unified command. Gradually she was able to overcome early losses and exert superiority on the Upper Rhine.

Toward the end of 1674 France persuaded Sweden to invade the Mark Brandenburg. Elector Friedrich Wilhelm hurried home from the Upper Rhine with his troops and in June of the next year triumphed over Sweden near Ferbellin. He used the opportunity, since Denmark had also turned against its neighbor, to conquer West Pomerania and Stettin, pursuing Swedish troops all the way to Riga. This war proved only to be a secondary offensive that did not disrupt French plans. It lessened the pressure against France on the Rhine, and Brandenburg did not gain Pomerania in the end because France would not abandon its old ally. Yet the offensive exposed the weak Swedish position on the German side of the Baltic and revealed that the electors of Brandenburg were a serious military factor in the north.

The decisive events in the great struggle with and around France occurred in the Mediterranean, on the Rhine, and in Flanders. France went everywhere on the offensive, only to learn that she could not gain the Netherlands. But France's opponents also collapsed, allowing peace negotiations to begin in 1677 in Nijmegen under English mediation. A number of individual treaties emerged from these negotiations. The States General emerged with almost no losses. The Spanish then were forced to accept the greatest losses – the bailiwick of Burgundy and thirteen border fortresses in the Spanish Netherlands. Finally the emperor and the empire were forced to accept that France retained Freiburg and the strategically important fortress of Hüningen. In practical terms, they also ceded Lorraine, since Duke Charles refused to accept the oppressive and dishonorable treaty conditions. Moreover, they agreed not to support any enemies of Sweden. With deep bitterness the elector of Brandenburg found himself forced in the Treaty of St. Germain-en-Laye (1679) to abandon most of his Pomeranian conquests. France extended her position in Flanders and on the Rhine. Nowhere was France forced to sacrifice gains or even to abandon her long-term goals in Spain. Louis XIV was at this moment at the height of his power. His actions predominently shaped European politics, especially the attitudes of the German imperial estates.

European diplomats understood full well that the Treaty of Nijmegen was only an armistice and knew where France would next attack. In 1673 the ten Alsatian imperial cities had incorporated the areas over which they had exercised legal jurisdiction (*Landvogtei*) since 1648. The peace of 1679 had avoided a final clarification of the situation in the Alsace. In the middle of this peace, it was here that Louis took imperial territories, using as a pretext a legal opinion based on medieval feudal law. Territories and places once subordinate to areas annexed by France should now belong to the French crown. In order to prove this claim, France set up special courts, the "chambers of reunion." As soon as these had identified such territories, all counterclaims and doubts were dismissed, and the possessors were challenged to swear an oath of fealty to the king of France or face occupation. In this manner the county of Mömpelgard, belonging to a Württemberg secondary line, was subordinated to the French crown as a Burgundian fief. The same occurred to territories of the bishop of Strasbourg and the archbishop of Trier, the counts of Salm and Lützelstein, and lands belonging to Saarbrücken, Zweibrücken, and others. Without any legal justification Strasbourg was commanded in November 1681 to subject itself to France, and after a short siege, it was occupied without a struggle. These events unleashed strong patriotic protests, but the military weakness of the empire and the divergent interests of the imperial estates meant that nothing could be done.

In the meantime the constellation of forces altered within the empire. The disappointed elector of Brandenburg joined forces with France, in order to acquire as an ally what had eluded him as an opponent. From the other side, Saxony and even Bavaria had distanced themselves from France. The imperial diet agreed to a reform of the imperial military system in 1681. The Frankfurt Association, formed in 1679, extended itself to the Upper Rhenish and Franconian imperial circles and concluded a defensive treaty with the emperor in Laxenburg (1682). In the following year the emperor also joined a coalition with Holland, Sweden, and Spain. A renewal of war seemed to await Europe, especially as Spain resisted French penetrations in the Netherlands. The emperor, however, was tied up in the east in war against the Turks, who put Vienna under seige for the second time in 1683. At this moment France once again demonstrated her military superiority by conquering the fortress of Luxemburg. In the truce of Regensburg (August 1684) that followed, the emperor accepted for a period of twenty years, dating from 1 August 1681, both the completed acts of reunion and the French conquests of Strasbourg and Luxemburg. The emperor hoped to buy peace in the west with this agreement, but this soon proved to be illusory. France pressured the western borders once again; this time the attacks were conducted so shamelessly that great bitterness was generated.

It was precisely in these years that Louis' power began to decline. The European balance of power also altered in a manner that, in retrospect, proved decisive. Louis overreached himself with the revocation of the Edict of Nantes (1685). Internally it was supposed to have made monarchical absolutism complete by unifying religious belief within the unitary state. Although it took until the end of his life for him to admit that he had not achieved his goals, Louis much sooner came to see the negative political consequences for his foreign policy. The flight of many Protestants unleashed discontent throughout Europe. In England the accession of the Catholic Stuart, James II, intensified the fears of a Catholic reconquest. In Germany they caused Friedrich Wilhelm of Brandenburg to abandon his French alliance and join the opposition. In the edict of Potsdam (1685) he offered haven to the Huguenots, and later in the year he renewed his alliance with the Netherlands. These were signs of the changing constellation of power in northern Germany, because Brandenburg also made peace with Sweden, the traditional ally of France, and with the emperor. As a confirmation of the new relationships, Brandenburg, Hanover, Sweden, and the emperor then successfully intervened in the occupation of Hamburg by France's Danish allies. In principal the same pattern was apparent in the Augsburg Alliance, formed in the same year between the emperor and the southern German imperial cities. The latter were militarily and politically insignificant, but their willingness to join in alliance signaled the growing awareness of the French threat.

The French soon increased pressure again. In 1685 the last Palatine elector from the house of Simmer died, to be succeeded by Philipp Wilhelm from the Catholic house of Neuburg. Louis XIV used the occasion to claim in the name of his sister-in-law Liselotte her brother's allodial inheritance, which consisted of a number of districts *(Aemter)*. He besieged a number of fortifications on the right bank of the Rhine in order to give weight to his demands. At the same time Louis increased pressure on the archbishopric of Cologne, where his supporter, Cardinal Wilhelm von Fürstenberg, was seeking the archbishop's chair. At the time of the divided election in 1688 he occupied the country, even as the pope, in league with the emperor, confirmed the appointment of the Bavarian prince Joseph Clemens. At this point Louis went on the offensive, demanding the permanent recognition of the reunions and the elevation of Fürstenberg into the electoral college. He also agreed to settle the claims in the Palatinate for a cash indemnity. This time, however, the emperor would not give ground and war began anew. Once again it assumed European proportions but under a different constellation of forces. In England the Stuart dynasty fell, and William of Orange, the great opponent of Louis XIV, ascended the throne. In the east in the meantime, the emperor's armies had already gone on the offensive against the Turks after victory at Kahlenberg (12 November 1683). The Turks soon suffered serious defeats at Ofen (1686) and Mohacs (1687). In September 1688 Belgrade was conquered. For Louis this was a sign to attack, since the Habsburgs had previously always been forced to pay attention to the east, and now the effective interplay with the Ottomans was threatened. The Habsburgs not only had a freer hand, although the war with the Turks still continued, but their self-confidence was greatly strengthened. In May 1689 the emperor and the empire concluded an alliance with Holland, and this broadened into a great coalition with the entry of England, Spain, Sweden, and Savoy. They agreed to restore Europe to conditions at the peaces of Westphalia and the Pyrenees.

The new war formed the first phase of a series of wars lasting until 1714 and was simultaneously the prelude to the war of the Spanish succession. (In Germany the conflict is called the Palatine War.) But it was only one aspect of a struggle between a great, though heterogeneous, coalition and an isolated but still mighty France, who had by no means abandoned her efforts to achieve hegemony on the continent. Claims against Palatine and Simmern territories provoked the war, and, consequently, the Palatine electorate became the victim. Faced with the constellation and placement of his opponents, Louis refrained from attacking beyond occupying electoral Cologne and conquering Philippsburg. Instead he systematically razed the fortresses and demolished the defendable cities and villages in the occupied areas and within reach of the French armies. Hardest hit were areas along the middle Rhine, the Moselle, and especially the Palatinate. Cities such as Mannheim and Heidelberg were badly burned. These were symbols of an arbitrary and false strategy, for the military advantage was small, but the political damage to French–German relations continued for a long time thereafter.

Eventually imperial troops reconquered Mainz, Bonn, and Kaiserswerth from the French, but they lacked the strength and decisiveness to counterattack. Mistrust among the imperial estates and the disparity of political interests prevented them from mobilizing their military potential for common action, even though it was a declared imperial war. If the thought of forming associations found renewed resonance among the foremost imperial estates as well as the smaller ones, it was treated in Vienna with great skepticism. In northern and middle Germany a plan for a third party made the rounds, and the Guelf Ernst August used the opportunity to demand the electoral rank for his house by entering into alliance with France. By agreeing (1692), the emperor was able to bind Hanover to Habsburg policies, but it brought dissension among the other electoral princes. Thus the war dragged on without a military decision, even on the fronts outside Germany. Since France could not be defeated decisively, the great coalition began to unravel, and France was able to enter into negotiations with her opponents individually. With Sweden mediating, France entered into peace discussions in Ryswick (September 1697) with Great Britain, Holland, and Spain. A few weeks later the emperor had little choice but to enter these talks for himself and the empire.

In the peace settlement, France and the maritime powers restored their conquered territories. Even Spain suffered only small territorial losses. France recognized William of Orange as the English king; she retained her Alsatian reunions and Strasbourg but returned the duchy of Zweibrücken, Philippsburg, Breisach, Kehl, Freiburg, and – upon receiving the right of troop passage – Lorraine to Duke Charles V in the contours of 1670. Finally, she dropped the candidacy of Cardinal Fürstenberg as the archbishop of Cologne.

Measured in terms of Louis' goals, the Peace of Ryswick was certainly a failure. But measured in terms of the expectations and goals of the great coalition, it demonstrated the power and defensive strength of the Bourbon monarchy. Nevertheless the coalition created by William of Orange had for the first time limited French expansion. Still it was neither able to force France to return to the status quo in 1648 and 1659, nor could it force France to abandon her claims to the Spanish succession. For this reason a new series of battles could be envisaged for the future. In these, however, the empire played only a secondary role. Austria, on the other hand, had interests separate from the empire as a European great power, and she did play a major role.

The Peace of the Pyrenees had made the political decline of Spain manifest, but the Westphalian settlement had not made it possible to foresee the political rise of Austria. Austria emerged due to events in southeastern Europe that were both independently and dynamically linked to the conflicts in western Europe. Turkish pressures in the east had long limited Austrian actions in the west, thereby aiding French policies. By the same token, as the Turkish threat began to dissipate, Austria engaged herself more intensively in the west. This possibility became real exactly at the moment the question of the Spanish succession became acute.

People in the seventeenth and eighteenth centuries were undoubtedly much more aware than we are today of the importance of the Ottoman Empire within the European system of states. As non-Christians and outsiders to the *jus publicum Europaeum,* the Ottomans had despotically ruled significant parts of Europe for hundreds of years. The Turks had managed to retain their European holdings after the death of Süleyman I (1566) and the naval defeat at Lepanto (1571). Dynastic struggles, decay within the army, domestic troubles, and conflicts with Persia all prevented them from attacking westward for quite some time. They ruled the largest part of Hungary, and exercised a disputed suzerainty over Siebenbürgen and the Moldau regions. The fronts began to move again after Grand Vizier

Mohammed Köprülü had restabilized state authority. The first Turkish attacks were repelled in 1664 at St. Gotthard a.d. Raab by the imperial general and important tactician Montecuccoli, but the victory was not exploited. However, Austria created twenty more years of relative peace for herself on this front, time which she desperately needed for battle with France, by entering in the same year into the Peace of Vasvar. In addition to this, Turkish attention turned away from Austria and toward Poland and Russia. Even so, the Habsburg parts of Hungary remained restless. The nobility in particular were provoked to resistance and revolt by Leopold I's insensitive centralizing and anti-Protestant policies. The French, of course, were there to stoke the fires. Emmerich Tököly, the leader of the revolt, sought ties with the Turks, who proceeded to attack the Austrian hereditary lands en masse in 1683. Again the French were involved in supporting the attack, but the great impulse came from Grand Vizier Kra Mustapha who was committed to destroying Habsburg power. In a short time a Turkish army of 200,000 men stood before the gates of Vienna. It was due largely to Pope Innocence IX that Poland stood with the emperor. In the empire, on the other hand, the supporters of France, among them the elector of Brandenburg, remained aloof. Vienna was held under siege for three months before the relief army led by the king of Poland, Johann Sobieski, defeated the Turks at Kahlenberg (12 September 1683). It was even more decisive that a ceasefire with France in the Truce of Regensburg made it possible for a large offensive force under Duke Charles of Lorraine to alter permanently the balance of forces in the east.

Emperor Leopold concluded a "Holy Alliance" with Poland, Venice, and the pope in March of the next year. After victory at Mohacz completely freed Hungary, Leopold persuaded the imperial diet in Pressburg to recognize the hereditary right of the Habsburg house to the imperial crown and to crown his son Joseph. Siebenbürgen also then subordinated itself to Habsburg rule. Max Emmanuel of Bavaria conquered Belgrade in September of the following year. Margrave Ludwig of Baden attacked Bosnia, even as the grand vizier fell victim to a revolt by Janissaries. At this moment, when Austria and the empire might have advanced even farther, France invaded the Palatinate. It was a proof of Austrian self-assurance and strength that she continued the Turkish War and thus allowed herself to be involved in a war on two fronts. Operations suffered because of the war in the west, especially because her coalition partners demanded that Austria retire from the Turkish War. There were defeats such as the loss of Belgrade, and there were victories such as that at Szlankamen (1691). Finally, however, Prince Eugene of Savoy reorganized the army and led it to a major victory at Zenta (1697) and further victories in Bosnia, forcing the sultan to accept an offer by the maritime powers to mediate a peace settlement. Austria also needed peace, since the issue of succession in Spain was fast approaching. In the Peace of Carlowitz (26 January 1699), the Ottoman Porte was forced to recognize Habsburg rule over all of Hungary, with the exception of Banat, over Siebenbürgen, and over large parts of Slavonia and Croatia.

The Ottoman Empire was never again a threat to middle Europe. A process of retreat had begun to set in that would last until the twentieth century. In the nineteenth century the disintegration of the Ottoman Empire became known as the oriental question since it concerned competition between the European powers for the inheritance of the "sick man on the Bosphorus." Thereafter Austrian foreign policy focused on southeastern Europe as one of her most important areas of interest. Furthermore, the extension of Austrian political power into the Balkans became fundamental to her position as a great power, which she came to assert in the war of the Spanish succession, even though the Austrian Habsburgs lost the largest part of the Spanish inheritance. In line with Austria's policies as a great power, particularly as Prince Eugene had asserted them, it was important that she once again begin war with the Turks after the end of the war of Spanish succession. When the Turks annexed the Venetian Morea, Prince Eugene attacked, defeating them at Peterewardein (1716), conquering Temesvar, and occupying Belgrade (August 1717). In the Peace of Passarowitz concluded the next year under the mediation of England, Holland, and Sweden on the basis of the war's results, Austria for the first time went beyond the boundaries of Hungary, acquiring the Banat, northern Serbia, and Wallachia.

The Turkish War was never simply a Habsburg war, even if it was hardly a struggle of the entire empire. Still the Austrian house carried the main burden in first repulsing the Turks and then attacking the Ottoman Empire, and it was the great winner in these struggles. The war partially retained the quality of a crusade and a struggle to defend occidental culture. Mercenaries and condottieri from many German and European states fought in these battles; many of the significant military leaders of the early eighteenth century received their education there. The imperial city of Vienna became more a European city than ever before, and imperial service gained in luster and attractiveness for the German and parts of the European nobility.

Certainly the rise of Austria belongs more to European than to German political developments. But it was of fundamental importance for the middle of Europe, the empire, and Germany that a political power center of independent weight emerged there. It gave support to the empire in the turbulent years of the first two thirds of the eighteenth century. That was particularly revealed in the war of the Spanish succession. This war encapsulated in many ways the political tendencies and potentialities for action within the European state system as the states struggled for hegemony or a balance of power.

THE EMPIRE IN THE EUROPEAN WARS
OF THE EARLY EIGHTEENTH CENTURY

The wars of the late seventeenth and early eighteenth centuries retained the character of "cabinet wars" in spite of the fact that they were European-wide conflicts and even became worldwide conflicts, extending to the oceans and overseas possessions. They were politically calculated undertakings, a means to achieve political goals by simply threatening troop movements, occupying a few strategically important points, constructing or besieging fortresses, or intersecting lines of operation. Military operations were held in check because the officers constantly had to deal with desertion and discipline, with massive illness, and with poorly fed and equipped mercenary troops. Military strategists were thus pressured to control their troops even in battle. For these reasons they had to force them to operate in the tightest formations possible and otherwise to live with the harshest of discipline. When these were standing armies, there were additional factors of cost and difficulty of replacement. The strictest calculation was therefore necessary in planning every action. One highly prized solution in this period was to substitute systematically constructed fortifications for the uncertainties of battle. In comparison with the Thirty Years War, all of these factors had the effect of lessening to some extent the consequences of war for the lands and populations beyond the battlefields themselves.

The art of war was similar to the rationalistic form diplomacy had assumed. Wars were declared mechanistically and then ended, peace treaties signed and then broken, alliances formed and marriages planned. If military leaders sought victory, diplomats sought gain, compensation, reparations, and maintenance of the balance of power. Equilibrium, concert, and agreement (*équilibre, concert, convenance*) were characteristic terms in the language of politics. Politics in this period was not simply dominated by egoistic thoughts of power but also attempted rationally to contain the labile and explosive forces within the European order. It was a politics of reason of state, *raison d'état*, or *Staatsräson*, that had evolved from a particular doctrine of interest. Every state was assumed to have special interests to pursue. Were the various interests to collide, compromises then had to be made on the basis of treaties or warfare. Governments oriented their own reason on a more or less temporary basis with whatever government happened to be in power, but it might serve their interest to conclude alliances and preserve the peace. In retrospect this seems to have been an age of continuous warfare but also an age of peace treaties and alliances. Indeed it often appears to have been an age of the diplomat more than the general.

The Peace of Ryswick had not resolved the question of the Spanish succession. The childlessness of Charles II (1665–1700)), however, brought the extinction of the Spanish Habsburg line ever closer. The collective experience of the last war indicated that one or more of the heirs apparent would go to war again to pursue claims to the collective inheritance. The diplomats were thus concerned to resolve the matter by dividing the inheritance before the death of Charles. Accordingly, the booty was distributed on paper before it became available.

There were a number of powerful heirs with hereditary claims. Louis XIV of France was the son of the eldest daughter of Philipp III and the husband of the eldest daughter of Philipp IV of Spain. Emperor Leopold I was son of the youngest daughter of Philipp III and husband of the youngest daughter of Philipp IV. Moreover, he was head of the Austrian line of the house of Habsburg. Electoral prince Joseph Ferdinand of Bavaria was the great grandson of Philipp IV and the grandson of Charles II. The claims of the women were also relevant, for though the mother and wife of Louis XIV had both renounced their claims to the Spanish throne, the Parisian Parlement had nullified their declarations. In addition, the agreed upon dowry had not been dispensed properly. Leopold's wife, on the other hand, had not renounced any claims. In the spirit of Habsburg policy, Leopold laid claim to the undivided inheritance for his second son, Charles. Louis, however, accepted a solution proposed by the naval powers England and Holland, agreeing to a division of the inheritance in the name of his second grandson, Philipp of Anjou. The treaty concluded in October 1698 to maintain the peace of Europe proposed to give Philipp Naples, Sicily, and hereditarily linked areas in Tuscany; Charles was only to receive the duchy of Milan; and Joseph Ferdinand was to acquire the lion's share, namely Spain, her colonies, and the Netherlands. It stayed only a minor episode when Charles II named the Bavarian prince his universal heir, because Joseph Ferdinand died in 1699. The treaty of division then lost its basis, so the naval powers and France replaced it by another in March 1700. In this version Philipp was to receive Milan in addition and exchange it for the duchy of Lorraine. Charles was to receive the share originally granted to the Bavarian prince. The emperor, however, rejected this apparently advantageous solution in the hope that Madrid would name the archduke universal heir. Instead French diplomacy managed to have the entire inheritance passed on to Philipp. Shortly thereafter Charles II died, and Louis XIV, ignoring the treaty of division, had his grandson, Philipp V, proclaimed king of Spain.

The emperor was determined to press his claims militarily, and he found support among the naval powers. The Hague Alliance of 1701 was the last achievement of William of Orange (he died on 19 March 1701) but his plans for a coalition to contain French hegemonial claims survived him. Portugal and later Savoy joined the alliance, as did most but not all of the imperial estates. The Wittelsbach electoral princes of Bavaria and Cologne, for instance, remained in the French camp. Once again, and not for the last time, the Wittelsbachs saw the greater danger to lie in Habsburg aspirations that limited their own expansionary plans. Quite different interests prevailed among the other participants: Hanover was already making plans for the English crown; Saxony-Poland needed to keep a watchful eye on the crisis in the north; and Brandenburg-Prussia, although it was indebted to the emperor for recognizing the Prussian royal title, was interested in the family inheritance of William of Orange.

In 1702 the empire declared war against France. Still the empire played only a subordinate role in the events that followed – how much so was revealed in exemplary fashion in the Peace of Baden (26 June 1717) in which the empire merely recognized the Peace of Rastatt negotiated between the emperor and France. Even this settlement (6 March 1714) was simply a sequel to the Treaty of Utrecht (1713), in which the other belligerents regulated the Spanish succession, to the bitter disappointment of the emperor. Austria and the empire attempted to continue the war alone, but with Prussia already having abandoned the war effort, their armies soon proved their weakness vis-a-vis the French.

We cannot follow the course of the war in any detail. It began with Austrian troops entering Milan and produced brilliant victories by Prince Eugene in coordination with John Churchill, Duke of Marlborough. It also saw French armies attack southern Germany and share operations with Bavarian contingents. There were failures of the imperial armies on the Upper Rhine, revolts in Hungary, and tensions between the imperial estates and the new emperor Joseph I (1705–11). In addition, the coalition armies were only able to enter French territory for brief periods. After the battle of Oudenaarde (1708), the decisive advantage appeared to fall to the alliance, but their extreme demands drove Louis to continue the war. As his situation worsened once again, he was saved by the beginning dissolution of the coalition. Marlborough fell from power in England, and a Tory party seeking peace opened secret negotiations with France (1710–11). Joseph I died without a male heir shortly thereafter, so that his brother Charles, who had been called to Spain as king, was named his successor and was now also named German emperor in the same year of 1711. These events made a return to the empire of Charles V a real possibility – a situation even more unpalatable to the other powers than the hegemony of France. English pressure forced the calling of a peace congress at the Hague in early 1712, even as the war still continued. A number of peace treaties emerged between France and England, Holland, Portugal, Savoy, and even Prussia. England managed to gain French recognition of the Hanoverian succession, a promise not to support the Stuarts, the razing of the fortifications at Dunkirk, and the acquisition of Gibraltar and enormous areas of Canada. Holland's agreements were negotiated in a complex set of exchanges based on Bavarian acquisitions. But essentially Holland received the right to occupy a number of fixed defensive sites in border areas of the Spanish

Netherlands called the Barrier that now were to belong to Austria. Prussia gained the Spanish part of Geldern, sovereignty over Neufchâtel and Valengin from the Orange inheritance, and recognition of the Prussian royal title. Savoy was promised the kingdom of Sicily and, in addition, the right to succeed the Bourbon line in Spain were it to die out. Austria, finally, acquired the Spanish dependencies of Milan, Naples, and Sardinia that Louis XIV had failed to acquire for Max Emanuel of Bavaria. France, however, also achieved a chief goal – that Philipp of Anjou be recognized as king of Spain. Nine months later the emperor found himself forced to join the Utrecht settlement. Territorial acquisitions, in addition, were restored to the year 1697, with the exception that France retained the city and fortress of Landau.

Neither the Habsburgs nor France had achieved its goals. The war ended much more in the interests of the sea powers, especially England, whose political pressure on the European states to maintain the balance of power proved decisive from thence onward. At the same time, the peace of Utrecht signaled a shift in power to Protestant Europe. Yet the old struggle between the Habsburgs and France remained intact, because Austria acquired the entire front from the Netherlands to Italy. The empire played only a secondary role as the large imperial estates pushed beyond its boundaries more than ever before. They began to engage in conflicts that were totally peripheral to the empire. This proved especially to be the case in the so-called Northern War, which ran parallel to but was independent of the war of the Spanish succession.

The unrest in the north and the northeast belongs to the great and lasting themes of the political development of Europe in the early modern period. At the end of the Thirty Years War, Swedish possessions surrounded the Baltic, and she had no serious competitor for domination of the sea (*dominium maris baltici*). Sweden had attacked Poland shortly after Charles X Gustavus, from the house of Palatinate-Zweibrücken, had succeeded to the throne in 1654 upon the abdication of his cousin, Queen Christiana. He had attacked Poland because of her growing weakness, but he was also disturbed by Russia's push westward to the Baltic, and sought to engage the army, the backbone of Swedish might, in struggle outside of his own lands. The success of the Swedish attacks and the collapse of Poland forced the elector of Brandenburg into the humiliating position of pledging the fealty of the duchy of Prussia to Sweden instead of Poland (January 1656). But the issue was not yet resolved. The Poles, not unexpectedly, revolted, the Russians appeared before Riga, Denmark and Austria intervened on Poland's behalf, and Sweden found herself isolated. She was forced to grant Brandenburg full sovereignty over Prussia and Ermland in the Treaty of Labiau (November 1656). Shortly thereafter, however, Friedrich Wilhelm changed sides, and through mediation by the emperor, Poland granted the same concessions (without Ermland) in the Treaty of Wehlau (1657). A series of battles and coalitions, French threats, Austrian exhaustion, renewed Swedish successes in Denmark, and the death of Charles X (1660) led to the Peace of Oliva. Brandenburg had the Treaty of Wehlau confirmed, but it was forced – with the bitter disappointment mentioned earlier – to evacuate West Pomerania. Sweden essentially retained political preeminence in the north and in northern Germany. In spite of later military victories by Brandenburg (Fehrbellin) in the wars against Sweden (1675–8), nothing fundamental altered. Still Brandenburg had become a visible force in the struggles for power in the north and the east. These areas became, then, the focal points of her ambitious foreign policy.

The Northern War cost Sweden her position as a great power and brought Russia directly into the arena of European politics. When Charles XII (1697–1718) came to power as a fifteen-year-old, he sought to redress the erosion of Swedish might. He attacked Denmark immediately, forcing the latter to conclude an alliance with Poland-Saxony that Russia also entered. The ensuing war was at first completely dominated by Charles's rapid and bold victories. These sparked wonderment throughout Europe. Denmark was forced to sue for peace, surviving only through the intervention of England and Holland. Sweden defeated the Russian army at Narva in the same year (1700). Thereupon Charles turned toward Poland, conquering both Warsaw and Cracow (1702). He had August the Strong dethroned and Stanislaus Leszczyński put in his place as king of Poland. But he was actually able to bring August to the point of surrender only after a lengthy struggle that took him into Saxony. In the Peace of Altranstädt near Leipzig (1706), August was forced to abandon his Polish crown and dissolve his Russian alliance. Saxony suffered from an oppressive Swedish occupation and billeting of troops until Charles left to attack his most dangerous opponent, Russia. Under Czar Peter I (1689–1725) Russia had been launched onto the path of forced modernization and expansion toward the Baltic. The Swedish army, unable to bring the Russian army into a decisive battle, diverted itself into the Ukraine, where it suffered a severe defeat near Poltava (1709). Charles, in turn, fled to Turkey. Sweden's enemies – Russia, Denmark, and Poland (where the Saxon king had been restored) – then joined forces; and Hanover, Bremen and Verden, and Prussia, who coveted the mouth to the Oder, added themselves to the alliance. When Charles returned and rejected the demands of the allies, war broke out again. Since the allies could not agree among themselves and were deeply concerned about Russia's westward advance, matters soon largely left the battlefield and entered the world of diplomacy. George I of England and Hanover played an important role in the complex negotiations that followed. Extraordinary alliance combinations were also put forward from the Swedish side. At this point, however, Charles XII died in battle before the fortress of Frederikshall in December 1718. Sweden immediately abandoned the war and made the way clear for the liberation of the north.

From this point onward, Russia's westward penetration came to replace a concern with Swedish might.

The peace treaties of Stockholm, Friedrichsburg, and Nystad were the northern parallels to the Treaty of Utrecht. They ended a lengthy era of war and confirmed an altered power constellation. Relations between Sweden and Denmark were clarified. Russia acquired the Swedish provinces of Livonia, Estonia, Ingria, and parts of Carelia. Poland was also drawn into the settlement with Russia, though the negotiations confirming August II of Saxony as king of Poland were not ended until 1729. Sweden transferred the duchies of Bremen and Verden to Hanover and thereby lost her position on the German North Sea coast. She was also forced to cede to Brandenburg-Prussia West Pomerania between the Oder and the Peena. Thus Sweden retained only a tiny portion of her German possessions: The area around Wismar, for example, still allowed Sweden a seat in the imperial and district diets. The most important consequences of the Northern War for German history were, on the one hand, the strengthening of Prussia and, in particular, the confirmation of the dynasty's self-confidence. On the other hand, it began Russian pressure on eastern middle Europe, and especially on Prussia, which increasingly had to include the czarist empire in its foreign policy calculations.

After Utrecht and Stockholm no large wars broke out among the European powers. Yet conflicts continued, and some required intense diplomatic activity to bring events back from the edge of war. New disturbances started in Spain where Elizabeth Farnese of Parma, the wife of Philipp V, claimed for her children the former Spanish principalities of Parma, Piacenza, and Tuscany that had now gone to Austria. What unfolded was a characteristic example of the constant effort to balance competing interests. The Spanish occupied Sardinia and Sicily (1718), threatening to overthrow the balance of power achieved with such great difficulty. At this point England formed an alliance (the Quadruple Alliance) with France and the emperor – and potentially also Holland – to maintain the peace settlement of Utrecht. The crisis ended after the destruction of a Spanish fleet and the retaking of Sicily. Austria retained control of Sicily, while the duke of Savoy acquired Sardinia and was elevated to the ranks of royalty. The Spanish prince Charles did not come away empty-handed either, acquiring a hereditary right to the imperial fiefs of Parma, Piacenza, and Tuscany.

After the Quadruple Alliance fell apart, the succession question among the hereditary Italian principalities prompted a congress of the great powers in Cambrai (1724). As a result, Austria and Spain allied themselves against France and the naval powers. The Austrian Ostend Company played a role in the unfolding hostilities since it was a thorn in the side of the maritime countries. The English organized a defensive alliance in response, the Defensive League of Herrenhausen (1725), with France, Hanover, and

Prussia. When Russia along with Saxony began to get close to the Austrian-Spanish camp, Prussia also joined the alliance in the Treaty of Wusterhausen (1726). In the meantime Holland, Sweden, and Denmark placed themselves on the side of England. A new European war thus appeared in the offing, one whose fronts threatened to divide the empire. Before it came to that, however, the great powers realigned themselves once more. Spain joined the side of the western powers in the hopes of greater gain and for a freer hand in invading the Italian principalities. On the other side, Austria sought to come to an agreement with England (1731) by proposing the marriage of Maria Theresia, the emperor's daughter, to a Bourbon prince and by offering to abandon its ties to the Ostend Company and prohibit trade by Habsburg subjects with India. Austria thus accepted a characteristic demand of England and Holland, in order to have England recognize the Pragmatic Sanction.

The failure of Charles VI to produce a male heir made the issue of a secure succession of fundamental importance to Habsburg foreign policy. Before the succession crisis actually occurred in 1740, there was another consequential complication that is somewhat falsely known as the "war of the Polish succession." Although the conflict was triggered in 1733 by struggle over the successor to August the Strong of Saxony-Poland, its deeper cause lay in French concern about Austrian plans to marry the emperor's daughter to Duke Frances of Lorraine. The father-in-law of Louis XV of France, Stanislaus Leszcyński, was elected king of Poland by a majority of the Polish diet. Russia and Austria, however, had supported the election of a regency government for the prince elector Friedrich August of Saxony, and they proceeded to invade Poland. France, then, supported by Spain and Sardinia, declared war on Austria. The sea powers remained neutral, and even though the empire entered the war on the side of Austria, they provided little actual aid. The war was fought on the Upper Rhine and in Italy: The French occupied Lorraine and conquered Milan, the Spanish Naples, and Sicily. Not much remained of Austrian military glory from the time of Prince Eugene. Even the intervention of Russian troops on the Rhine could not affect events. The naval powers once again sought to mediate but were kept at a distance as Austria and France negotiated directly. The preliminary peace of 1735 in Vienna confirmed an astounding exchange: Stanislaus Leszyński had to abandon the Polish crown to a Saxon prince for a second time. As compensation he received first the duchy of Bar and then the duchy of Lorraine; both were to pass to France upon his death. The duke of Lorraine (and husband of Maria Theresia), on the other hand, followed the last Medici as the grand duke of Tuscany (1737). With this agreement, confirmed by an imperial memorandum in 1736, the empire permanently lost Lorraine. Austria received Parma and Piacenza, while ceding Naples and Sicily to the Spanish Prince Carlos, who formed a secundogeniture there. Sardinia, in addition, acquired a few districts in

Lombardy. This distribution of property, strengthening Austrian power in upper and middle Italy, ultimately survived until the penetration of the French revolutionary armies.

Viennese diplomats could not, on the whole, have been dissatisfied with the results. By gaining Saxon ascent to the Polish throne, the rounding off of their Italian possessions, and French recognition of the Pragmatic Sanction, they were able to clarify many of the areas of opposition with their old enemy. In spite of this, Paris, where Cardinal Fleury held the strings of power, was the real center of European political activity during these years. This was even more the case because Austria entered Russia's war against the Turks (1736), partly to gain recognition of the Pragmatic Sanction by Czarina Catherine I but also to acquire Bosnia and Wallachia. After an unfortunate campaign and inadequate cooperation among the allies, Austria disengaged itself from the war, ultimately to sign, on the basis of French mediation, a separate Peace of Belgrade (1739). Austria lost to Turkey control over the areas south of the Donau and the Save, including Belgrade. Thus, with the exception of Banat, Austria returned to the borders of 1699. It was never able to recover from this serious blow to its prestige in the Balkans as Russia increasingly became the dominant opponent of the Ottomans there.

The death of Charles VI (20 October 1740) tested Austria severely, threatening her existence as a state. Austria was attacked militarily and politically at his death and revealed at that moment an incapacity to mobilize fully her economic and financial resources due to faulty central institutions and governmental energy. It became clear at once how little the diplomatic efforts to confirm the Pragmatic Sanction were worth. Elector Karl Albert of Bavaria raised claims to a part of the Habsburg inheritance on the basis of his descent from emperor Ferdinand I and his marriage to emperor Joseph I's younger daughter Maria Amalia – this even though the archduchess had accepted the succession settlement and had abandoned old hereditary claims. He sought the imperial crown, in addition, and acquired French support for his effort. In 1738 France agreed contractually that its recognition of the Pragmatic Sanction did not affect Bavarian hereditary claims. With French support from the rear and an alliance with Spain (1741), Karl Albert had seized a conflict with Austria as a pretext for war. His actions were shaped, moreover, by a second military action, the Prussian invasion of Silesia (1740).

The year 1740 was a fateful year for Germany and Europe. In this year Maria Theresia succeeded to the throne in Austria, unleashing a European war concerning the succession, and Friedrich II succeeded in Prussia, only shortly thereafter to invade Silesia and begin the first Silesian war. These events generated a far-reaching reorientation of political forces. With the reversal of alliances (*renversement des alliances*) in 1756, the old Habsburg-French opposition was transcended. In northern Germany Prussia emerged as the second German great power. Out of this emerged the Austrian–Prussian dualism that remained a dominant factor in German political history until 1866. At the same time Austria and Prussia together gave a new political significance to middle Europe. If French influence thereby declined significantly, the opposition between the two German powers created maneuvering space for Russia in its efforts to advance farther westward. The significance of this pattern was first made clear in 1762 when the Russian shift of allegiance – *le miracle de la maison de Brandenbourg* – decided the outcome of the Seven Years War.

Both powers emerged inwardly modernized from the first phase of their rivalry. The slow economic growth in both lands, clearly perceptible by the 1760s, was not hindered in any fundamental manner by the results of war. The opposite was in fact the case. In both countries the wars mobilized substantial energies to intensify financial and military capacity, increase administrative efficiency, and thus to reconstruct and reform in the postwar years.

THE RISE OF PRUSSIA AND GERMAN DUALISM

Prussia played such an extraordinary and decisive role in German history since the second half of the eighteenth century, but especially in the nineteenth century, that historians have often searched for the presuppositions and conditions of Prussia's rise to preeminence. Its small size and population level, its disadvantageous geographical location, the relatively low cultural achievement of its population – all these made Prussia seem a far less likely candidate for the status of great power than, for instance, electoral Saxony. Still, if we look more carefully at the potentialities, the margravate of Brandenburg was already a substantial territory in northern Germany before the middle of the seventeenth century. Unlike the house of Braunschweig-Lüneburg, moreover, its possessions were not widely separated, and the margrave was one of the imperial electors. In the east the Brandenburg Hohenzollerns also inherited (1619) the duchy of Prussia that was still under Polish suzerainty, but the Hohenzollerns had already been jointly invested in 1569 and had controlled the administration since 1605. Similar developments had occurred in the west, where they had taken control of Cleves, Mark, and Ravensberg between 1609–14.

In the Westphalian settlement Brandenburg acquired the bishoprics of Halberstadt, Minden, and Cammin, the county of Hohenstein, eastern Pomerania, and the expectancy for the archbishopric of Magdeburg that was then possessed by Elector Friedrich Wilhelm in 1680. The pattern of further expansion – the directions, desires, and attempts – was thus shaped, but the acquisitions also created new defensive imperatives that could not be avoided by a state committed to playing an independent role in foreign affairs. Since the great elector the Hohenzollerns were indeed committed to such independence, and we cannot overemphasize how important their collective will and ambition was for the future of Brandenburg-Prussia. This state did not rise or expand in the normal sense but was actually formed and stamped by the monarchy.

Let us first consider matters in the west. Both Brandenburg and Palatinate-Neuburg had hereditary rights to Jülich-Cleves, and both maintained claims to the indivisibility of these lands. In 1651 Brandenburg attempted unsuccessfully to acquire Jülich and Berg; in 1660 it concluded a definitive treaty of division, whereby in the event one line were extinguished the lands would fall to the other house. Concerned with the eventual death of the childless duke of Neuburg, Friedrich Wilhelm I later renewed these claims with the emperor in the treaties of Westerhausen and Berlin (1726 and 1728). In 1740 Friedrich II attempted to gain the support of France and England for the acquisition of Berg, but he abandoned these claims two years later in favor of the Palatinate-Sulzbach line. This happened partly because the center of the Prussian state already had shifted to the east for quite some time. Friedrich Wilhelm's temporary if intense engagement in the west had been conditioned by his admiration for the economic might of the northern Netherlands, but it had remained an episode. Acquiring west Pomerania had been more important to Friedrich Wilhelm, and he had been bitterly disappointed when he had not gained it in 1648 in spite of a hereditary treaty from 1637. In the Peace of St. Germain-en-Laye (1679), he had also been able only to acquire the left bank of the Oder and had failed to gain Stettin and the islands of Usedom and Wollin. These were not acquired until the Treaty of Stockholm in 1720. By then, however, Brandenburg-Prussia controlled the mouth of the Oder and a usable western harbor on the Baltic, even though the Prussians were no longer pursuing the maritime policies that had interested Elector Friedrich Wilhelm. In this regard, even the acquisition of the principality of East Frisia with Emden (1744) did not turn Prussia toward the sea. It remained a land power, as was clear in its military posture. It was a country with lengthy borders, difficult to defend, and with indefensible western outposts, as the Seven Years War demonstrated.

At the accession of Friedrich II, Prussia was not viewed as a considerable power because of its territorial acquisitions, but because it had a sizable war chest and a well-trained and well-equipped army of about 80,000 men. Friedrich Wilhelm I, *roi sergeant* and tyrannical patriarch, had placed his lands under an enormous burden in order to construct this army. By making the army the absolute first priority, moreover, he had created the institutional context for Prussia's military successes and its ability to survive three wars over Silesia. He had also militarized social life so deeply that under altering circumstances it continued to remain a fundamental feature of Prussian life. Friedrich was responsible for preventing Prussia from merely becoming a barracks wasteland and an oppressive autocracy. The philosopher king (*roi philosophe*), general, and enlightened absolutist believed that discipline could be united with justice, obedience with freedom, and power with spirit.

At first Europe only listened to his military and political successes and to the new style that made the Prussian court attractive. Friedrich Wilhelm had been a stingy ruler after the extravagance of his father, Prussia's first king. Friedrich Wilhelm had attempted to increase royal income, using the strictest controls, in order to maintain a growing army independent of foreign subsidies. Though he had avoided war because of its costliness, his son engaged the army to invade Silesia in his first year of power, not two months after the death of Charles VI.

The appeal to hereditary claims in Silesia was more than a mere excuse, but it was not the main motive for the attack. In 1621, after the Bohemian war, the emperor had appropriated the Hohenzollern duchy of Jägerdorf and given it to the Liechtensteins. The duchies of Liegnitz, Brief, and Wohlau also were not passed onto the Hohenzollerns after the extinction of the Piastic dukes in 1675, in spite of a treaty, because emperor Leopold I as overlord had retained them himself. Shortly before his death, Elector Friedrich Wilhelm had abandoned these claims in exchange for the district of Schwiebus, but his successor was forced to return the property. The twenty-eight-year-old Friedrich did not forget this humiliating transaction. Even more importantly, he desired to make a name for himself and exploit the favorable situation he recognized so quickly. When the Austrian succession became actual, Charles VI's lengthy efforts to have the *sanctio pragmatica* recognized could not prevent the outbreak of war, because latent and new tensions came to the fore: the Habsburg–Wittelsbach rivalry, the old opposition between Habsburgs and France, and the competition between England and France for trade and overseas colonies. Cardinal Fleury attempted at precisely this moment to replace the English–Dutch vision of a European balance of power with a French one. England, on the other hand, sought to exclude France completely from India and North America. In any case, it seemed clear that the first to act in this situation would not remain completely isolated or experience unified rejection by the great powers. The rapid Prussian attack was risky in spite of this assessment because it was completely uncertain whether France would support Bavarian claims. And Friedrich himself certainly could not have foreseen the dangerous long-term situation he led Prussia into by his lightninglike invasion of Silesia. The annexation of Silesia, he thought, would make Prussia the definitive leading power in northern Germany and would not threaten Austria's existence. But in making these calculations, he underestimated Maria Theresia's commitment to defending Silesia.

The Prussian victory at Mollwitz (10 April 1741) proved decisive for the further course of the war. Only then did France openly support Bavaria and conclude an alliance with Prussia (June 1741), in which Friedrich abandoned claims to Jülich-Berg and agreed to support the Wittelsbachs as imperial candidates in exchange for support in annexing Lower Silesia, including Breslau. At the end of July Bavarian troops occupied Passau, and the French began their advance on the Upper Rhine. The Prussian attack on Silesia, beginning as a limited operation, unleashed a Europeanwide war for the Austrian succession. Bavaria, Saxony, the Palatinate, Cologne, and Spain began to operate together with France. Sweden was persuaded to attack Russia, and even George II of England agreed to support the election of Karl Albrecht as emperor as the condition for respecting Hanoverian neutrality. That election occurred (14 January 1742) after Bavaria and France had invaded Bohemia, conquered Prague, and allowed Karl Albrecht to crown himself as the king of Bohemia. How little Friedrich II saw his invasion of Silesia as part of the war for the Austrian succession is revealed by the temporary military truce with Austria he concluded in October 1741. Austria had already gone on the offensive by this time, occupying Bavaria. England meanwhile began to pressure France, but simultaneously encouraged Vienna to conclude a separate peace with Prussia. Maria Theresia accepted the loss of Lower Silesia, the largest part of Upper Silesia, and the county of Glatz, only after new military victories by Prussia, in order to have a free hand to fight her other enemies (Preliminary Peace of Breslau, 11 June 1742).

Prussia could credit this exceptional gain to the extremely favorable political situation more than to the will of her king and the strength of her armies. She was threatened, however, as soon as the tide shifted in the struggle for the Austrian succession. Austria drove the French from Bohemia and forced Saxony to sue for peace. England and Savoy entered the war together and constructed a "pragmatic" army from English, Dutch, Hanoverian, and Austrian contingents, and they defeated the French at Dettingen am Main (1743). Maria Theresia thought to compensate herself for the loss of Silesia by annexing Bavaria and formed a new alliance with England and Sardinia. France, which had only supported Bavaria until then, renewed her familial treaty with Spain at this point and declared war openly against Austria. Even more importantly, France formed a new offensive alliance with Prussia.

Friedrich II had watched the growing strength of Austria and the debacle of Emperor Charles VII with the greatest concern. When the Austrians crossed the Rhine, he invaded Bohemia in the middle of August 1744. Yet he soon had to abandon Prague and retreat into Silesia, because Maria Theresia halted the campaign in the Alsace, France failed to follow, and Saxony joined the Austrian side. Austria, Saxony, England, and Holland then formed the Warsaw Quadruple Alliance for the liberation of Germany (1745), and Russia appeared inclined to join. During this situation Charles

VII died, and his son Max Joseph signed a treaty (Peace of Füssen, 22 April 1745) relinquishing all hereditary claims for himself and his heirs to the Austrian succession. He also promised to support the husband of Maria Theresia, Archduke Franz Stephan of Tuscany, in the imperial election. For this he was able to recover his hereditary lands.

In the continuing war Friedrich defeated Austria in battle at Hohenfriedberg, but the election of Franz I as emperor, the French reticence to commit further because of English pressure, and the hope of Russian intervention encouraged Maria Theresia, with the aid of Saxony, to invade Brandenburg. When Friedrich forestalled her plans by defeating the Saxon army at Kesselsdorf, she accepted English mediation to end the war. The peace treaty signed in Dresden at Christmas 1745 guaranteed Prussian possession of Silesia, but it also recognized Franz I as emperor. Thereby the second Silesian war confirmed the results of the first. In addition, Prussia removed herself from the struggle over the Austrian succession without achieving her goal of preventing the election of another Austrian emperor and strengthening Bavarian power at the expense of Austria. Austria remained the most powerful state within the empire, although she was only able to mobilize her superior power to a limited extent because of her diverse European interests and involvements and because of her comparatively loose administrative system. Most importantly, Austria's military weakness was apparent, particularly when compared to the smaller Prussian military state. For the first time Austria had acquired a strong rival within the empire. Prussia was able to pursue her own interests while also exploiting the inherent tension between emperor and empire, by speaking for the opposition within the imperial estates. In the eighteenth century the fronts were no longer clearly drawn between Catholic and Protestant German states, since the smaller imperial estates simply attempted to maintain their independence from the great powers. In spite of this, Prussia became to a certain extent the protagonist of a Protestant Germany against the preeminence of Catholic Austria. This was particularly true in the political consciousness of the German people who saw the rise of Protestant Prussia alongside imperial Catholic Austria as a significant factor in their own age. Moreover, the emergence of Prussia, together with England and Russia in the wings, also increased the political weight of northern Germany and intensified the changes in the European constellation of power.

The Peace of Dresden completed the negotiations in Germany to end the war. Due to Austria's defensive alliance with Russia (1746), Friedrich no longer dared to reenter the war, and England supported his neutrality. Maria Theresia continued the struggle with France, but this war had long since become a struggle between England and France that went far beyond Europe itself. Spectacular French successes in Italy and the Austrian Netherlands were met by overwhelming English superiority on the seas, until finally in 1748 the war came to a stalemated conclusion with the Treaty of Aachen. Austria was forced, against her will, to join the understanding worked out between the sea powers and France. She had to accept the loss of Parma to a Spanish prince. France, on the other hand, returned the occupied territories but kept her own possessions and survived as the most powerful continental power. France, however, like Prussia, failed to influence the Austrian succession. England acquired from France recognition of the Hanoverian succession, the promise that the Stuart pretender would receive no support, and the guarantee of Hanover's German possessions. But the Peace of Aachen proved to be only a ceasefire elsewhere, for it was not able to resolve the great maritime and colonial conflict between the two powers.

The guarantee of Prussian ownership of Silesia was the most important aspect of the peace settlement for Germany. Europe essentially recognized the shift in forces and elevated Prussia into the ranks of preponderent powers. The consequences of this development for the European states system were soon revealed when the entire system of alliances transformed itself in 1756. For Germany the consequences became clear in the Seven Years War, when a declared imperial war proved unsuccessful against its most powerful member. If contemporaries had thought in 1745 and 1748 that compromise between Austria and Prussia could produce lasting peace, they soon came to understand that a tension-filled rivalry had been born in Germany, a bipolarity that we refer to as *dualism*. This struggle would ultimately be fateful for German history, even though events in the next years did not weaken the conflict. The Seven Years War, the French Revolution, and the Napoleonic conquest of Germany only helped to shape the independent political existence of two states of European rank, whose rulers hardly saw themselves any longer as princes of the empire. The empire to which they both belonged became increasingly less significant.

Friedrich's prestige was enormously enhanced after the Peace of Dresden. He was not so much concerned thereafter to develop new policies but to produce a new style of rule that would place absolutist policies within the goals and framework of the European Enlightenment. In these years he developed the style of enlightened absolutism that became paradigmatic for Germany. But Austria also undertook significant changes in these years. Already before the Peace of Aachen, Austria had energetically begun to modernize the central institutions. The "Theresian reforms" that peaked in 1749 were supposed to allow Austria to catch up with absolutist reforms elsewhere and to increase her military and economic potential. Although the results were at first somewhat limited, Austria had acquired a new internal dynamic that was later intensified in the reform movement of "Josephenism," even though this movement also failed because too many presuppositions were still lacking.

THE SEVEN YEARS WAR

In spite of the peace, both Austria and Prussia increased the fighting power of their armies. Maria Theresia was not prepared to accept the loss of Silesia permanently, and Friedrich felt Prussia needed new acquisitions to consolidate his position. However, renewed war between Austria and Prussia was not unavoidable. Under the measured influence of Count Kaunitz, Austrian diplomats sought to come to terms with France in order to isolate Prussia, but at first this policy met with little success. Increasing tensions between France and England over trade and expansion in North America and India proved decisive in renewing the war. In order to protect Hanover, England attempted to bring Austria to its side. Kaunitz, on the other hand, again renewed his overtures to France in order to separate Prussia. His final success was due to Friedrich's decision to ally himself with England, thereby hoping to free himself from Russian pressure and to isolate Austria in turn. Friedrich calculated that Austria would be unable to come to an arrangement with France. In the Treaty of Westminster (January 1756), however, each partner promised to maintain the peace in Germany and come to the defense of the other in case of invasion by a foreign power. This treaty thus caused the reversal of alliances (*renversement des alliances*) that generated the Seven Years War. On May 1 at Versailles, France and Austria concluded a treaty of defense and neutrality that was transformed one year later into an offensive alliance. According to their agreement, Austria was to reacquire Silesia, and Prussia was to be completely partitioned. Don Philipp, the son-in-law of Louis XV, was to acquire the Austrian Netherlands, and Austria Parma and Piacenza. The empire joined "Kaunitz's coalition" with the exception of Hanover, Braunschweig, Hesse, and Gotha. France also concluded individual treaties with Württemberg and with the Wittelsbach states of Bavaria, the Palatinate, and Cologne. Earlier, Czarina Elizabeth had also joined the alliance along with Poland, pressuring the allies for a quick attack. In a later treaty (1760) she received the promise of East Prussia at the end of the war. Sweden also joined the alliance, receiving a future claim to Pomerania. The encirclement of Prussia had thus become apparent with the signing of the first Austrian–French treaty. But before it could be completed and in order to prevent it, Friedrich himself declared war by invading Saxony on 29 August 1756. The Seven Years War that would bring Prussia close to extinction had begun as a Prussian preventive war.

The preventive war was a political disaster. The Austrian–French alliance was transformed into a war coalition of crushing proportions. Prussia had England as an ally, but the English remained largely inactive, particularly because Hanover wanted to remain neutral. Only in 1758 did England engage herself more fully on the continent, but even then she essentially provided only financial aid; the Hanoverian army under the Duke of Braunschweig provided only indirect support. With the elder Pitt's fall in 1761, England once again left Prussia to its own fate. For England it was important that Prussia tie down French forces, but otherwise the continent was only a secondary issue. From the other side, England's overseas war brought Prussia little relief, because her chief opponents – Austria and Russia – were uninvolved. Hence, even though both wars were complexly interrelated, they functioned in military terms largely independently.

The first three years of the war on the continent were dominated by Prussia. The Saxon army capitulated in the fall of 1756 after Prussia had turned aside an Austrian relief column. Thereby Prussia prepared herself to invade Bohemia early in the next year, but a victory over the Austrians near Prague proved indecisive. Friedrich then suffered his first defeat near Kolin by a relief army under Daun, and it proved to be very dangerous. Bohemia was liberated, the Austrians invaded lower Silesia and the Lausitz, the Russians entered East Prussia, the Swedes invaded Pomerania, the French defeated and dissolved a defending Hanoverian army near Hastenbeck, and, finally, a French army joined the imperial army. These events produced the first severe crisis for Prussia in the war. In spite of the forces placed against him, Friedrich defeated the French and imperial armies at Rossbach, and shortly thereafter (early December 1757) he won a victory at Leuthen over the Austrians under Charles of Lorraine. He was unable, however, to force his opponents to sue for peace.

In 1758 Friedrich invaded Moravia without achieving any results. He was then forced to turn away from Moravia in order to fight the Russians, who were defeated but not conquered near Zorndorf. In the meantime Ferdinand of Braunschweig successfully defeated a French army near Krefeld. Friedrich drove the Austrians and Saxons from Silesia, the Russians from East Pomerania, and the Swedes from the Mark Brandenburg. But the Prussian army entered the third year of war sorely tried. Still attacking, Friedrich suffered his greatest defeat in August 1759 at Kunersdorf against a combined army of Russians and Austrians. He was perhaps only saved because his enemies did not exploit their victory. The bleak picture for Prussia was not lightened by the first real successes in the west, for in the late campaigns of 1760, Austria suffered a severe defeat at Torgau. Friedrich waited for his enemies to become tired of the war. His opponents, on the other hand, awaited his collapse, and though they did not conduct any large-scale operations against him, they were able to make their winter quarters on Prussian soil. After the collapse of Pitt, meanwhile, the English sought to come to terms with France. They recommended that Friedrich abandon Silesia and stopped the payment of subsidies. Prussia was unexpectedly saved in this desperate situation by the death of Czarina Elizabeth I at the beginning of 1762. Her successor, Duke Peter (III) from the

Holstein-Gottoper line, concluded peace with Prussia and shortly thereafter an alliance. Catherine II, who seized power in the same year, refused to accept the agreement but did not choose to reenter the war. With Russia abandoning the war, Sweden, too, decided to conclude peace with Prussia. These peace treaties freed Prussia to invade Silesia and Saxony once again, even as the imperial diet, meeting in Regensburg, declared the neutrality of the empire. The French and English also decided to end hostilities, and in November 1762 they agreed to a preliminary treaty at Fontainebleau. (The definitive peace was signed in Paris on 10 February 1763). Austria found herself incapable of continuing the war for Silesia alone. It is significant that the Peace of Hubertusburg, signed five days after the Peace of Paris, was mediated not by one of the great powers, but by Saxony. It had become a German affair. In the settlement the two powers returned to the status quo ante. Silesia remained Prussian, and no other territorial changes took place. Both partners mutually guaranteed to respect the sanctity of their holdings and included Saxony in the agreement. In a secret article Prussia promised to cast its Brandenburg electoral vote at the imperial elections in favor of Archduke Joseph.

Fought with much greater bitterness than earlier wars, this seven year struggle brought enormous suffering to both states. In this sense the results may seem absurd though just. King Friedrich had used every means at his disposal to preserve the existence of the Prussian state. His lands and people had been required to make extreme sacrifices, even to the point of threatening the achievements of his predecessors. The final success was purchased at great cost and was a matter of luck, but it could also be seen as justifying that sacrifice. Prussia's reputation increased dramatically in the prestige-conscious world of that era. But Austria, too, had developed more military and political strength. She had revealed an energy in government not seen since the days of Prince Eugene. Both states, moreover, developed an even greater sense of their independent existence.

CONCLUSION

GERMANY AT THE END OF
THE SEVEN YEARS WAR

Just as the seven-year-long double war burst the bonds of cabinet wars, so, too, did the peace settlements of Paris and Hubertusburg go far beyond the framework of cabinet foreign policy in their collective historical significance. The first confirmed England's triumph over France in the colonial world and guaranteed English supremacy on the high seas until the end of the nineteenth century. The second confirmed Prussia's emergence as a competing power with Austria on German soil. Unlike the Peace of Paris, that of Hubertusburg did not cause borders to be recast or rulers to be changed. Austria could not regain Silesia and, even with her allies, she was not able to destroy Prussia. Prussia had triumphed but was not able to prevent the lengthy Russian occupation of East Prussia. She also had been unable to destroy her enemies and gained no new territories for all her sacrifices in the war.

Prussian plans with Hanover–England to secularize the bishoprics of northwest Germany had come to naught after the death in 1761 of the archbishop of Cologne (and bishop of Münster, Paderborn, and Hildesheim). Not all imperial estates had supported the declaration of an imperial war against Prussia, but those who had joined the war had failed, and Prussia remained "unpunished." In spite of this the imperial system remained intact: the Prussian king was still an imperial prince as the elector of Brandenburg. In any event it was still expected that the struggle between Prussia and Austria would weigh heavily on the empire and would even paralyze imperial institutions, especially the imperial diet. But there was no likelihood that the imperial estates would divide themselves into a Prussian and an Austrian party. There was simply too much mistrust among the smaller states, such as Hanover and Bavaria, of their mighty neighbors. Saxony might have been inclined to support Habsburg policies. It had lost the Polish crown in 1763 after the death of Friedrich August II, largely because the czarina, with the aid of the Prussian king, engineered the election of Stanislaus Poniatowski. But Saxony felt itself more threatened by Prussia than by Austria and therefore stayed clear of the dangerous waters of Habsburg foreign policy.

Viennese attempts to develop more active imperial policies had always been treated with the suspicion that they were merely intended to serve Habsburg interests. But in the future such plans could always be resisted by Prussia, and the other imperial estates could resist the emperor's goals and find Prussian support. The existence of the empire was much more threatened by the possibility that the two powers might act in consort and divide the empire into spheres of influence or rule. This, however, was not very likely. The last war had demonstrated that neither power could alter inner German relations without the aid of one or more of the European great powers. Such an eventuality was so fraught with internal and external complications that an intensive struggle in middle Europe could not have appeared worthwhile.

In addition, France's chief allies no longer threatened Germany. The Turks had been driven back, and the Swedes had lost control over the Baltic. The emergence of Prussia and the westward expansion of Russia had largely cost France its influence in middle Europe. By the end of the Seven Years War France had been practically excluded from internal German decisions. English interest in this area was largely confined to the security of Hanover. The Russians, as long as their expansion plans were focused on the Black Sea, were mostly concerned with exerting influence in Poland. Thus middle Europe found itself free from external pressure for the first time in many years.

The foreign policy realignment contributed to a new phase in which German governments concerned themselves much more strongly with domestic policies. They were partly motivated – especially Prussia and Saxony – by the need to overcome the effects of war. In Prussia there was a renewed effort to reconstruct. The example of Prussian – and Austrian – reform activities shaped other German states. Although the most significant and effective impulses in social and political life still largely came from above, public opinion, as carried by the middle social strata, began for the first time to exert an ever greater pressure in economic and cultural affairs. The internal German war had awakened an understanding that there were more serious tasks to solve than simply for Germans to fight among themselves. Individuals became particularly aware that they needed to tap the undeveloped resources within the German people in order to overcome the relative material backwardness with respect to western Europe.

In the narrowness and oppressiveness of German political relations, the martial experiences of the Seven Years War – mainly the Prussian victories over the French, the appearance of gifted leaders within the Prussian and Austrian armies, but especially the figure of the Prussian king – became a focus for patriotism and national pride. From the middle of the century these feelings began to find literary expression. Gleim's songs of war, Ewald von Kleist's glorification of the Prussian army, Thomas Abbt's tract *Vom Tode fürs Vaterland (On Dying for the Fatherland)*, and even the arrogant pride of Prussians after the war – all these were signs of a patriotism with a clear political character. At the same time other positive and negative voices emerged, who were challenged by the war and stimulated by a renewed interest in history. They sought not the ideal form of the state but the proper historical form for Germany. In comparison with western Europe, they sought to create a national consciousness that among some could be termed imperial patriotism, among others cultural nationalism. Friedrich Karl Moser's book of 1765, *Von dem deutschen Nationalgeist (Concerning the German National Spirit)*, was typical of the form political discussion assumed at the end of the Seven Years War. Moser was filled with the political views of a jurist and official trained in the legal traditions of southwest Germany, in territorial and imperial law. He was sharpened by the struggles carried by the Württemberg estates and shaped by Swabian pietism. His book was thus emotional and moral-pragmatic, tied directly to a pride in the past, filled with trust for the German future, and a lament concerning German disunity. He wrote,

We are one people with one name and language. We live under a common head of state, under one set of laws that determine our constitution, rights, and duties, and we are bound together by a common and great interest in freedom....In our internal power and strength we are the first empire in Europe..., and, yet as we are now we still remain a puzzle as a political system, the booty of our neighbors, disunited among ourselves, feeble by our divisions, strong enough to hurt ourselves, but powerless to save ourselves. [We are]...a great and at the same time a despised people, one who has the potential to be happy but is actually very lamentable.

Who was responsible for this misery? According to Moser, it was princely absolutism supported by standing armies.

State patriotism, imperial patriotism, and national consciousness form different strands in the political consciousness of Germany in the last third of the eighteenth century. They were not necessarily mutually exclusive, because they could act in combination with the natural rights thinking in the Enlightenment or corporatist thought based on the study of history. If some placed their hopes in enlightened governments, others sought to reawaken estatist institutions and structures. Both hoped, however, that reforms would occur in social and political life. For that, they thought, the time had come.

CHRONOLOGY

1635–7	Emperor Ferdinand III
1640–88	Elector Friedrich Wilhelm I of Brandenburg
1647/9–73	Johann Philipp Count of Schönborn, elector and archbishop of Mainz
1648	Westphalian Peace
1649	Friedrich Spee: *Trutznachtigall (Defiant Nightingale)*
1652	Founding of the Leopoldinisch–Carolinische Academy of Natural Sciences in Schweinfurt
1654	Recent Imperial Recess Otto von Guericke's demonstration of an air pump at the imperial diet in Regensburg
1657	Treaty of Wehlau Angelus Silesius: *Cherubinischer Wandersmann (Cherubic Wanderer)* Andreas Gryphius: *Deutsche Gedichte,* Part One *(German Poetry)* Heinrich Schütz: *Zwölf geistliche Gesänge (Twelve Spiritual Hymns)*
1658–1705	Emperor Leopold I
1658	Rhenish Alliance (First Rhenish League)
1659	Peace of the Pyrenees
1660	Peace of Oliva
1663	The "Eternal Imperial Diet" meets in Regensburg
1663–4	Turkish War

1664	Construction begun on the Theatiner Church in Munich (Antonio Barelli; after 1674, Enrico Zucalli)
1667	Samuel von Pufendorf: *De statu imperii germanici* (*The State of the German Empire*) Johann Joachim Becher: *Politischer Diskurs* (*Political Discourse*)
1668–9	Hans Jacob Christoffel von Grimmelshausen: *Der Abenteuerliche Simplizissimus* (*The Adventurous Simplizissimus*)
1669–73	Anton Ulrich von Braunschweig: *Aramena*
1672	Christian Weise: *Die drei ärgsten Erznarren* (*The Three Worst Arch-Fools* Samuel von Pufendorf: *De iure naturae et gentium* (*The Law of Nature and Humankind*)
1675	Brandenburg Victory at Fehrbellin Philipp Jacob Spener: *Pia Desideria*
1678	Peace of Nijmegen Opening of the Hamburg Opera
1679	Peace of St. Germain-en-Laye Establishment of Chambers of Reunion by Louis XIV
1679–1726	Elector Maximilian II Emanuel of Bavaria
1681	French Occupation of Strasbourg Military Agreement for the Defense of the Empire
1682	The *Acta Eruditorum* began to appear in Leipzig
1683–99	Turkish Wars
1683	Siege of Vienna by the Turks; Battle at Kahlenberg First great settlement of German immigrants in North America Founding of a Brandenburg colony on the west coast of Africa
1684	Holy League against the Turks
1685	Edict of Potsdam
1686	Gottfried Wilhelm Leibniz: *Discours de métaphysique*

	Abraham a Santa Clara: *Judas, der Erzschelm (Judas, the Arch-Knave)* [Appears until 1695]
1687	Hungarian Imperial Diet in Pressburg
1688–97	Palatine War
1692	Duke Ernst August of Braunschweig-Lüneburg (1694–8) became elector of Hanover
1693	Destruction of Heidelberg. Resettlement of the Imperial Cameral Tribunal from Speyer to Wetzlar
1694	Founding of the University of Halle Construction begun on Schloss Schönbrunn in Vienna (Johann Bernhard Fischer von Erlach)
1695	August Hermann Francke founded the *Armenschule* (Poor School) in Halle
1697	Prince Eugene of Savoy assumed supreme command in the Turkish war; victory at Zenta Elector Friedrich August I of Saxony (1694–1733) became king of Poland Peace of Ryswick Frankfurt Association Recess
1698	Construction begun in Berlin of Schloss and equestrian statue of Great Elector (Andreas Schlüter)
1699	Peace of Carlowitz
1699–1700	Gottfried Arnold: *Unparteiische Kirchen-und Ketzergeschichte (Nonpartisan History of the Church)*
1700–21	Northern War
1700	Founding of the Academy of Sciences in Berlin The Gregorian calendar introduced in the Protestant areas of Germany
1701–14	War of the Spanish Succession
1701	The Grand Alliance of The Hague Elector Friedrich III of Brandenburg (1686–1713) became king in Prussia (Friedrich I)
1702	Construction begun on the abbey of Melk (Jacob Prandtauer)

	Founding of the University of Breslau
1703	Phlogiston theory developed by Georg Ernst Stahl
1704	Victory of Prince Eugene and Marlborough at Höchstädt
	Construction begun on the Fulda cathedral (Johann Dientzenhofer)
1705–11	Emperor Joseph I
	Christian Thomasius: *Fundamenta iuris naturae et gentium* (*Fundamental Laws of Nature and Humankind*)
	Georg Friedrich Händel: *Almira*
1706	Imperial ban on the electors of Bavaria and Cologne
	Peace of Altranstädt
	Christoph Semler founded the first German secondary school based on modern subjects (*Realschule*)
1708	Battle at Oudenaarde
1709	Battle at Malplaquet
	Mass emigration of Germans to North America begun
	Permanent Secret Conference founded in Vienna
	Fabrication of hard porcelain by Johann Friedrich Böttger
1710	Gottfried Wilhelm Leibniz: *Essai de Théodicée*
	Construction begun on the monastic church in Banz (Dientzenhofer)
	Founding of the Charité in Berlin
1711–40	Emperor Charles VI
1711	Construction begun on the Schloss Pommersfelden (Dientzenhofer) and the Zwinger in Dresden (Matthias Daniel Pöppelmann)
1712	Christian Wolff: *Vernünftige Gedanken von den Kräften des menschlichen Verstandes* (*Intelligent Thoughts Concerning the Powers of the Human Understanding*)
1713–40	King Friedrich Wilhelm I of Prussia
1713	Peace of Utrecht
	Pragmatic Sanction

1714	Peace of Rastatt and Baden Electoral Prince George of Hanover (1698–1727) became king of England Gottfried Wilhelm Leibniz: *Monadologie* Gottfried Silbermann constructed the organ in the Freiburg cathedral
1715	Construction begun on the abbey church of Weingarten (Franz Beer) Founding of Karlsruhe by Margrave Karl Wilhelm of Baden
1716	Austrian victory at Peterwardein
1717	Conquest of Belgrade by Prince Eugene Compulsory school attendance in Prussia Construction begun on the Charles's Church in Vienna (Johann Bernhard Fischer von Erlach)
1718	Peace of Passarowitz Quadruple Alliance of London Founding of the Viennese porcelain manufactory
1719–20	Peace treaties of Stockholm
1720	Construction begun on the princely residence in Würzburg (Balthasar Neumann)
1721	Johann Sebastian Bach: Brandenburg Concerti Johann Jacob Bodmer and Johann Jacob Breitinger: *Discourse der Mahlern (Discourse on Painters)* [until 1723]
1722	Founding of the Herrnhut Community of Brethren Johann Sebastian Bach: *Well-Tempered Clavier*
1723	Creation of the General Directory in Brandenburg-Prussia Christian Wolff exiled from Halle Johann Sebastian Bach became cantor of the Thomas Church in Leipzig
1725	Treaty of Herrenhausen
1726	Secret treaty of Wusterhausen Construction begun on the *Frauenkirche* in Dresden (Georg Bähr)
1727	Chairs for the cameral sciences established at the

	universities of Halle and Frankfurt an der Oder Acting company of Friederike Caroline Neuber started in Leipzig
1729	Johann Sebastian Bach: *St. Matthew Passion* Johann Christoph Gottsched: *Versuch einer kritischen Dichtkunst (Attempt at a Critical Poetics)* Albrecht von Haller: *Die Alpen (The Alps)*
1731	Imperial legislation regulating handicrafts Expulsion of Protestants from Salzburg
1732	Johann Heinrich Zedler (publisher): *Grosses vollständiges Universallexikon (Large Complete Universal Dictionary)* [completed in 1754]
1733–5	War of the Polish Succession
1735	Peace of Vienna Peace of Belgrade
1736	Death of Prince Eugene of Savoy Archduchess Maria Theresia married Duke Franz Stephan of Lorraine
1737	Founding of the University of Göttingen Johann Jacob Moser: *Teutsches Staatsrecht (German Constitutional Law)* [completed in 1754] Founding of the first German freemasonic lodge in Hamburg
1738	Georg Friedrich Händel: *Xerxes, Saul*
1739	Georg Friedrich Händel: Twelve Concerti Grossi
1740–80	Maria Theresia, queen of Bohemia and Hungary, archduchess of Austria
1740–86	King Friedrich II of Prussia
1740–42	First Silesian War
1740	Johann Christoph Gottsched: *German Schaubühne (German Stage)* [appears until 1745]
1741	Construction begun on the Berlin opera house (Georg Wenzeslaus von Knobelsdorff)
1742–5	Emperor Charles VII
1742	Peace of Breslau Georg Friedrich Händel: *Messiah*

1743	Founding of the University of Erlangen Construction begun on the stairwell at Schloss Brühl and the pilgrim church Vierzehnheilige (Balthasar Neumann)
1744–5	Second Silesian War
1745	Prussian victory at Hohenfriedberg Peace of Dresden Peace of Füssen
1745–6	Emperor Franz I Construction begun on Schloss Sanssouci in Potsdam (G. W. von Knobelsdorff)
1746	Construction begun on the pilgrimage church Wies (Dominikus Zimmermann) Friedrich II: *Histoire de mon temps (History of My Age)*
1747	Andreas Markgraf discovered the sugar content in beets Christian Fürchtegott Gellert: *Das Leben der schwedischen Gräfin von G. (The Life of the Swedish Countess of G.)*
1748	Peace of Aachen Friedrich Gottlieb Klopstock: *Messias (Messiah)* [the first three hymns]
1749	Austrian state reforms Johann Sebastian Bach: *Art of the Fugue*
1751	The Prussian Trading Society formed in Emden Founding of the *Vossische Zeitung (Voss Newspaper)* in Berlin
1752	Gotthold Ephraim Lessing: *Miss Sara Sampson*
1753	Wenzel Anton Count von Kaunitz became director of Austrian foreign policy
1755	Hereditary Compromise in Mecklenburg Johann Heinrich Gottlieb Justi: *Staatswirtschaft (Economy of the State)* Joseph Haydn: First String Quartet
1756	Westminster Convention Johann Heinrich Gottlieb Justi: *Grundsätze der Policeywissenschaft (Principles of the Science of Public Welfare)*

1756–63	Seven Years War
1757	Austrian victory at Kolin; Prussian victories at Rossbach and Leuthen Albrecht von Haller: *Elementa physiologiae corporis humani*
1758	Prussian victory at Zorndorf and defeat at Hochkirch; Russian occupation of East Prussia Johann Wilhelm Ludwig Gleim: *Lieder eines preussischen Grenadiers* (*Songs of a Prussian Grenadier*)
1759	Prussian defeat at Kunersdorf Caspar Friedrich Wolf: *Theoria Generationis* Founding of the Bavarian Academy of Sciences in Munich Gotthold Ephraim Lessing: *Briefe die neueste Literatur betreffend* (*Letters Concerning the Most Recent Literature*) [appear until 1766]
1760	Johann Heinrich Lambert: *Photometria*
1761	Thomas Abbt: *Vom Tode fürs Vaterland* (*On Dying for the Fatherland*)
1762	Christoph Willibald Gluck: *Orfeo et Euridice* Christoph Martin Wieland: Shakespeare translations
1763	Peace of Hubertusburg Johann Joachim Winckelmann: *Geschichte der Kunst des Altertums* (*History of the Art of Antiquity*) Prussian General–Provincial School Code

BIBLIOGRAPHY

The following bibliography is meant to be a preliminary guide for further reading, in English, on Germany in the age of absolutism. It is a shortened and altered version of the lengthy bibliography of French, German, and English works that accompanies the second German edition. The reader should note that the German edition contains citations in topics neglected in English and that certain of the English-language works listed here reside in historiographical and interpretive traditions that run counter to Professor Vierhaus's argument. The reader of French and German will, for these reasons, still find the German bibliography valuable.

This book is the first work of Rudolf Vierhaus to be translated into English. Professor Vierhaus has written numerous essays and books dealing with early modern and modern German history. Of those most closely related to the themes of this book are his *Staaten und Stände. Vom Westfälischen bis zum Hubertusberger Frieden 1648–1763,* in Propyläen Geschichte Deutschlands, 5 (Berlin, 1984); *Deutschland im 18. Jahrhundert. Politische Verfassung, soziales Gefüge, geistige Bewegungen. Ausgewählte Aufsätze* (Göttingen, 1987). Also pertinent are certain works edited by him: *Eigentum und Verfassung. Zur Eigentumsdiskussion im ausgehenden 18. Jahrhundert,* in Veröffentlichungen des Max-Planck-Instituts für Geschichte, 37 (Göttingen, 1972); *Deutsche patriotische und gemeinnützige Gesellschaften,* in Wolfenbütteler Forschungen, 8 (Munich, 1980); *Bürger und Bürgerlichkeit im Zeitalter der Aufklärung,* in Wolfenbütteler Studien zur Aufklärung, 7 (Heidelberg, 1981).

JONATHAN B. KNUDSEN

GENERAL SURVEYS

The New Cambridge Modern History. Vol. 4, *The Decline of Spain and the Thirty Years War, 1609–48/59*. Edited by J. P. Cooper. Cambridge, 1970. Vol. 5, *The Ascendancy of France, 1648–88*. Edited by F. L. Carsten. Cambridge, 1961. Vol. 6, *The Rise of Great Britain and Russia, 1688–1715*. Cambridge, 1970. Vol. 7, *The Old Regime, 1713–1763*. Cambridge, 1957.

Anderson, Matthew S. *Eighteenth Century Europe. The 1680s to 1815*. 2d ed. London, 1976.

Bruford, W. H. *Germany in the Eighteenth Century: The Social Background of the Literary Revival*. Cambridge, 1959.

Dunn, Richard S. *The Age of Religious Wars, 1559–1689*. 2d ed. New York, 1979.

Holborn, Hajo. *A History of Modern Germany*. Vol. 2, *1648–1840*. New York, 1964.

Hufton, Olwen. *Europe: Privilege and Protest 1730–1789*. Ithaca, 1980.

Krieger, Leonard. *Kings and Philosophers, 1689–1789*. New York, 1970.

Ogg, David. *Europe of the Ancien Régime, 1715–1783*. New York, 1965.

Pennington, D. H. *Seventeenth Century Europe*. London, 1970.

Rabb, Theodore K. *The Struggle for Stability in Early Modern Europe*. New York, 1975.

Rudé, George. *Europe in the Eighteenth Century. Aristocracy and the Bourgeois Challenge*. Cambridge, 1985.

Sagarra, Eda. *A Social History of Germany, 1648–1914*. New York, 1977.

Woloch, Isser. *Eighteenth-Century Europe: Tradition and Progress, 1715–1789*. New York, 1982.

GERMANY AFTER THE THIRTY YEARS WAR

Evans, R. J. W. "Culture and Anarchy in the Empire, 1540–1680." *Central European History* 18 (1985): 14–30.

Kamen, Henry. "The Economic and Social Consequences of the Thirty Years War." *Past and Present*, no. 39 (1968): 44–61.

Parker, Geoffrey. *The Thirty Years War*. 2d ed. London, 1987.

Polišenský, J. V. *The Thirty Years' War*. Translated by Robert Evans. Berkeley, 1971.

Rabb, T. K. "The Effects of the Thirty Years' War on the German Economy." *Journal of Modern History* 34 (1962): 40–51.

ECONOMIC DEVELOPMENT

GENERAL WORKS

Cipolla, Carlo M., ed. *Fontana Economic History*. Vols. 2–4. London, 1973–4. *Before the Industrial Revolution, European Society and Economy, 1000–1700*. 2d ed. New York, 1980.

Davis, R. *The Rise of the Atlantic Economies.* London, 1973.

Kriedte, Peter. *Peasants, Landlords and Merchant Capitalists. Europe and the World Economy, 1500–1800.* Translated by Volker R. Berghahn. Leamington Spa, 1980.

Rich, E. E., and Wilson, C. H., eds. *The Cambridge Economic History of Europe.* Vols. 4–5. Cambridge, 1967–77.

Wilson, Charles, and Parker, Geoffrey. *An Introduction to the Sources of European Economic History 1500–1800.* Ithaca, 1977.

DEMOGRAPHY

Glass, D. V., and Eversley, D. E. C., eds. *Population in History. Essays in Historical Demography.* London, 1965.

Sharlin, Allan. "Natural Decrease in Early Modern Cities: A Reconsideration." *Past and Present,* no. 79 (1978): 126–38.

Wrigley, E. A. *Population in History.* London, 1969.

AGRICULTURE

Abel, Wilhelm. *Agricultural Fluctuations in Europe from the Thirteenth to the Twentieth Centuries.* Translated by Olive Ordish, foreword and bibliography by Joan Thirsk. New York, 1980.

Slicher van Bath, B. H. *The Agrarian History of Western Europe, A.D. 500–1850.* London, 1963.

INDUSTRIAL ECONOMY AND TRADE

Henderson, William O. *Studies in the Economic Policy of Frederick the Great.* London, 1963.

Kriedte, Peter; Medick, Hans; and Schlumbohm, Jürgen. *Industrialization before Industrialization. Rural Industry in the Genesis of Capitalism.* Translated by Beate Schempp. Cambridge, 1981.

MERCANTILISM

Coleman, D. C., ed. *Revisions in Mercantilism.* London, 1969.

Heckscher, Eli F. *Mercantilism.* Translated by M. Schapiro. 2 vols. rev. ed. London, 1955.

SOCIETY

PRINCES AND COURTS

Dickens, A. G., ed. *The Courts of Europe. Politics, Patronage and Royalty, 1400–1800.* New York, 1977.

Elias, Norbert. *The Court Society.* Translated by Edmund Jephcott. New York, 1983.

The Civilizing Process. Translated by Edmund Jephcott. 2 vols. New York, 1982.

OLD AND NEW NOBILITY

Goodwin, Albert. *The European Nobility in the Eighteenth Century.* New York, 1953.
Johnson, Hubert C. *Frederick the Great and His Officials.* New Haven, 1975.
Rosenberg, Hans. *Bureaucracy, Aristocracy, and Autocracy. The Prussian Experience, 1660–1815.* Cambridge, Mass., 1958.

RURAL POPULATION

Barnett-Robisheaux, Thomas. "Peasant Revolts in Germany and Central Europe after the Peasants War: Some Comments on the Literature." *Central European History* 17 (1984): 384–403.
Berkner, Lutz. "Inheritance, Land Tenure and Peasant Family Structure: A German Regional Comparison." In *Family and Inheritance. Rural Society in Western Europe, 1200–1800,* edited by Jack Goody, Joan Thirsk, and E. P. Thompson, 71–95. Cambridge, 1976.
"Peasant Household Organization and Demographic Change in Lower Saxony, 1689–1766." In *Population Patterns in the Past,* edited by Ronald Demos Lee. New York, 1977.
Blum, Jerome. *The End of the Old Order in Rural Europe.* Princeton, 1978.
Huggett, Frank. *The Land Question and European Society Since 1650.* London, 1975.
Roth, James. *The East Prussian "Domänenpächter" in the Eighteenth Century: A Study of Collective Social Mobility.* Ph.D. dissertation, Berkeley, 1979.
Link, Edith M. *The Emancipation of the Austrian Peasant 1740–1798.* New York, 1949.
Medick, Hans, and Sabean, David, eds. *Interest and Emotion: Essays on the Study of Family and Kinship.* Cambridge, 1984.
Sabean, David. *Power in the Blood: Popular Culture and Village Discourse in Early Modern Germany.* Cambridge, 1984.
Wunder, Heide. "Peasant Organization and Class Conflict in East and West Germany." *Past and Present,* no. 78 (1978): 47–55.

RURAL ARTISANAL AND MANUFACTURING LABOR

Barkhausen, Max. "Government Control and Free Enterprise in Western Germany and the Low Countries in the Eighteenth Century." In *Essays in European Economic History 1500–1800,* edited by Peter Earle, 212–73. Oxford, 1974.
Kellenbenz, Hermann. "Rural Industries in the West from the End of the Middle Ages to the Eighteenth Century." In *Essays in European Economic History 1500–1800,* edited by Peter Earle, 45–88. Oxford, 1974.

Kisch, Herbert. "The Textile Industries in Silesia and the Rhineland: A Comparative Study in Industrialization." *Journal of Economic History* 19 (1959): 541–64.

Prussian Mercantilism and the Rise of the Krefeld Silk Industry: Variations upon an Eighteenth-Century Theme. Transactions of the American Philosophical Society, n.s. 58/7. Philadelphia, 1968.

"From Monopoly to Laissez Faire: The Early Growth of the Wupper Valley Textile Trades." *Journal of European Economic History* 1 (1972): 298–407.

Klíma, Arnost. "Agrarian Class Structure and Economic Development in Pre-Industrial Bohemia." *Past and Present,* no. 85 (1979): 49–67.

"Industrial Development in Bohemia, 1648–1781." *Past and Present,* no. 11 (1957): 87–99.

THE URBAN POPULATION

Friedrichs, Christopher R. *Urban Society in an Age of War: Nördlingen, 1580–1720.* Princeton, 1979.

"German Town Revolts and the Seventeenth-Century Crisis." *Renaissance and Modern Studies* 26 (1982): 27–51.

Liebel, Helen P. "Laissez-Faire versus Mercantilism: The Rise of Hamburg and the Hamburg Bourgeoisie against Frederick the Great in the Crisis of 1763." *Vierteljahrschrift für Sozial- und Wirtschaftsgeschichte* 52 (1965): 207–38.

"The Bourgeoisie in Southwestern Germany, 1500–1789: A Rising Class?" *International Review of Social History* 10 (1965): 283–307.

Soliday, Gerald L. *A Community in Conflict: Frankfurt Society in the Seventeenth and Early Eighteenth Centuries.* Hanover, N.H., 1974.

Walker, Mack. *German Home Towns.* Ithaca, 1971.

EXCEPTIONAL AND MARGINAL GROUPS

Altmann, Alexander. *Moses Mendelssohn. A Biographical Study.* University of Alabama, 1973.

Graupe, H. M. *The Rise of Modern Judaism. An Intellectual History of German Jewry, 1650–1942.* New York, 1978.

Israel, Jonathan I. *European Jewry in the Age of Mercantilism 1550–1750.* Oxford, 1985.

"Central European Jewry During the Thirty Years War, 1618–1648." *Central European History* 16 (1983): 3–30.

Pollack, Hermann. *Jewish Folkways in Germanic Lands (1648–1806). Studies in Aspects of Daily Life.* Cambridge, Mass., 1971.

Shulvass, M. A. *From East to West. The Westward Migration of Jews from Eastern Europe during the Seventeenth and Eighteenth Centuries.* Detroit, 1971.

Stern, Selma. *The Court Jew. A Contribution to the History of the Period of Absolutism.* Philadelphia, 1950.

CULTURAL LIFE

GENERAL WORKS

Bossenbrook, William J. *The German Mind.* Detroit, 1961.
Cobban, Alfred, ed. *The Eighteenth Century. Europe in the Age of the Enlightenment.* New York, 1969.
Hauser, Arnold. *The Social History of Art.* 2 vols. New York, 1951.
Hertz, Frederick. *The Development of the German Public Mind.* 3 vols. New York, 1957–75.
Kann, Robert A. *A Study in Austrian Intellectual History. From Late Baroque to Romanticism.* London, 1960.

CONFESSIONAL COEXISTENCE

Allison, Henry E. *Lessing and the Enlightenment. His Philosophy of Religion and Its Relation to Eighteenth-Century Thought.* Ann Arbor, Michigan, 1966.
Barth, Karl. *Protestant Theology in the Nineteenth Century: Its Background and History.* Valley Forge, Pa., 1972.
Cragg, G. R. *The Church and the Age of Reason, 1648–1789.* The Pelican History of the Church, vol. 4. Harmondsworth, Eng., 1960.
Drummond, A. L. *German Protestantism since Luther.* London, 1951.
Frei, Hans W. *The Eclipse of Biblical Narrative. A Study in Eighteenth and Nineteenth Century Hermeneutics.* New Haven, 1974.
Gawthorp, Richard, and Strauss, Gerald. "Protestantism and Literacy in Early Modern Germany." *Past and Present,* no. 104 (1984): 31–54.
Grossmann, Walter. "Religious Toleration in Germany, 1648–1750." *Studies on Voltaire and the Eighteenth Century* 201 (1982): 115–41.
Midelfort, H. C. Erik. *Witch Hunting in Southwestern Germany 1562–1684. The Social and Intellectual Foundations.* Palo Alto, 1972.
Stroup, John. *The Struggle for Identity in the Clerical Estate.* Studies in the History of Christian Thought 33. Leiden, 1984.
Whaley, Joachim. *Religious Toleration and Social Change in Hamburg, 1529–1819.* Cambridge, 1985.

RELIGIOUS AND SECULAR BAROQUE

Argan, Giulio C. *The Europe of the Capitals, 1600–1700.* Translated by Anthony Rhodes. Cleveland, 1965.
Bazin, Germain. *Baroque and Rococo.* Translated by Jonathan Griffin. New York, 1964.
The Baroque. Translated by Pat Wardroper. New York, 1968.
Benjamin, Walter. *The Origin of German Tragic Drama.* Translated by John Osborne. London, 1977.
Bourke, John. *Baroque Churches of Central Europe.* London, 1958.

Bukofzer, Manfred F. *Music in the Baroque Era.* New York, 1947.

Geiringer, Karl. *The Bach Family.* New York, 1954.

Johann Sebastian Bach. New York, 1966.

Held, Julius Samuel. *Seventeenth- and Eighteenth-Century Art: Baroque Painting, Sculpture, Architecture.* New York, 1971.

Hempel, Eberhard. *Baroque Art and Architecture in Central Europe.* London, 1965.

Moser, Hans Joachim. *Heinrich Schütz: His Life and Work.* Translated by Carl Pfatteicher. St. Louis, 1959.

Otto, Christian. *Space into Light: The Churches of Balthasar Neumann.* New York, 1979.

Petzoldt, Richard. *Georg Philipp Telemann.* Translated by Horace Fitzpatrick. New York, 1974.

Powell, Nicolas. *From Baroque to Rococo.* London, 1959.

Spitta, Philipp. *Johann Sebastian Bach.* 3 vols. in 2. New York, 1951.

SCIENCE, CULTURE, EDUCATION

Beck, Lewis White. *Early German Philosophy. Kant and His Predecessors.* Cambridge, Ma. 1969.

Bödeker, Hans Erich; Iggers, Georg; Knudsen, Jonathan; and Reill, Peter, eds. *Aufklärung und Geschichte. Studien zur deutschen Geschichtswissenschaft im 18. Jahrhundert.* Göttingen, 1986.

Copleston, Frederick. *A History of Modern Philosophy.* Vol. 4, *Modern Philosophy: Descartes to Leibniz.* Vol. 6, *Modern Philosophy: The French Enlightenment to Kant.* Westminster, Md., 1946–75.

Gierke, Otto. *Natural Law and the Theory of Society 1500–1800.* Translated by Ernest Barker. 2 vols. in 1. Boston, 1957.

Grafton, Anthony. "The World of the Polyhistors: Humanism and Encyclopedism." *Central European History* 18 (1985): 31–47.

Koestler, Arthur. *The Watershed. A Biography of Johannes Kepler.* Lanham, Md., 1985.

McClelland, Charles E. *State, Society and University in Germany 1700–1914.* Cambridge, 1980

Meyer, Robert W. *Leibniz and the Seventeenth-Century Revolution.* Translated by J. P. Stern. Cambridge, 1952.

Paulsen, Friedrich. *The German Universities: Their Character and Historical Development.* Translated by Edward Perry. New York, 1895.

German Education, Past and Present. Translated by T. Lorenz. London, 1908.

The German Universities and University Study. Translated by Frank Thilly and William Elwang. New York, 1906.

PIETISM

Fulbrook, Mary. *Piety and Politics. Religion and the Rise of Absolutism in England, Württemberg and Prussia.* Cambridge, 1983.

Pinson, Koppel. *Pietism as a Factor in the Rise of German Nationalism.* New York, 1934.

Stoeffler, F. Ernest. *German Pietism during the Eighteenth Century.* Leiden, 1973. *The Rise of Evangelical Pietism.* Leiden, 1965.

ENLIGHTENMENT

Cassirer, Ernst. *The Philosophy of the Enlightenment.* Translated by Fritz C. A. Koelln and James P. Pettegrove. Princeton, 1951.

Gay, Peter. *The Enlightenment. An Interpretation.* 2 vols. New York, 1966–9.

Heitner, Robert R. *German Tragedy in the Age of Enlightenment.* Berkeley, 1963.

Porter, Roy, and Teich, Mikuláš, eds. *The Enlightenment in National Context.* Cambridge, 1981.

Reill, Peter Hanns. *The German Enlightenment and the Rise of Historicism.* Berkeley, 1975.

Venturi, Franco. *Utopia and Reform in the Enlightenment.* Cambridge, 1971.

THE WORLDVIEW AND VALUES OF THE BURGHER CLASS

Blackall, Eric A. *The Emergence of German as a Literary Language.* Cambridge, 1959.

Fabian, Bernhard. "English Books and Their Eighteenth-Century German Readers." In *The Widening Circle: Essays on the Circulation of Literature in Eighteenth-Century Europe,* edited by Paul Korshin, 117–96. Philadelphia, 1969.

Melton, James Van Horn. "From Image to Word: Cultural Reform and the Rise of Literate Culture in Eighteenth-Century Austria." *Journal of Modern History* 58 (1986): 95–124.

Menhennet, Alan. *Order and Freedom. Literature and Society in Germany from 1720 to 1805.* New York, 1973.

Ward, Albert. *Book Production, Fiction and the German Reading Public 1740–1800.* Oxford, 1974.

POLITICAL ORGANIZATION

Blanning, T. C. W. *Reform and Revolution in Mainz, 1743–1803.* Cambridge, 1974.

Carsten, Francis L. "The Great Elector and the Foundation of Hohenzollern Despotism." *English Historical Review* 65 (1950): 175–202. *Princes and Parliaments in Germany from the Fifteenth to the Eighteenth Century.* Oxford, 1959.

Clasen, C. P. *The Palatinate in European History 1559–1660.* London, 1963.

Dorwart, Reinhold A. *The Administrative Reforms of Frederick William I of Prussia.* Cambridge, Mass., 1953.

The Prussian Welfare State before 1740. Cambridge, Mass., 1971.

Evans, R. J. W. *The Making of the Habsburg Monarchy 1550–1700: An Interpretation.* Oxford, 1979.

Fauchier-Magnan, Adrien. *The Small German Courts in the Eighteenth Century.* London, 1958.

Frey, Linda, and Frey, Marsha. *Frederick I: The Man and His Times.* East European Monographs, 166. New York, 1984.

Gagliardo, John. *Enlightened Despotism.* New York, 1967.

Gross, Hanns. *Empire and Sovereignty. A History of the Public Law Literature 1599–1804.* Chicago, 1973.

Ingrao, Charles, ed. *Politics and Society in the Holy Roman Empire, 1500–1806.* Supplementary issue. *Journal of Modern History* 58 (1986).

Krieger, Leonard. *The German Idea of Freedom.* Boston, 1957.

"Germany." In *National Consciousness. History and Political Culture in Early-Modern Europe,* edited by O. Ranum, 67–97. The Johns Hopkins Symposia in Comparative History, vol. 5. Baltimore, 1975.

The Politics of Discretion: Pufendorf and the Acceptance of Natural Law. Chicago, 1965.

An Essay on the Theory of Enlightened Despotism. Chicago, 1975.

Meinecke, Friedrich. *Machiavellism. The Doctrine of Raison d'Etat and Its Place in Modern History.* Translated by David Scott. London, 1957.

Oestreich, Gerhard. *Neostoicism and the Early Modern State.* Edited by Brigitta Oestreich and H. G. Koenigsberger. Translated by David McLintock. Cambridge, 1982.

Raeff, Marc. *The Well-Ordered Police State. Social and Institutional Change through Law in the Germanies and Russia, 1600–1800.* New Haven, 1983.

Ritter, Gerhard. *Frederick the Great.* Translated by Peter Paret. Berkeley, 1968.

Roberts, Michael. *The Swedish Imperial Experiment 1560–1718.* Cambridge, 1979.

Schevill, Ferdinand. *The Great Elector.* Hamden, Conn., 1965

Vann, James A., and Rowan, Steven, eds. *The Old Reich: Essays on German Political Institutions 1495–1806.* Brussels, 1974.

Vann, James A. *The Swabian Kreis: Institutional Growth in the Holy Roman Empire.* Brussels, 1975.

The Making of a State: Württemberg 1593–1793. Ithaca, 1984.

Walker, Mack. *Johann Jakob Moser and the Holy Roman Empire of the German Nation.* Chapel Hill, N.C., 1981.

WARS, CRISES, AND CONFLICTS

Behrens, C. B. A. *Society, Government, and the Enlightenment. The Experiences of Eighteenth-Century France and Prussia.* New York, 1985.

Carsten, Francis L. *The Origins of Prussia.* Oxford, 1954.

Fay, Sidney B., and Epstein, Klaus. *The Rise of Brandenburg-Prussia to 1786.*
  rev. ed. New York, 1964.
Kann, Robert A. *A History of the Habsburg Empire, 1526–1918.* Berkeley,
  1974.
Parry, Geraint. "Enlightened Government and Its Critics in Eighteenth-
  Century Germany." *Historical Journal* 6 (1963): 178–92.
Wangermann, Ernest. *The Austrian Achievement 1700–1800.* London, 1973.

INDEX